Taken by Adolph Dittmer in 1913, the front cover photograph shows a view from the turret of the former Rochester Hotel, now the Post Office at Chapman and Lemon.

The house in the center is still at Maple and Olive, and two of the high school buildings, now Chapman University are still present although the large white building has moved.

A Tour Of
Old Towne Orange
— *Founded in 1871* —

by
Douglas Paul Westfall

Featuring
Steven G. McHarris
as the author of the application to the
National Register of Historic Places

Produced in cooperation with
The Old Towne Preservation Association
of Orange.

ASSOCIATION

The Paragon Agency
Publishers
1999

A Tour Of
Old Towne Orange
—Founded in 1871—

Westfall, Douglas Paul, 1949—

Published by
The Paragon Agency
Orange, California, 1999

1. Old Towne Orange, 1871–1940
2. Preservation, architectural
3. Heritage, historical
4. Walking Tours
   I. Steven G. McHarris, editor
   II. Title

ISBN: 1–891030-09-4

2k•r1
Printed in USA

A Tour Of
Old Towne Orange
— *Founded in 1871* —

A comprehensive walking tour of:
Architecture,
Heritage,
History,
& Preservation.

Covers 1,500 structures and 26 miles.
— all within a one square mile area —

This is a Heritage book.

*Anyone wishing to contribute information or photgraphs
to future versions of this book, please contact:
The Paragon Agency
P.O. Box 1281• Orange, CA • 92856*

Any errors or omissions within this publication
are purely unintentional.

Acknowledgment

Many people and significant organizations contribute to the preservation of a historic town like Orange. It takes a concerted effort to just keep our heritage for our children.

The Old Towne Preservation Association of Orange, is a nonprofit organization established in 1986. It's mission is *"To preserve and enhance the unique Old Towne Orange area through education, communication and community involvement."*

The writing of the nearly 500 page application took over four years. Although everyone supporting the effort can not be recognized, the following people should receive special attention for their work.

Steven G. McHarris, with a professional background in city planning, is the author of the NRHP application. He spent untold hours in completing and perfecting it and so deserves a place on the title page as a kind of editor of this publication.

Others with invaluable contributions are:
　　　　Shannon Tucker (OTPA President 1994-1995)
　　　　Anne Siebert (OTPA President 1996)
　　　　Gloria Boice (OTPA Historian)
Special thanks for her coordination of this project:
　　　　Joan Crawford (OTPA President 1997-1998)

For their special preservation work in Orange:
　　　　Orange County Supervisor Todd Spitzer, 3rd Dist.
　　　　Orange County Supervisor Cynthia Coad, 4th Dist.
　　　　The Orange County Historical Commission
　　　　The Orange Community Historical Society
　　　　The Orange City Council
　　　　The Orange Public Library
Also:
　　　　Al Remyn, Arborist — for all the trees
　　　　Craig B. Wheeler, Architect — for all the buildings
　　　　Casey Williams — for all the support

Dedication

This book is dedicated to two people whom I love.
*My oldest friend in Orange, **Kenneth Claypool,** who passed*
away at 96 in 1995 and my youngest friend in Orange,
***Jonathan Matthew Chambers,** my grandson, who will be*
one year old this summer.

Heritage is when there is something to inherit.

CONTENTS

ILLUSTRATIONS

Preface

This book represents my home town, where I live. The contents of this book list only some of the many wonderful architectural structures but most of those within Old Towne.

Contained in this publication is the narrative that is included within the actual application for nomination to the National Register of Historic Places. The remainder of the application lists and identifies all properties in the NRHP district. This book notes those properties within the listings and year of nomination. Many other structures are noted as well.

The National Historic Preservation Act of 1966 established that the Secretary of the Interior of the US is authorized to expand and maintain a National Register of Historic Places.

The Plaza Park and the Plaza Historic District in Orange, were honored with this distinction in 1978 and 1982 respectively. Other significant buildings have been listed as well. It has been a long range goal for the OTPA to gain National Register status for the residential area. State registry was attained on February 14, 1997 and the Federal registry on July 11, the same year. The new NRHP residential district is joined with the Plaza Park and Plaza Historic District and is collectively known as Old Towne Orange — the largest historic district within the state of California.

After two years of collating three independent data bases, walking routes to verify houses, reviewing hundreds of photographs and visiting with trees, this volume has come into being. To me, the OTPA is about preserving my town for my grandson. Orange is a special place and I plan to stay.

Douglas Westfall, April 1999

Foreword

In our rush to the future, we could lose the valuable ties to our past. The ties that tell us who we are and tell us where we came from. What sets one city apart from another is the story of its past. It's a story told by its buildings, its homes and its neighborhoods.

This is the story of my city and how in looking to its past, begins to define its future. We have the roots that are represented by what's called a "Built" environment, those buildings and homes that makeup Historic Old Towne Orange.

Historic structures are reminders of yesterday. They give us a sense of place, a sense of identity and a sense of pride. They are a part of the legacy from those who came before us, and are a gift to our children. These places and the memories they represent, are a vital part of our community and our neighborhoods. Not just because they are old, but because they contain so much of ourselves.

By telling us the story of our past, they show us where we came from and help us to understand where we are going. They point the way to a future that builds on a solid foundation. We leave behind the thoughtful consideration of what to preserve, because when we do, we honor those who came before us and we set an example for our children to follow in the future.

Orange City Councilman
Mike Alvarez, April 1999

CHAPTER 1

AN INTRODUCTION TO OLD TOWNE ORANGE

A wooden stake, driven into the ground in July of 1871 marked the center of a new town soon to be called Orange. William T. Glassell, brother to one of the town's founders, surveyed the land into 25 x 50 foot lots. The town at that time was but eight square blocks — now designated as the *Plaza Historic District*. In 1875, eight dedicated lots formed the town *Plaza Square*, measuring 292 by 330 feet.

First known as Richland, the town was laid out in 1871 by Alfred Beck Chapman and Andrew Glassell, two lawyers who received the land as a payment for services.

The Orange Plaza about 1890

Whether or not the city is named for oranges is still undetermined, partially because orange trees didn't come to the area until the 1870s.

Orange County had plenty of oranges when carved out of Los Angeles County in 1889. In fact, oranges had made the area so well-known: *"This county is given its name by the Legislature because of the orange groves for which it is justly famous."* While the Orange groves are now mostly regulated to backyard trees, a packing house is still active in the community.

Not *orange groves* but Orange *City* groves. grapefruit, avocado, olive, lemon, almond, walnut and yes, orange groves. The variety seemed endless, and with the orange — even more so. What seemed an endless flow of fruit-bearing trees has been reduced to a few commercial groves and private backyard lots. Tops among all of course is still the orange and it came with greater assortment and long-lasting grove trees.

The groves of Orange, in the late teens

The Orange Plaza about 1890

During the 1870s, A.B. Chapman, one of the founders of Orange, obtained Valencia seedlings from Thomas Rivers. Chapman's plantings made him the "Father of the Valencia Industry." By 1873 Patterson Bowers of Orange, obtained Navel orange seeds from the US agriculture department in Washington DC, creating the "Washington Navel." Many orange varieties were tried: St. Michaels, Mediterranean Sweets, and others.

Actually, there were six Orange Counties throughout the U.S. by 1880 and the burgeoning town received its Post Office in 1873, officially named Orange. The city incorporated in 1888 with the population boom, brought on by low railroad fares from the east. By now the town expanded to beyond the *Old Towne* borders of a square mile to Santiago Creek, both South and East.

The land for The Plaza Park measures 170 by 200 feet. Therefore The Plaza is *not a circle*, it's an oval. Pepper trees were the first to be planted in 1881 and by 1886 the present form took shape. Most of the trees were planted prior to 1900.

The Victorian fountain, now at 330 E. Chapman, came in 1887. The Norfolk Star Pine Tree planted in 1903, is the city Christmas Tree and in 1937 the electric fountain replaced the Victorian fountain. The Plaza Park itself was placed on the National Register of Historic Places in 1978 and is the oldest dedicated parkland in Orange County.

The NRHP district of Old Towne Orange, does not include the entire square mile and has small extensions outside the square. These are indicated in the listings as: Out of Old Towne.

All structures with the NRHP designation are shown as: NRHP and the year. Buildings not within the NRHP district and buildings which are nonconforming to the requirements for listing are designated in the listings as: NONC. In addition, the OTPA has also designated special homes with a plaque. These houses are shown as: OTPA.

The classifications for structures within the NRHP are:

1. Domestic single and multiple dwellings.
2. Commerce & Trade business, professional, organizational, financial, stores, restaurants and warehouses.
3. Government Post Office
4. Educational schools.
5. Religious schools, churches, and manse.
6. Cultural theaters, outdoor recreational parks, sports facilities and monument markers.
7. Agricultural processing and storage facilities.
8. Industrial manufacturing facilities and industrial storage.
9. Landscaped parks, trees, street objects and The Plaza.
10. Transportation, both rail and road-related.

In addition, the entire NRHP District retains its early 20th century character with mature street trees, early period street lighting and interesting street artifacts.

CHAPTER 2

TOURS OF OLD TOWNE ORANGE

Old Towne Orange is a perfect square mile, divided into 4 perfect quarters, with the *oval Plaza Park* at the center. Roads labeled *street* run north & south, and roads labeled *avenue* run east & west. Odd numbered addresses are on the *north & east* sides, and the even numbered addresses are on the *south & west.*

A Map of Orange about 1912

Each quarter is divided in the center by a primary thoroughfare, these being Palm & Palmyra avenues running east & west and Shaffer street & the Atchison, Topeka & Santa Fe Railroad running north & south. Montgomery (Place), runs adjacent to the railroad tracks for a short distance and at one time, extended the entire way with the name of Grant Street.

Chapman Avenue and Glassell Street divide the quarters of Old Towne and converge at Plaza Square. Old Towne's perimeter-surrounding avenues are Walnut & La Veta running east & west, and the surrounding streets are Batavia & Cambridge running north & south. Only the Nutwood addition of 1922 is actually outside and south of the square of Old Towne.

Long blocks run north/south as there are twice as many streets as there are avenues. There are also many exceptions to the Old Towne layout adding interest and variety to driving around. Examples are the Chapman University complex and Atchison Street at the railroad station.

Take a drive around and discover a street or avenue you never knew, for Old Towne is a perfect square mile.

If every road is covered once, the distance is 26 miles.

Style in reference to buildings is sometimes obvious and many times quite ambigious. Most people know what Victorian means and some may know the difference between Craftsman and Bungalow. Although somewhat limited in Orange, the styles of the WPA & PWA during the depression are significant.

Moderne and Spanish Colonial are two styles of architecture that came from the great depression in the U.S. (1929-1939.) Likewise, there were two government programs that helped to get the country back on its financial feet. The PWA (Public Works Administration) built schools, libraries and post offices to give work to laborers. Most of these structures are referred to PWA Moderne.

The WPA (Works Program Administration) created art projects as an innovative way to give work to artists. Many of these are referred to as WPA Spanish Colonial (not Mission.) Actually, both the PWA and the WPA built many of both styles across America, of both Moderne and Spanish Colonial design. A unique example is the Orange Train Depot which is a combination of Spanish Colonial and Moderne.

For a better definition of architectual style and terminology, see the glosary in the back of this book.

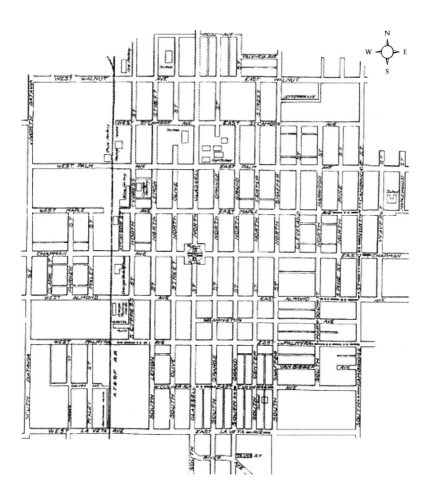

Map of Old Towne Orange - 1935c

The Plaza Park — Tour
(Business)
Plaza means place in Spanish, a central meeting place.

The Plaza Square consists of an oval park with a WPA style fountain dating from 1937 along with trees, shrubbery, and rose gardens. Four memorial plaques adorn the fountain and the park forms a rotary from which Chapman Ave. and Glassell Street radiate outward in four directions.

It is one of few places left in California around which a plaza can still be driven. While most buildings face the Plaza and are addressed there, four buildings described here are presently addressed to their spoke street. These are listed here however, and have access doors to both the Plaza and the respective spoke street.

1 Plaza Square — *1886 Victorian Park*   NRHP:1978

The Plaza Park is the oldest dedicated parkland in Orange County. The parkland itself is 170 by 200 feet, central to which is the WPA style electric fountain. The original Victorian fountain is now at 300 E. Chapman Ave.

The Plaza in 1908

8

The Plaza Square is centered in the eight block Plaza District.

Although the original town in 1871 covered but these original eight blocks (40 acres,) by the time of incorporation in 1888, the City of Orange ran from Collins on the *North*, Batavia on the *West*, La Veta on the *South* and the Santiago Creek on the *East*. The Plaza Park was created in 1886 and the Victorian fountain came the following year.

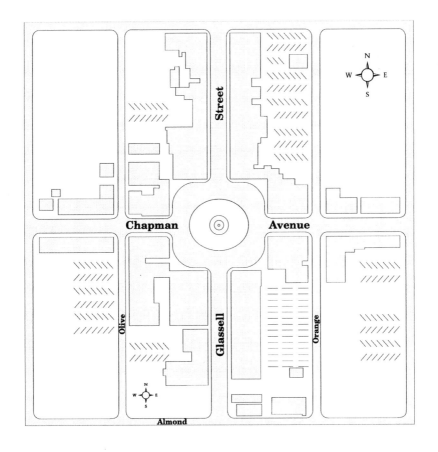

The Plaza District

During the days of the Works Program Administration (WPA,) art projects were created starting in 1935, mostly of Spanish Colonial Revival architecture. The second Plaza Fountain here, is of this design although was paid for by the city, not the WPA. The present fountain has colored lights and a rhythmic water jets and is best seen at night.

The 1937 Electric Fountain

Walk toward the east, to the Norfolk Star Pine.

The east-end Norfolk Star Pine planted in 1903, is the city Christmas Tree. There are two; its sister Star Pine is in the North-West corner of the park.

The City Christmas tree in 1939 (looking West on Chapman)

The 1886 Plaza Park

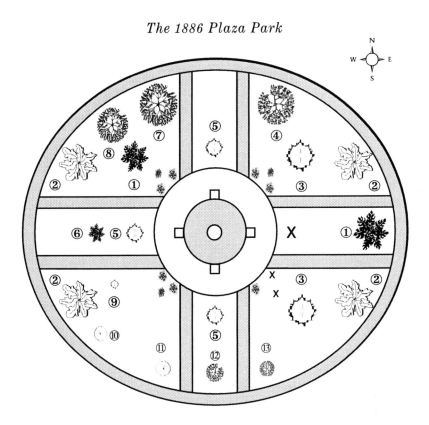

The Trees of the Plaza Park.

① Norfolk Star Pine *Araucaria heterophylla*   (2)   1903
② Magnolia *(Magnolia grandiflora)*   (4)
③ Date Palm   (2)   1890c
④ California Sycamore   (1)   1950c
⑤ California Fan Palm   (3)   1890c *(1 died)*
⑥ California Coast Redwood   (1)
⑦ Avocado   (1)
⑧ Orchid Tree   (1)   1910c
⑨ Sago Palm   (1)   1900c (1"/Yr)
⑩ Crepe Myrtle   (1)
⑪ Rose of Sharon   (1)
⑫ Valencia Orange   (1)   1969c
⑬ Chinese Flowering Magnolia   (1)   1976c

The Plaza Park 1900c (looking West on Chapman)

—*The Plaza District Tour continues with the Plaza Square.*—

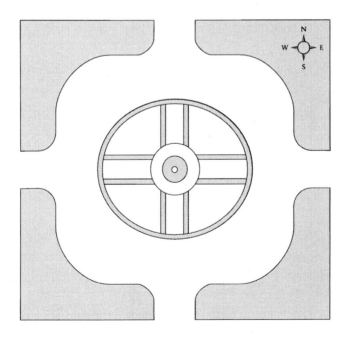

The Plaza Square

THE PLAZA SQUARE — TOUR
— From the Star Pine tree in the Plaza Park —
Looking East on Chapman Ave. to the right.
(Follow the park sidewalk clockwise.)

Chapman Ave. from the Plaza Park, looking East – about 1934

10 Plaza Square — *1898 Brick Commercial*   NONC
Carpenter Bank Building   11,050 sq. ft.   *(+ adjacent bld.)*
The first location of the National Bank of Orange,
dating from 1906. Heavily modified, this building is
actually combined with the adjacent structure on E.
Chapman Ave. The bank vault & safe are still intact.
A two story brick building, the present wood siding
hides the original brick structure, although they are
still visible from an interior garden area. Beautifully
restored interior of oak woods.

20 Plaza Square — *1922 Brick Commercial*   NRHP:1982
The Orange Building & Loan   2,100 sq. ft.
A Mediterranean style brick, typical for commercial
buildings of the 1920s. Three large arched transoms
with ornamental iron grates grace the facade. A bank
vault and original woodwork is still present inside.

26 Plaza Square — *1902 Brick Commercial*   NRHP:1982
M.L. Willits Building   6,000 sq. ft.   Pharmacy
Once known as the Mission Pharmacy, this building
actually held one of four pharmacies located in town.

A still was discovered in the 1980s, showing the method used to support so many drug stores during prohibition.

A brick, 1902 structure with an Art Deco exterior veneer, dating from 1935 with two floors.

Looking South on Glassell to the right.

Glassell Street from the Plaza Park, looking South

36 Plaza Square — *1905 Brick Commercial*   NRHP:1982

M.C. Cuddleback Building   7,650 sq. ft.   Sanitarium

> Completed the same year as the adjacent building began construction, this building is surrounded by the larger structure on two sides. A business now resides in the small previously adjacent 'alley' immediately to the South.
>
> Two story Brick and concrete block with veneer and cornices.

42 Plaza Square — *1907 Brick Commercial*   NRHP:1982

Ehlen & Grote Building   4,800 sq. ft.   Motorcycles

> This section of the building located on South Glassell, contained a bicycle store until about 1912, when Judson Carriker began carrying motorcycles. The business, now on Katella, is the oldest, continuously operated motorcycle shop in the US.
>
> This, the largest commercial building in historic

Orange, this part of the 'Big White Store' is also built from the white glazed brick, giving it the name.

44 Plaza Square — *1909 Brick Commercial*   NRHP:1982
The Orange Daily News   4,500 sq. ft.   Newspaper
Originally, the location of the Orange Post newspaper, W.O. Hart [see Hart Park, 701 S. Glassell] along with Justice Craemer moved the Orange Daily News here in 1922. The North side *'news alley'* is where the *'newsies'* would fold their papers for delivery.
Brick with veneer, modified in 1930 to its present appearance.

Orange Daily News & News Alley

48 Plaza Square — 1888 Brick Commercial   NONC
Ainsworth Block   11,250 sq. ft.   Mercantile
Lewis Ainsworth settled in Orange during 1901. He and his sons operated the Ainsworth Lumber Company and purchased the 1888 Armor building, enlarging the structure in 1907.
Brick veneer, wire glass skylighting and a second floor. [see the Ainsworth House, 414 E. Chapman Ave.]
Note the iron support post stamped:
1888 Baker Iron Works - Los Angeles.

Looking West on Chapman to the right.

55 Plaza Square — *1912 Brick Commercial*   NRHP:1982

Jorn Building   15,300 sq. ft.   Insurance
    ARCT: C.B. Bradshaw
    Insurance Salesman Carl Jorn, built this building and
    had his offices on the second floor. E.H. Smith's
    Jewelry store stood on the first level.
    Yellow brick veneer with stone cornices & skylight.
    The 1920 adjacent addition on W. Chapman follows the
    same style architecture.

58 Plaza Square — *1910 Brick Commercial*   NONC
    375 sq. ft.   Business Building

60 Plaza Square — *1889 Brick Commercial*   NRHP:1982
Pixley Newspaper Office   2,800 sq. ft.
    Two story brick commercial; modestly decorated front.

75 Plaza Square — *1912 Brick Commercial*   nrhp:1982
D.F. Campbell's Opera House

Looking North on Glassell to the right

77 Plaza Square — *1905 Brick Commercial*   NRHP:1982
N.T. Edwards Block   44,000 sq. ft.   Mortuary
    With the USO on the first floor, a mortuary operated
    in the basement. A young woman, going to see a dead
    relative, died herself in an elevator accident. Her
    white framed ghost, to this day, is supposedly still
    seen by the residents on the second floor.
    Two story brick veneer with cast iron post

reinforcement, wire glass skylight and full basement. *Note the awning bell on the cast iron support post on Glassell.*

80 Plaza Square — *1928 Beaux Arts Commercial*   NRHP:1982
First National Bank   11,050 sq. ft.
    ARCT: Morgan, Walls & Clements
    Formed in 1906, the First National Bank of Orange grew to absorb the old Bank of Orange and the original bank building on the site had opened in 1887 and razed in 1927. Opened in 1928 with an original cost of $47,500, high ceilings and a second floor add to this remarkable structure. A step inside, provides a special treat with the vaulted ceiling's carved inlay woods.
Note the historic plaque on the South West corner.

The Plaza Park

—To continue the Plaza District Tour—

Follow the spoke streets for the first two blocks on Chapman.

Then follow the first block on Glassell.

Orange Union High School — Tour
— *Chapman University since 1954 at 333 N. Glassell St.*—

Orange Union High School, as it is and was in 1930c

The new high school on Shaffer St. came in 1953 and Chapman University took over this complex the following year. The five original Neo-classics structures did not start in this configuration. *Wilkenson Hall* came first, somewhat closer to Glassell St. in 1904. *See the front cover photograph.*

Smith & Reeves Halls were both built in 1913 but as seen on the front cover, not at the same time.

Wilkenson Hall - moved in 1920

To build *Memorial Hall,* Wilkenson had to be moved some 300 off of Glassell in 1920, leaving the sunken lawn. Memorial hall, completed the following year, contains the 999 seat auditorium. *Roosevelt Hall* was built last in 1928.

Memorial Hall - filled with 999 students

The Sisters of St. Joseph — Tour
— Sisters of St. Joseph Sanctuary is at 480 S. Batavia St.—

St. Joseph's Hospital

Ask permission at the office before entering the grounds.
The *Order of the Sisters of Saint Joseph* came to Orange
County in 1922; building the hospital on Main St. in 1929.

Grounds and Buildings

The Sanctuary and grounds are much the same after 70 years – with the exception of the large Craftsman Home, now gone. The grounds and the interior court, offers a pause for retrospect.

Front entrance, interior court

The Sanctuary still contains the same ambiance as when built. The Sisters of St. Joseph continue to provide for the community.

St. Joseph's sanctuary, chapel

Organ loft and chapel

The Sisters have a history room with artifacts of their past and also an extensive photographic collection, dating from the construction of the Mission Revival hospital in the 1920s.

View from back, interior court

Music Hall

Industrial — Tour
— Anaconda Wire & Cable came to 200 N. Cypress.—

Anaconda Cable

Orange had quite a large industrial community aside from oranges. Three cordage factories here still give testiment to this. The Anaconda Cable building covers almost 100,000 sq. ft.

Braiding machine

Interior cotton yarn mill

— Western Cordage Company on 545 W. Palm.—

Western Cordage Company, Inc.

Inside Western Cordage

*A-1-inch rope and
A-2½-inch drilling cable*

Spinning department

Orange, nuts and other fruit packing houses were extensive; three packing houses are still in Orange. *Villa Park Orchards* on Palm continues operation. Contact the main office for visitation.

— *Red Fox Orchards at 128 S. Cypress.*—

This packing house is still intact — although used today for another purpose. Another is located at 426 W. Almond

Orange Packing

City Park — Tour
— W.O. Hart Park today can be entered at 701 S. Glassell —

The Park and Tree tour involves three parks:

Plaza Park *(1886)* in the Plaza Square
Depot Park *(1888)* on Atchison St. &
The City Park *(Hart Park — 1936)*

The first two parks are the oldest parkland in Orange County, actually pre-dating the county's formation in 1889. Most trees have the designation: 30", 20', 25' representing the dimeter - height - spread, respectively of each tree. Refer to each park location for tree details, and be sure to view the trees as they are found in the street listings.

In Hart Park, the Plunge, Band Shell and Horse Shoe Club are all WPA Spanish Colonial architecture. Constructed between 1935 and 1937, the pool building and surrounding courtyard are still enjoyed today as they were during the depression.

Near the Plunge

Young trees, here in 1935, are mature today.

Other entrances to Hart park include:
- The south end of Shaffer St. *(driving)*
- The south end of Grand St. *(walking)*
- The south end of Orange St. *(walking)*

If the park is entered from Glassell or Shaffer, access is into the Santiago Creek. Now paved, the park terraces are built out of river rock and allow parking in the creek bed. Entrance via Grand and Orange street is by foot and offers a view of the Bandshell from Orange St. and a very large Moreton Bay Fig tree from Grand.

Henri F. Gardner was a noted horticulturist, an Orange City Councilman and a founder of the Santa Ana Valley Irrigation district. His 20 acre ranch along Santiago Creek boasted many varieties of plants as well as trees and the family lived on south Glassell. Henri F. Gardner planted the Moreton Bay tree on Glassell as he did its twin here on Grand St. The Moreton Bay is a historical landmark and one of few found in California.

The Spanish Colonial architecture of Hart Park

Wide walkways and river rock show the 1930s influence.

CHAPTER 3

THE NARRATIVE DESCRIPTION FOR
THE NATIONAL REGISTER OF HISTORIC PLACES

The Old Towne Orange Historic District, located between five major freeways in the center of urban Orange County has withstood the pressures of growth throughout the decades. Once a small agrarian community surrounded by citrus groves, farmland, and ranching operations, Orange rapidly developed in the 1960's and 70's into a highly urbanized setting, leaving its historic downtown business district and surrounding original neighborhood community primarily unchanged. Unlike many Southern California communities, Orange never experienced significant redevelopment or modernization of its original town area and thus retained its original charm and character. This proposed National Register nomination is the most significant of many preservation efforts for Old Towne Orange. The District consists of the original residential community, central business district, and industrial area of Orange.

The District retains its early 20th century character with mature street trees, early period street lighting, subdivision monumentation, early period parks, train depot, churches and the downtown commercial business district. There are few intrusive non-contributing buildings in comparison to the number and variety of contributing resources, with most having had little modification through the years.

The District is composed of historically interdependent buildings which still exhibit the special ambiance associated with their time and place in history. On the whole, the homes and buildings are in a well-maintained condition and retain their original architectural integrity. District buildings dating from the late 1880's, when the population was 866, through 1940 are present and exhibit styles and architectural details unmatched in our present day housing tracts and planned communities. The complete stock of downtown commercial buildings, industrial buildings, and surrounding residential homes and buildings, which are a part of the original town settlement, remain in active use today, and represent a rare and important reminder of the small town character once prevalent across the Southern California region.

The District core is represented by the Plaza and the Plaza Historic District buildings which consists of the original four-block commercial business district. These buildings, constructed largely during the 1905-1920 economic growth period, reflect the mode of construction and design style popular in the Southern California region prior to 1925. The Plaza District acreage was originally set aside in 1871, but it was not until 1886 that it was improved and the original fountain constructed (the original cast bronze fountain now sits in front of City Hall and the current fountain at the Plaza dates to 1936). Commercial buildings of the Plaza Historic District are largely comprised of brick or concrete construction and veneer. The contributing early commercial buildings are primarily historic brick commercial with various examples of Mission Revival and one example of Corinthian columned Beaux Arts.

Surrounding the Plaza Historic District are four historic quadrants or neighborhoods which comprise the slightly larger than one square mile of original development in the City of Orange. This area is documented in the City of Orange General Plan as a local district with historic significance. Here a diversity of architectural styles, building types and neighborhood characteristics are represented. Homes and buildings from the 1880's through 1940 are still present in nearly the same concentrations as they existed prior to 1940. The streets are laid on a north-south east-west axis, supported by four spoke streets which radiate from the central Plaza and business district. Many of the residential streets have prominent homes situated on corners which provide a focal point from street to street. Streets lined with numerous varieties of canopy trees or palm trees provide countless beautiful neighborhood views and examples of traditional hometown character.

In general, there are four primary architectural periods and styles represented in the District: Victorian (1871-1900), Classical Revival (1900-1910), Craftsman and Bungalow (1910-1925), and Mediterranean Revival (1922-1935). While not every house or building is a pure example of its period, most draw heavily from the influences popular at the time of construction. The majority of the District houses have wood frame construction covered by wood siding or shingles with double-hung or casement windows and hipped and/or gabled roofs. They are built on raised foundations of cut stone, brick or cement and steps typically lead up to a front porch. Although numerous early detached garages still exist, they are not counted as contributing because many were not typically well constructed. Those remaining are generally in fair condition. The street lights, installed in the 1920's, are cast in cement and have fluted shafts on a octagonal base with a collar beneath the acorn shaped luminaries.

Most of the original houses have had only minor alterations such as concrete steps or composition shingles replacing the original wood steps or siding. More drastic alterations, such as enclosing front porches, stuccoing wooden siding and replacing windows with aluminum, are less common. A few houses were covered with asbestos shingles but as the District continues to be rehabilitated, more are having the asbestos shingles, and other inappropriate alterations removed. Some single family homes were converted to duplexes. These conversions seldom affected the outside appearance as most of these homes were originally built with two front doors. Some of the larger homes with a main hallway entrance were also converted to multi-family use without exterior alterations. Some of the homes once multi-family have been or are presently being converted back to single family residences.

The dwellings in the proposed District also include former boarding and lodging houses, apartment buildings and cottages as well as estate homes. Most of the Districts estate homes are located along the larger spoke streets of Chapman Avenue and Glassell Street, while the Nutwood Place Subdivision and northwest quad/ industrial area contain some of the most modest homes. The apartment buildings are closer to the Plaza Historic District as were the lodging and boarding houses. Overall, the District houses are predominantly one, one and one half, and two story, that are between 1000 and 2500 square feet in size.

The location of the Atchison Topeka & Santa Fe (AT&SF) rail line three blocks from the center of the business district provided opportunities for the development of industrial facilities for the receipt, packing and shipping of locally raised agricultural products. In 1900, the most important business was the fruit packing and shipping operations. Approximately 350 carloads of oranges were shipped out yearly, as well as lemons, walnuts, dried fruit, potatoes, peanuts, grapes, and cabbage. There are two historic packing house complexes that survive within the District. The earliest building is the Villa Park Orchard's Association Packing House complex which was built in 1919. The Richland Walnut Association building was constructed in 1924. In both cases the packing houses were constructed immediately adjacent to the rail line.

In 1914 the Orange Contracting and Milling Company built their yard and mill on Lemon Street. The false front industrial building consists of a wood frame sheathed with corrugated iron panels. The other false front industrial building within the District is the structure at 145 North Lemon Street that features pressed metal panels on the wall of the street facade.

During the 1920's larger industrial operations moved into the District's industrial area. In 1927 the Western Cordage Company, a rope manufacturer established in 1923, moved into the Richland Walnut Association Building. In 1928 the California Wire Company (became the Anaconda Wire Company in 1930) built a complex of industrial buildings adjacent to the rail line between Palm Avenue and Maple Avenue. The buildings feature industrial steel windows and skylights to light the interior work areas. A cotton mill was originally established as a separate business to supply cotton yarn for the manufacture of weather proof wire and later became the California Cordage Company. It was located directly opposite the wire plant along the east side of Cypress (later used by Anaconda as the bare wire drawing mill). After 2 years of operation, machinery was sold and moved to a location on Lemon Street to start another mill. Another important early industrial business was the Ainsworth & Butler Lumber Company (1902 - 1914) at the corner of Maple Avenue and Cypress Street which supplied the majority of lumber and building materials to the growing Orange community during this period of growth.

Preservation Planning Background

In 1981, the City Council authorized preparation of a historic survey to identify, evaluate and document all pre-1940 buildings existing throughout the City. The purpose of the survey was to gather data needed to prepare a Historic Preservation Element of the City's General Plan. This survey was completed in 1982. The Council subsequently authorized an update and computerized listing of the original survey to further assess the City's historic resources. When the update was completed, it was presented to the City Council and Planning Commission in May 1992, at which time the Council took action to receive and file the report. Based upon the results of the original 1982 Orange Historic Survey and the updated 1992 Building Inventory, the City of Orange determined that there are special areas of historic importance in Orange that warrant preservation and conservation.

In 1982, the downtown Plaza Historic District was placed on the National Register of Historic Places. In 1983 the Historic Preservation Element was adopted into the City's General Plan. Included in the Element was the framework for a three-tiered planning approach to address the preservation needs of the adjacent historic residential neighborhood. The three concepts include: (1) adoption of design (by ord. '86) and demolition review (by ord. '88) processes in conjunction with sensitive land use planning, (2) the stimulation and promotion of neighborhood pride through a committed effort to revitalization, and (3) incentives for property owners to ensure ongoing preservation and revitalization efforts.

The District lies primarily within a larger area commonly known as "Old Towne" since July 1982. Old Towne encompasses the downtown area bounded by Walnut Avenue to the north, La Veta Avenue to the south, Cambridge Street to the east, Batavia Street to the west, and includes the Nutwood Place Subdivision and Hart Park south of La Veta Avenue. The Old Towne Orange Historic District proposes a more accurate and contiguous area which appears as it did during the period of documented significance. The proposed District contains a total of 1,237 contributing resources including numerous historic homes, six historic church sites (three historic buildings), three historic parks, three historic educational sites, several early industrial buildings, and includes the 35 historic buildings within the central business district. It is for this reason that the Old Towne neighborhood distinguishes itself from any other original settlement area within the City and County of Orange. The above mentioned 1992 Building Inventory reports finding a variety of architectural styles within the District. The predominant styles included: Bungalow, Hip Roof Cottage, Craftsman Bungalow, Craftsman, Mediterranean Revival, Victorian, Spanish Colonial Revival, Vernacular, California Bungalow, and Provincial Revival. Other notable but less frequent architectural examples include, Classic Box, Dutch Colonial Revival, Gothic, Italiante, Japo-Swiss/

Craftsman, Moderne, Period Apartment Bldg., Prairie Influence, Victorian Cottage, Queen Anne Victorian, and Stone Bungalow.

The Plaza Historic District National Register Inventory reports a variety of brick commercial style buildings within the District. One notable bank of Corinthian columned Beaux Arts style is also present. Mission Revival style is also present within the District.

Narrative Statement of Significance

<u>Historical Background and Significance:</u>

The Old Towne Orange Historic District in the City of Orange, California, is nominated under National Register Criteria A and C. Under Criterion A, in the area of exploration/settlement, the District is the original community development which evolved from a pioneer settlement into an established center of the Orange County citrus industry during the years 1888 to 1940. These 52 years represent the period of development in which Orange began as a agricultural-based township and developed into a thriving small-town community, represented by distinct styles of architecture and methods of construction and craftsmanship which quickly diminished after 1940. The downtown Plaza marked the initial core of commercial development from which simultaneously evolved the surrounding early residential neighborhoods. Industrial development quickly followed suit with citrus and construction-related material yards, packing plants, and shipping/receiving businesses flourishing within the three short blocks between the Plaza and the Santa Fe rail line. Interdependent to one another, commerce, industrial, and residential served the original Orange settlement. Under Criterion C, in the area of architecture, the District represents a large intact collection of early Southern California residential, commercial, and industrial buildings constructed during the years 1888 to 1940, with the majority maintained as such to present day. As discussed in more detail below, the significance in the District lies within the retention of so many early-period residential, commercial, and industrial structures which collectively retain the original town settlement architectural character and ambiance, and remains a central focus of community and civic pride to present day.

The town settlement of Orange traces its early beginnings to the breakup of the 1810 Spanish land grant Rancho Santiago de Santa Ana. When this sprawling cattle ranch was subdivided in the late 1860's, a Los Angeles lawyer, Alfred B. Chapman represented several parties in the partition suit. He took about four thousand acres as payment for his fees. Farm lots were first surveyed in the fall of 1870 ranging in size from ten to forty acres and divided in 1871, under the supervision of William T. Glassell (1827-1901). Four ten-acre lots were divided into eight 5-acre blocks with 20 lots in each block. These lot parcels were approximately 50 by 150 feet each, many with rear alley access.

The allocation of eight town lots in the center as a public square created the original Plaza Square. Walnut St. (now named Maple Ave.), bounded it on the north, Grape St. (now called Grand St.), on the east, Almond St. on the south and Lemon St. on the west. The two main intersecting streets were named Chapman Avenue and Glassell Street. The original name of the town was Richland, but this was changed to Orange by January 1875, when Mr. Chapman had the map recorded. The name had to be changed because there was another Richland in the State and the federal government refused to grant a duplicate post office. The town was incorporated April 6, 1888, as a sixth class city within Los Angeles County. Historic periodicals suggest that the reason for the early incorporation was to prevent saloons from coming to Orange and one of the first ordinances passed, was to prohibit the sale of intoxicating liquors. The size of the town at the time of incorporation was about three square miles, with a population of approximately 600. Additions to the town were made by subdividing the acreage tracts surrounding the original townsite, and naming such additions and their streets after the owner: such as Peter J. Shaffer and Nathan D. Harwood, Dewitt Clinton Pixley, and Charles Z. Culver. Other streets were named after their hometowns such as Palmyra and Batavia, New York. Daily life for most of Orange's early residents centered on small family ranches surrounding the townsite. Ten acres was a common size, at an average cost of $300 per acre.

Like most Southern California communities, Orange was strongly affected by the Great Boom of the 1880's, especially since the Santa Fe Railroad (later AT&SF) entered Orange about four blocks west of The Plaza in August 1887. This land boom spurred the most important improvements to The Plaza. In 1886 the circular park pattern was designed and surveyed. Plantings (some of which still exist) and a central fountain completed the park. A number of the first brick commercial buildings also were constructed at this time, including the C. M. Woodruff store (1885) and the D. C. Pixley store (1886). These and other boom era brick buildings, or portions thereof, still stand and add to the District's sense of age and continuity. Water, a valued resource from the Orange Water Works, was delivered through a stove-pipe to what is now the Plaza and people hauled water in barrels to their homes. Flocks of sheep were allotted thirty minutes to drink at the fountain place.

Construction lay dormant in the aftermath of the great boom for over ten years. After 1900, another building period saw the construction of many of the most important structures in the Plaza Historic District. Examples of this early twentieth century building era are the N. T. Edwards Block (1905), the Ehlen & Grote Building (1907) and the Kogler Hardware Building (1916). The construction period slowed with the onset of World War I. The final building period influencing the composition of the District occurred during the 1920's. Notable buildings representing this period are the Orange or Pantages Theater (1928), the W. O. Hart Post Office (1926) and the former First National Bank Building (1928). This was the fourth and last construction period to have added buildings which now contribute to the District's historic significance. In later years, front and interior remodeling have altered some of the buildings, and some post World War II buildings mildly intrude.

The original crop of Orange's agricultural era was not citrus, but grapes. Even at the time the city was named Orange, citrus crops were not abundant. Disaster hit the grape industry in 1886, when a blight destroyed all vineyards. Other crops such as apricots and walnuts were also successful, but were superseded by the citrus industry. By the late 1920's, Orange was one of the largest citrus producing areas in the State. This is reflected in the functions of at least two of the Plaza District's buildings. The first is the Santa Ana Valley Irrigation Company building of 1931. This 1877 cooperative water venture (through 1977) had its headquarters at this site. The Santa Ana Valley Irrigation Company served the farmers of Orange, Santa Ana and Tustin. Its control of water rights and extensive system of canals contributed significantly to the economic development of this area of Orange County. The second building of agricultural importance is the Orange County Fruit

Exchange or Sunkist Building. The Orange County Fruit Exchange was one of the original members of the 1893 Southern California Fruit Exchange. This group marketed the citrus product of Orange County under the famous "Sunkist" brand.

Southern California Fruit Exchange

The Plaza Historic District was the commercial and social hub of the Orange Community and at one time held the principal banks, newspapers, stores and public institutions of Orange. Such business centers included the former Orange Building and Loan Bank, the Ehlen & Grote Building, the former First National Bank, the M. Dobner Block, and Watson's Drug Store. Many of these buildings have specific associations with early community leaders, including businessman D. C. Pixley, newspaperman W. O. Hart, and state senator N. T. Edwards. Social and humanitarian organizations also had their community headquarters here, such as the 1920's Elk's Building which continues to serve this benevolent order.

The Orange Public Library and the Orange Tribune, the first local newspaper were founded in 1885. Orange Postmaster Robert E. Tener (1850-1931) served as librarian, thus the library itself was originally housed in the Post Office Building on South Glassell. The Tribune was founded by Bill Ward (1842-1930), a Gold Country pioneer who made his opinions clear throughout the pages of the Tribune. A cautious believer in the "Boom", he left Orange at the end of 1887, selling the Tribune to Fred W. Clemons. Later revived as the Orange Post, the paper endured a succession of owners, operated for many years as an adjunct of the later Orange Daily News until 1946.

Acquired by the City in 1894, the Main Library operation and its outlying branches served the community to this day. Ward and Tener were both strong supporters of the efforts to create the Plaza park in 1886 and '87. By 1888, the Plaza was under construction. Mrs. Samuel Armor, wife of city councilman and former county supervisor, organized the Women's Christian Temperance Union in the development of the Plaza. They raised $200 through sponsoring community dinners, jubilees, and staging a play. Another highlight of 1886 was the formation of Orange's first bank, a state-chartered institution known simply as The Bank of Orange. Though not all of the bank's capital came from Orange, local businessmen like D.C. Pixley and Jesse Arnold, who sat on the bank's Board of Directors, helped guide the bank's emergence as a major force in the community. It merged and was renamed the First National Bank of Orange in 1906. The bank survived until 1977. Today the building is occupied by a Wells Fargo branch office.

In August of 1887 Orange's Santa Fe depot opened alongside the tracks near West Chapman Avenue. The original building was replaced in 1938 by the present depot (closed since 1971 and subsequently purchased by the City of Orange for future preservation and reuse). The depot rail yard was recently improved in 1995 with the addition of a new platform and parking with period-style lighting and railings for the newly established Metrolink service. Orange's Depot Park, first developed in 1891, still survives as the oldest park in Orange. This park was recently improved and rededicated in 1996. Orange's other two railroads in 1888 were actually horse-drawn street cars: the Orange, McPherson & Modena and the Santa Ana, Orange & Tustin lines. The former was a short-lived line which ran from 1888 until 1891. The Santa Ana, Orange & Tustin line, which reached Orange in February of 1888, survived through various changes of ownership until it was finally taken over by the Pacific Electric line in 1906.

As late as 1881, the town still had only two organized churches. By 1888, that number had grown to six. Each of those pioneer churches continue to serve Orange today. The first congregation to organize in Orange was the Methodist Episcopal Church (now the First United Methodist Church of Orange) in 1873. They also built Orange's first church in 1875 on land donated by Chapman & Glassell on the east side of South Orange. This same land is owned by the church today. The only other church founded during Orange's first decade was the First Presbyterian Church, founded in 1874. Their first church (1881) was also built on land donated by Chapman & Glassell. In 1888 the Rev. Alexander Parker was the church's pastor and a well-known figure in the community, serving from 1883-1917. The next church to be founded in Orange was St. John's Lutheran Church, organized in 1882 by the Rev. Jacob Kogler, who would serve the congregation until 1917. Both the church and Rev. Kogler were mainstays in the lives of Orange's many German pioneers in the early days. Commonly known as the "German Church" in the 1880's, St. John's has also maintained a private school since its founding. The existing grandiose, Gothic church building was dedicated in 1914 and placed on the National Register on October 16, 1991.

St. John's Lutheran Church

The First Christian Church of Orange was founded in 1883 with 19 charter members. From 1887 until 1963, their church was located at the southeast corner of Chapman and Grand. The First Baptist Church was founded in 1886. Their 1893 chapel at the corner of Almond and Orange is the oldest surviving church building in Orange. The newest congregation in 1888 Orange was the Trinity Episcopal Church. Its members met in a small church near the corner of Chapman and Lemon. It 1909, a year after Trinity became recognized as a separate church, a new church was built at the northeast corner of Maple and Grand, and presently serves as the

Chapman University Chapel.

Another important civic institution was the Orange Intermediate School/Grammar School founded in 1872. After the old school had burned in the spring of 1886, Orange built a two-story school near the southeast corner of Sycamore Avenue and Glassell Street. This property had been donated to the Richland School District by Chapman and Glassell in 1872. The school housed K - 8 grades for approximately 40 years and then became the Orange Intermediate School. This structure was placed on the National Register on April 13, 1993. This building was recently acquired in 1996 by Chapman University for the expansion of their law school program. In 1888 the school's five teachers were under the leadership of Principal George Weeks who instituted many progressive changes and formalized the school's eight grades. The graduating class of 1888 consisted of just six students. At that time the closest high school was located in Los Angeles.

Settlement History

The Old Towne Orange Historic District is significant under Criterion A, in the area of exploration/settlement, because the area reflects an original community development that evolved historically into a cohesive neighborhood where the professional and trades people lived and did business. Many early residents were doctors, lawyers, and merchants. They developed the original downtown business district and resided in the adjacent subdivisions or ranches close to their shops and offices. Residents often worked, shopped and socialized in the downtown plaza area where the following services were rendered: Four excellent hotels, dry goods, clothing, grocery, hardware, pharmacies, four physicians, confectionery, saddle and harness, millinery and dressmaking, feed store, wood and coal dealers, water companies offices, blacksmiths and wagon makers, boot and shoe makers, bankers, real estate, architects, surveyors, civil engineers, carpenters, painters, furniture shop, barbers, book and stationery, artists, musicians, and three theaters.

Early Settlers & Community Leaders

A brief profile of eleven prominent District residents, who aided in establishing the community within the proposed District prior to the turn of the century through 1940, is as follows.

Sam Armor (1843-1933) arrived in 1875, and worked as a rancher, school teacher and carpenter until the mid-1880's when he built a wooden store building near the southwest corner of the Plaza, and opened a book and stationery store. In 1888 he replaced his first store with a new brick building, portions of which still stand today as part of the Ainsworth Block (100 W. Chapman). With the creation of Orange County in 1889, he served on the first Board of Supervisors, then later served on the Orange Board of Trustees. He also served as Orange's Justice of the Peace. His wife, Alice (1848-1939) served as editor and publisher of the Orange Post from 1892 to 1915. In his later years he prepared the first real history of Orange County in 1911 and helped to found the Orange County Historical Society in 1919. His home can still be found in the District at 363 S. Orange Street.

DeWitt Clinton Pixley (1857-1937) was Orange's most successful 19th century businessman. An 1881 arrival in Orange, he started in business here by purchasing one of Orange's first general merchandise stores, Robert L. Crowder & Co. In 1886 he built his own brick store building at 122 N. Glassell which still stands today. Pixley was also associated with many of Orange's early financial institutions including the Orange Building and Loan Association (founded 1887) and The Bank of Orange. Pixley served one term on the Orange County Board of Supervisors (1899-1903). He also served several terms as Orange's City Treasurer. His home can still be found in the District at 288 N. Olive Street.

Cornelius B. Bradshaw (1840-1932) was involved with each of these pioneer businessmen and was the city's only architect. Bradshaw's first major project in Orange was D.C. Pixley's new brick building in 1886. His last was the Kogler Hardware Co. store (143 N. Glassell) in 1916. In between, he designed virtually every major business block and many of the private homes in Orange. Among the best-surviving examples of his work are the I.O.O.F. Hall (112-120 E. Chapman) which opened in 1901, the Ehlen & Grote Company's "Big White Store" (108-126 S. Glassell), built in 1908, the Edwards Block (101-123 N. Glassell), built in 1905, and the original Orange Union High School Building (1905), now a part of Chapman University. Many of his downtown Orange buildings are now listed within the Plaza Historic District - National Register of Historic Places.

Albert S. Hamilton ran the Orange Livery stable, located midway down the block on the east side of North Glassell. Hamilton settled here in 1876 and in 1878 went into the livery business. Beside board and care for horses, Hamilton's livery kept a line of buggies for sale or rent. He also provided regular Omnibus service from the Santa Fe depot to the Palmyra Hotel. In mid-1888 the Orange Livery burned to the ground. Rather than rebuild, Hamilton had the St. James livery stable moved onto the site. Hamilton left town during the depression of the 1890's having declared bankruptcy early in 1895.

William Blasdale (1834-1892) settled in Orange in 1875, on a ranch at the northeast corner of Chapman and Tustin. He grew a variety of orchard crops including oranges, peaches and plums. In the late 1880's Blasdale had a two-story house built on his ranch. As development encroached, the house was moved to the northwest corner of Center and Santiago Blvd. in Villa Park, a neighboring community, where it stands today. The old Henry Grote house (169 N. Shaffer) was built by the same builder, and is a virtual twin to the original Blasdale house. Blasdale served as a director of the pioneering Orange Fruit Growers Association in 1880. In 1884 he was elected by the stockholders to his first term as a director of the Santa Ana Valley Irrigation Co. which conveyed water from the Santa Ana River to the Orange township and surrounding communities. He served two additional terms in 1888-89 and 1889-90 and, during each of his terms, acted as president of the water company. In 1888, shortly before the incorporation of Orange, he was appointed to fill an unexpired term on the Orange School Board. Blasdale served as Orange's first mayor from April, 1888 to September, 1890.

Dr. Orville P. Chubb (ca. 1830-1894) was one of the leading figures in the drive to incorporate Orange. He arrived in Orange in the mid-1880's, best remembered for the Orange, McPherson & Modena Street Railway and the Hotel Rochester. Chubb helped to back the line which linked the three communities during 1888 and '89 and served as its president. But the collapse of the "Boom" brought the end of the mule-drawn cars. The Hotel Rochester was also subject to the collapse of the "Boom." Built on Chubb's property at the southwest corner of Chapman and Lemon, the three story brick building dominated Orange's sparse skyline for decades, beginning in 1888 until the building was finally razed in 1931. He served three years from 1888 - 1891 on the Board of Trustees. His son, Mont. P. Chubb was also active in city affairs and served a term as City Marshall in the mid-1890s.

Charles Z. Culver (ca. 1849- 19??), born in Palmyra, New York, had moved to Orange in 1881 and established himself as one of the area's many prominent raisin grape growers. In 1885 he entered the real estate business, opening an office in Los Angeles and declaring himself the "Santa Ana Valley Immigration Agent." Most of his immigrants were recruited from around his old hometown, as were many of his business partners. But Culver continued farming, until the winter of 1886-87 when he began work on Orange's Palmyra Hotel. When completed in July 1887, the large, two-story building had cost $40,000, much of it supplied by ·Culver's many partners and investors. Some of Culver's other local projects included the Culver Hotel Tract, the Culver Home Tract (which featured its own tiny Plaza at the intersection of Orange and Washington), a number of small rental cottages and the surviving Palmyra Hotel Annex (205 E. Palmyra), listed on the National Register of Historic Places. But in 1888, as the "Boom" began to falter, so did Culver's finances. Shortly thereafter, on June 18, 1888, Culver resigned from the Board of Trustees. In October, Culver set off for Baja California never to return.

Henri F. Gardner (1852-1918) arrived in Orange in 1873 and began construction of a home on his 20-acre ranch along Glassell Street near the Santiago Creek. Gardner was involved with the Santa Ana Valley Irrigation Company from the time of its incorporation in 1877. He acted briefly as a Director of the company in 1880, was its Secretary/Treasurer in 1881-82 and beginning in 1892 served as Superintendent of the entire system for several years. When the collapse of the "Boom" left him heavily in debt, Gardner was careful to preserve the home ranch on Glassell. Portions of that land are still owned by his descendants to this day. Prior to his election as one of Orange's original City Trustees, Gardner's only elective office had been as a member of the Orange School Board. His first term as a City Trustee was only for two years, but in 1890 he won re-election to a four year term. In his later years Gardner divided his time between his property in Orange, Richfield and Los Angeles.

Peter J. Shaffer (1823-1907) was one of Orange's earliest pioneers, buying land in A.B. Chapman's Richland Farm Lots tract which surrounded Orange in 1871, and in 1874 building a substantial two-story home that stands today. Shaffer cultivated a wide variety of crops including almonds, apples, apricots, figs, walnuts, acres and acres of grains, and oranges. By 1881 he owned some 250 acres locally. Like most of the prominent ranchers in town, he was concerned with the success of the Santa Ana Valley Irrigation Company and served a term on its Board of Directors in 1878-79. Shaffer received one of the two four-year terms on Orange's new Board of Trustees, but did not seek re-election in 1892. In his later years he moved back and forth between Orange and Santa Ana. His home is considered the oldest remaining in Orange, built in 1874 at a cost of $2,500. It is located in the District at 221 N. Orange Street.

Walter M. Scott (1842-1910) was born in Batavia, New York and raised in Wisconsin, settling in Orange where he acquired a substantial orange grove. Like many prominent men in Orange, Scott went into the real estate business during the "Boom", forming a partnership with Dr. Frank Seeber about 1886 that lasted several years. He served as Marshall in 1888 until retiring in April, 1892. He was appointed to Orange's Board of Trustees to fill the remaining two years of William Blasdale's second term. That same month he also received his commission as Orange's sixth Postmaster. He served in this dual role until the spring of 1894. Scott later moved to Santa Ana in the fall of 1894 to serve as Orange County Recorder until the end of 1902. He later served the county between 1907-1910 as the new County Assessor.

Andrew Cauldwell (ca. 1831-??) moved from New York state to Orange shortly after 1880, and established himself as a grower of the area's first major cash crop - raisin grapes. In 1883, along with his son and W.L. Witherbee, another local vineyardist, he founded Orange's first packing house at Maple and Grand. Initially, Cauldwell & Co. only packed and shipped raisins, but after the grape blight they moved into Orange packing. In 1889 they moved their building to the new Santa Fe tracks to simplify shipping. Under the supervision of Cauldwell's son, attorney A.B. Cauldwell, the packing house remained in operation until 1893. Andrew Cauldwell was active in the drive for Orange's incorporation and served as a Judge at the April 6th election where he was also elected our first City Clerk. In 1887-88, Cauldwell served a term as President of the Santa Ana Valley Irrigation Company. He also served as founding

President of the Orange Board of Industries, organized on December 8, 1888. The Board of Industries was the first attempt to form a local Chamber of Commerce. Cauldwell served on the five-member Board of Commissioners which oversaw the election that separated the area from Los Angeles County and created Orange County on June 4, 1889. In late 1890, Cauldwell moved back East, perhaps to Washington D.C. where he had family.

Historic Resources

The homes and buildings included in the proposed Old Towne Historic District are those built prior to 1940 which still retain the majority of their original architectural integrity. The majority of the addresses are residential. Of these, a variety of historic architectural styles are present, but most are from the Craftsman period (1910-25). Those constructed between 1910-15 tend to be fully Craftsman while those built after 1925 are the bungalows which were a derivative of the Craftsman style. These Craftsman period houses are complemented by a strong representation of pre-1900 Victorian era homes which formed the original residential character of Orange. These are typically located on corner lots, but originally served as grove and ranch houses. In addition, a portion of the listings are from the Classical Revival period (1900-10) and are predominantly one story and simple in character. There are also some homes from the Mediterranean Revival period (1922-35) and they are generally located on the fringes of the District. The proposed District is unique among Orange County cities in that 1,237 properties remain intact.

The District has been evaluated and photographed by its four major spoke streets (Chapman Avenue and Glassell Street) which radiate from their intersection at the downtown commercial Plaza Historic District. The spoke streets create four distinct quadrants from which much of the District has been delineated. A description of the four quads, the spoke streets, and the Plaza Historic District follows. The later photo-documentation of typical street settings within the District identified these areas with the letters A - E preceding each photograph number.

The **Northeast Quad** is generally bounded by Chapman Avenue, Glassell Street, Waverly Street and Walnut Avenue. Homes and buildings located along Chapman and Glassell are presented in the later section entitled Spoke Streets.

The southwestern most portion of the quad is part of the original 1871 platt for the City of Orange. The remaining portion of the quad is part of subdivisions that date primarily to after the turn of the century. Subdivisions in this quad include: Library Tract - 1908, Bonnie Brae Tract - 1905, Cole's Sub. - 1901, Davis Cole's Add. - 1904, C.C. Honey's Sub. - 1905, W.H. Clayton's Tract #215 - 1905, Tract 480 - 1923, Marx's Sub. - 1923, Craddick's Sub. - 1906, Welch and Harrod's Resub. - 1908, Welch and Harrod's Add. - 1909, Cottage Home Tract - 1907, Maplewood Tract #202 - 1920, Maplewood Tract #136 - 1920, Henry Grote's Add. - 1887, Angelino Tract - 1887, and Valencia Park Tract - 1906. This quad, along with the others, served as an in-town neighborhood. Only four square blocks of this quad were subdivided in the late 1880's (streets generally bounded by Shaffer Street, Chapman Avenue, Cambridge Street and Maple Avenue). The remaining portion of the quad was subdivided largely after 1905 with much of it not subdivided until 1920. This contrasts greatly with the other quads which were subdivided primarily in the late 1880's. Thus, there are primarily Craftsman era homes with several of those in the Classical Revival period, and a wide array of Craftsman bungalows, which are the most abundant selection in the proposed District.

The **Southwest Quad** is generally bounded by AT&SF railroad, Chapman Avenue, Glassell and La Veta Avenue, and also includes the Pixley/Parker street neighborhood. Homes and buildings located along Chapman Avenue, Glassell Street, and the Plaza Historic District are presented later in this section. The northeastern most portion of the quad is part of the original 1871 platt for the City of Orange. The remaining portion of the quad is part of the subdivisions that date primarily to the boom of the 1880's. Subdivisions in this quad include: Chas. E. Spotts Sub. - 1913, Kordes Tract - 1887, Chubbs Add. - 1886, Beach's Add. - 1885, Palmyra Square - 1896, La Veta Home Tract -1923, McCoys Add. - 1887, Phelps Tract - 1887, and Gardners Add. - 1887. This quad served as an in-town neighborhood. The influence of the railroad produced some of the earliest remaining homes. Similar to the other quads, this one contains large anchor homes which housed the earliest, and usually the most prominent settlers. Some homes from the Classical Revival period and many from the Craftsman period were infilled in the early part of this century after the removal of the large groves. The homes which do remain are primarily good, intact period examples.

The **Northwest Quad** is generally bounded by Chapman Avenue, Glassell Street, Walnut Avenue and the AT&SF rail line. Homes and buildings located along Chapman Avenue, Glassell Street and the Plaza Historic District are presented later in the section. The southeastern most portion of the quad is part of the original 1871 platt for the City of Orange. The remaining portion of the quad is part of subdivisions that date primarily to the boom of the 1880's and just after the turn of the century. Subdivisions in this quad include: Spotts Villa Tract #965 - 1933, Hollister's Sub. - 1906, G. H. Pirie's Home Tract - 1907, Caudwell and Wetherbee Add. - 1887, Richland Farm Lots - 1883, Arthur West Add. - no date, Longfellow Tract - 1887, Davis Tract - 1887, and Halladay Tract - 1886. This is one of four quads which make up the original township of Orange. The majority of contributing homes in this quad are Craftsman bungalows from the period 1915-25. The railroad packing house and industrial buildings of the quad interface with modest houses that were built on the western edge of the District. These houses largely located on Pixley, Cypress and Lemon Streets, are one story wood frame residences that provided homes for workers who were occupied by the industrial facilities and packing houses in the area. Mrs. Carrie Martinez, who lived at 177 North Cypress Street, and Mr. Bernardino Martizes, who lived with his wife Frances at 185 North Cypress Street, were identified in the 1907 Directory as laborers. Mr. and Mrs. M.C. Cuddelback lived at 177 North Cypress. Mr. Cuddelback was listed as a retired builder. Their homes were typical small square box design wood frame residences with a hipped or pyramidal roofs and a projecting front porch. This turn-of-the-century style of residence was replaced by the bungalow style of home. An example of this type of house was the residence at 155 North Lemon Street built in 1920 by Rebecca Gillogy, the widow of a carpenter. The bungalow style house features a large front porch, low pitched roof with projecting eaves. This quad is also home to the 1938 Santa Fe Depot which represents the transition between the Spanish Colonial Revival style and the Moderne style. The exterior of the building, with its arcaded outdoor Waiting Room, plaster walls and red tile roof, represents an architectural idiom that was soon to pass out of favor. The Streamline Moderne details of the entrances and the Waiting Room are indicative of architectural design and development in this industrial age. The 1891 park adjacent to the train station retains a number of trees that were planted by the citizens who originally created the park. The trees represent species that were particularly popular in the late nineteenth century.

The **Southeast Quad** is generally bounded by Chapman Avenue, Glassell Street, La Veta Avenue/Santiago Creek and Waverly Street. Homes and buildings located along Chapman and Glassell are presented in the later section entitled Spoke Streets. The northwestern most portion of the quad is part of the original 1871 platt for the City of Orange. The remaining portion of the quad is part of subdivisions that date primarily to the boom of the 1880's. Subdivisions in this quad include: Shaffer's Add. - 1886, C.Z. Culver Home Tract - 1887, C.Z. Culver Hotel Tract - 1887, Grand Ave. Add. - 1887, George Atchison Sub. - 1905, Harwood's Add. - 1887, Kogler and Geiger's Add. - 1887, Cosart Add. - 1904, A.L.C. Bibbers Resub. - 1906, Palm Place - 1908, Hartwicks Sub. - 1910, Lockwoods Add. - 1886, Craddick's Home Tract - 1906, and the Nutwood Place Sub. - 1906. Historically, this quad, along with the others, served as an in-town neighborhood. The quad also contains the Nutwood Tract subdivision, located south of La Veta Street immediately adjacent to W.O. Hart Park. The Nutwood Tract was subdivided in 1906 as a distinct neighborhood entity known as Nutwood Place. The streets offered the first departure from the regular grid street pattern and are narrower than in the District area to the north. These streets remain in place today and are still oriented toward the Santiago Creek river bed in W.O. Hart Park. This neighborhood was the first to have paved streets, even before street paving in the Plaza. The neighborhood contains a variety of homes which are predominantly larger Craftsman and smaller Bungalow homes from the 1910-25 period. The neighborhood is identified by prominent arroyo stone entry markers which announce "Nutwood Place" on either side of all the entry streets. Similar to the other quads, this one contains large anchor homes which housed the earliest, and usually the most prominent, settlers. Most of the homes are of the Classical Revival and Craftsman styles. This quad represents the most solid concentration of early homes in Orange. Very few newer houses or intrusions exist, particularly in the northern and western most portions of the quad. Nearly one example of every architectural style which evolved in Orange exists in this quad. The vast majority, however, are of the Craftsman and bungalow styles.

The **Spoke Streets** historically served as main arterials to and from downtown Orange to this day. Chapman Avenue and Glassell Street are the only two streets which radiate from the Plaza. The Spoke Streets contain some of the largest homes built in the early years of Orange. Before the days of the modern automobile, it was advantageous to live close to the downtown and, therefore, the lots along Chapman Avenue and Glassell Street were at a premium. Generally, both North and South Glassell Street as well as East Chapman Avenue contain the prominent residences of the City's pioneers and date from the turn of the century to the Craftsman period. Homes that are farther from the downtown, particularly along East Chapman Avenue, are large, affluent Mediterranean Revival homes. Many doctors, contractors, merchants and others of wealth and prominence lived along these Spoke Streets. Several average-sized homes were also constructed amongst the larger ones. In the 1920's new commercial buildings were being erected on Chapman Avenue, west of the Plaza. These one story buildings featured large glass display windows and glazed entrance doors set into a facade veneered with decorative brick and terra cotta. A good example of the 1920's vernacular commercial buildings is the structure at 401 West Chapman Avenue. During this period, Southern California became an active market for the sale of cars in the 1920's. There are two buildings along West Chapman Avenue that were designed expressly to serve this new form of transportation. The new vernacular commercial building at 402 West Chapman Avenue served as the home in 1924 for O.A. Haley Company, which is believed to be the first auto dealership in Orange. The service station at 237 West Chapman Avenue is believed to be the first gas station in Orange. The restrained Streamline Moderne details of the building indicate that it may date from the late 1920's or early 1930's . Additionally, in 1935 the Post Office was erected at 305 West Chapman Avenue. Designed in the Spanish Colonial Revival style, the Post Office introduced a new architectural note to the vocabulary of building types on Chapman Avenue. Most of these early buildings are in well-maintained condition and retain their original architectural integrity. The Plaza Historic District contains fifty-three buildings of which thirty-five are historic and contributing to the significance of the district. The majority of these are brick commercial in style, however a few concrete buildings may also be found. The district centers upon The Plaza, a public square. The Plaza was laid out in 1886 and has been in continuous use since that date. The circular park in the center of The Plaza holds a fountain dating from 1937 and a number of mature trees, some of which date from the park's creation. Brick sidewalks and planters were added to the corners in 1970. The Plaza is the hub from which two streets radiate in four directions. The north-south street is Glassell Street and the east-west street is Chapman Avenue. The buildings within the first block north and south and the first one and one-half blocks east and west of The Plaza include most of the Plaza Historic District. Almost all of the buildings within the Plaza District adjoin one another to form a continuous row of structures. Few breaks appear between buildings giving the District a distinct appearance as a single commercial area. While a few of the District's building facades have been altered over the years in almost all such instances, the rear portions of these buildings have successfully preserved the original brick construction style and appearance. The Plaza District presents its component parts in a holistic manner by not simply focusing on facades or store fronts as measures of the degree of historic integrity. Currently the District maintains its commercial uses primarily within the Plaza area although these have changed in recent years as the agricultural economic base of Orange has been replaced with increased urbanization. A number of antique dealers are located in this area taking advantage of the historic atmosphere. Also, several office professional firms specializing in engineering, architecture and planning have located here. These examples of present District occupants reflect the changes that have affected the district and reinforce the importance of preserving the character and ambiance of small town America on the rapidly evolving Southern California landscape.

Boundary Description

The Old Towne Orange Historic District is located in the City of Orange. The District is located in the original downtown area and incorporates the existing National Register Plaza Historic District. The proposed boundaries follow property lines, streets and a rail line, and are roughly bounded by Walnut Avenue on the north, Atchison, Topeka and Santa Fe (AT&SF) rail right-of-way, and

Clark, Parker and Glassell Streets on the west, La Veta Avenue and Santiago Creek to the south, and Cambridge and Waverly Streets on the east. Precise boundaries are located on the accompanying base map.

Boundary Justification

The boundaries of the proposed Old Towne Orange Historic District delineate the original residential, industrial, and business community of Orange from the late 1880's through 1940. The District incorporates the heart of the historic downtown commercial and business center (circa 1905-20). The proposed boundaries reflect the early downtown subdivisions of Orange which originated from the first building boom of the late 1880's, again occurring just after the turn of the century, and continuing through the 1920's. The District experienced a steady infill of building construction during the 1930's. Much of the area outside the proposed boundary experienced either a loss in architectural integrity or was under citrus cultivation into the 1950's and 60's before subdivision occurred, thus being excluded from District consideration. This is particularly noticeable in the area west of the AT&SF railway where substantial "newer" construction and concentrations of altered, non-contributing structures depart from the continuity and pre 1940's context within the proposed District. Only the South Clark, Parker, Pixley, and West Culver Street neighborhood remains intact as an exception and is included in the proposed District. The remaining boundaries follow a distinct development pattern occurring after 1940, primarily in the 1950's and 60's. The proposed District boundary provides a distinct delineation between the original historic Orange community and the neighborhood sprawl and suburban character of later development periods. The proposed District contains a comprehensive array of 1888 to 1940 residential, industrial, and commercial building types and various architectural styles which make this area almost as eclectic and independent as it was originally. The values enlisted under Criterion A are addressed in the historic quintessence of Orange and the City's founding, the demonstration of early Southern California appearance and lifestyle, and the amiable values of its citizens. The principles of Criterion C are exhibited in the physical Old Towne Historic District contributing buildings which are interdependent in function and location within the overall District and still display a special ambiance associated with their time and place in history.

CHAPTER 4

LISTINGS BY STREET

Streets are listed alphabetically with south and east listed first. Of the four quadrants, the south-east contains a greater number of NRHP listings.

Remember:

Roads labeled *street* run north & south, and roads labeled *avenue* run east & west.

Odd numbered addresses are on the *north & east* sides, and the even numbered addresses are on the *south & west*.

Listings on the National Register Historic Places include:

Orange Union High School	1975
The Plaza Park	1978
Plaza Historic District	1982
C. Z. Culver House	1986
Parker House	1989
St. John's Lutheran	1992
The French Inn	1995
Baptist Church	1996
Old Towne Orange	1997

This is a comprehensive walking tour of some 1,500 structures, 100 trees, many artifacts and contains over 100 photographs taken before 1940. These listings include architecture, heritage, history and Preservation.

Welcome to Old Towne Orange.

Almond Avenue — East

— Almond is named for an agricultural grove tree —

102 E. Almond — *1910c Classic Box*   NONC
Coffey Funeral Home
Originally, the funeral home of C.W. Coffey, this structure has been heavily modified and is now a part of the church building to the west.

Coffey Funeral Home

135 E. Almond — *1920c Craftsman*   NONC
School related to the Baptist Church on Orange, now attached. Note the river rock from Santiago Creek.

215 E. Almond — *1915c Craftsman*   NRHP:1997
A one and one-half story Craftsman house with single side-facing gable roof and contrasting front facing gable dormer. Main roof extends forward to form full-width porch supported by brick piers connected by a brick porch wall.

218 E. Almond — *1929c Bungalow*   NRHP:1997
Single-story and single-gable bungalow with main roof being comprised of a side-facing gable. A contrasting front-facing gable forms entry porch overhang supported by Colonial-like columns.

230 E. Almond — *1920c Bungalow*   NRHP:1997
Single-story clapboard bungalow with L-plan and tri-gable roof. Main entry is at center front slightly

recessed beneath main facade of house.

414 E. Almond — *1909 Hip Roof Cottage* NRHP:1997
Single-story house with steep-pitched hip roof and clapboard siding. Small hipped dormer is on front portion of roof; a smaller hip extension of main roof, forms entry porch overhang supported by characteristic Classical columns.

422 E. Almond — *1905 Hip Roof Cottage* NRHP:1997
This single-story house has both Classical Revival and Craftsman bungalow influences. The house is single-story has clapboard siding and a hip roof. It is built on a box plan. An unusual feature for the period is a smaller gable projection pedimented and embellished with fish scale singles. Below the porch supports are treated in the Craftsman manner.

430 E. Almond — *1910c Stone Bungalow* NRHP:1997
Anna McNeil although not the original resident sold this house to John Stinson a shoemaker. Heavily remodeled the next year in 1931, Stinson created a most unusual home.

What makes this bungalow home unusual is the stone facing used throughout. The format of the house incorporates classic bungalow formatting built on a rectangular plan with double front-facing gable. The stone facing makes it a one-of-a-kind house in Orange.

501 E. Almond — *1929 Mediterranean Revival* NRHP:1997
St. John's Lutheran School
This is a one-story school building in the Mediterranean Revival style. The building features a symmetrical design which includes a central entry flanked by windows and a projecting corner wing on either side. The building is constructed in brick and has an adobe tiled roof. The main entry includes an arched parapet and an inner entry arch. This same arch is repeated again in the transom above the double door entrance. Terra cotta molding outlines both the inner and outer arch. Six sash windows with six-over-

six panes are located·on either side of the entrance; each of these windows has a reliever arch with a fanlight transom. The projecting corner walls are embellished with corner quoins and a diamond arrangement of contrasting brick. The building is in excellent condition and maintains its original architectural integrity.

506 E. Almond — *1905c Hip Roof Cottage*   NRHP:1997

TREE: Italian Stone Pine *Pinus pinea*. This tree is 105 feet high and has a spread of over 95 feet.
Box plan house with steep-pitched hip roof and circular wrap-around porch. The circular porch is complemented by a pedimented gable face adjacent which features a large transomed picture window. Classical columns support the porch overhang.

514 E. Almond — *1922 Bungalow*   NRHP:1997
Small single-story bungalow with single shallow-pitched side-facing gable roof and smaller front-facing gable attic dormer. Main entry is via a former porch recessed beneath main portion of house; this porch is supported by an elephantine pier articulated by ornamental bricks at the base.

515 E. Almond — *1929 Mediterranean Revival*   NONC

524 E. Almond — *1904 Hip Roof Cottage*   NRHP:1997
Single-story house built on a box plan with clapboard siding and a steep-pitched hip roof. A smaller front-facing gable is above the corner porch and serves as an attic dormer. Main entry is beneath the recessed corner porch supported by wood posts.

530 E. Almond — *1914 Craftsman Bungalow*   NRHP:1997
A single-story bungalow with single front-facing gable roof. The house has clapboard siding at the base but the upper portion of the gable face is sheathed in shingles. A full-width porch is recessed below the main portion of the house. This porch overhang is supported by characteristic elephantine piers with arroyo stone bases.

535 E. Almond — *1923 Craftsman Bungalow*   NRHP:1997
Single-story clapboard bungalow with shallow-pitched double front-facing gables. Forwardmost gable forms entry porch overhang supported by tapered piers.

540 E. Almond — *1908 Hip Roof Cottage*   NRHP:1997
A single-story box plan house with pyramidal roof and clapboard siding. Corner porch is recessed beneath main portion of the house and is supported by characteristic classical column.

601 E. Almond — *1913 Craftsman Bungalow*   NRHP:1997
Single-story clapboard bungalow with double front-facing gable roof. Forwardmost gable forms entry porch overhang supported by tapered piers.

604 E. Almond — *1909*   NONC

607 E. Almond — *1913 Craftsman Bungalow*   NRHP:1997
Single-story clapboard bungalow with double front-facing gable roof. Forwardmost gable forms entry porch overhang supported by wide piers. Added embellishment is provided by ornamental purlins beneath the eaves and by dentils along the frontmost gable face.

612 E. Almond — *1909 Hip Roof Cottage*   NRHP:1997
Single-story box plan house with clapboard siding and pyramidal roof. No porch is present. Entry is at center flanked by a large double-hung window on either side.

615 E. Almond — *1913 Craftsman Bungalow*   NRHP:1997
Single-story clapboard bungalow with double front-facing gables. Smaller forwardmost gable forms entry porch overhang supported by wide piers. Vertical slatting and purlins at the eaves ornament the house.

618 E. Almond — *1905 Hip Roof Cottage*   NRHP:1997
A single-story box plan house with clapboard siding and steep-pitched hip roof. Small hipped dormer is located on front portion of roof. Entry is via a corner recessed porch supported by Classical columns.

624 E. Almond — *1914 Bungalow*   NRHP:1997
Single-story clapboard bungalow with double front-facing gable roof. Frontmost gable forms entry porch overhang supported by wide piers. Ornamental purlins grace the eaves. The front facade is adorned by a large 3-part picture window.

638 E. Almond — *1909 Hip Roof Cottage* NRHP:1997
TREE: Australian Tea *Leptospermum laevigatum*. The tree is 35 feet high.
A single-story clapboard house with box plan and steep-pitched hip and gable roof. The house sits on a corner lot and a large corner wrap-around porch defines the entry; main door is also on the corner. The porch roof is supported by ornate turned columns with jigsawn brackets at the top. Two gabled dormers have ornamental shingles and vented transoms.

708 E. Almond — *1904 Victorian*   OTPA
BLDR: Edwin Honey
TREE: Incense Cedar *Libocedrus decurrens*,
Lodgepole Pine *Pinus murrayana*
Italian Stone Pine *Pinus pinea*
Edwin & Clarissa Honey, *(Rhymes with pony)* were pioneers of early Orange and each came here during the 1870s. Honey owned the Orange Water Company in town. The large Stonepine Tree planted by him, came from the High Sierra Nevada mountains in his horse's saddlebags. It is 95 feet high.

A Modified Queen Ann style Victorian with inset gable and heavy overlaying porch with columns. The house itself is more of a transitional style showing elements of later designs.

— *Outside Old Towne* —

1010 E. Almond — *1937 Transitional Revival* NRHP:1997
A single story clapboard L-plan house with double front facing gabled roof and a single side gable. A portion of the forward most front gable forms a small

porch. The porch pier is formed by a concrete base and a classical wood post on top. The backward front gable is adorned with shingles. An ornamented brick chimney is present.

1012 E. Almond — *1905 Victorian*   NRHP:1997

A one and one-half story clapboard rectangular plan house. A steep front and back facing gable forms the main portion of the roof. Two side facing dormers are accented with shingles as is the front facing gable. A large open porch running the full length of the house is placed on the side of the house. It is supported by simple wooded 4x4's. A small front porch is placed over the entry door and a window. The porch is supported by purlins. Both porches have a roof similar to a hipped roof. The eaves articulated with ornamental rafter tails.

1014 E. Almond — *1905 Victorian*   NRHP:1997

A single story box plan house with wide lap siding and a steep-pitched hipped roof. A small hipped dormer is present on the front facade. A small concrete unroofed porch forms the entry to the house. The entry door is accented by two narrow windows. The wide eaves are embellished with ornamental rafter tails.

ALMOND AVENUE — WEST

206 W. Almond — *1902 Classic Box*   NRHP:1997
This eclectic home combines features from both the Classical Revival style and the Craftsman style. Boxy formatting hip roof and dormers and rotund columns suggest Classical Revival. Arroyo stone columns on corner porch and brick on first story suggest Craftsman influences. Also notable is a large recessed corner porch and arched windows on front and side facades.

229 W. Almond — *1910c Rock Bungalow*   NRHP:1997
This rectangular plan house has a single-gable roof. Most notable is the arroyo stone on the first floor below the roof line. A corner recessed porch is supported by a large stone pier. Ornamental bargeboard is on front-facing gable.

237 W. Almond — *1915c Craftsman Bungalow* NRHP:1997
Built with a rectangular plan this house has a double front-facing gable. The front porch is supported by wide elephantine piers common to Craftsman styling. Beneath the eaves are ornamental purlins. An ornamental transomed window is in the frontmost gable and a large transomed picture window is near the entry.

305 W. Almond — *1923 Vernacular*   NRHP:1997
This is a small single-story clapboard church with a single gable roof. The corner entry is articulated by a rectilinear entry tower with a pyramidal roof. Casement windows around the building are arranged in pairs and each is crowned with a large stained glass transom. These arched windows are repeated in the entry tower. Triangular bracket supports are located beneath the eaves on the front gable face. The church was built adjacent to a small Classical Revival style house which still forms part of the church. These two are connected in such a way that together they appear as one building. The church shows slight Crafts-

man influence but is more a vernacular adaptation incorporating structural and economic pragmatics. The arched windows and entry tower are characteristic of small rural churches. The building is well-maintained and exhibits its original architectural integrity.

426 W. Almond — *1924 Mediterranean Revival* NRHP:1997
ORANGE PACKING HOUSE
A large rectangular plan industrial building located adjacent to the railroad tracks incorporates brick on the sides and a front facade with Mission influences. A characteristic Mission-like parapet is at the front entry. Below fenestration incorporates recessed rectangular windows of which centermost windows have recessed arches.

609 W. Almond — *1915c Bungalow*   NONC

721 W. Almond — *1920c Bungalow*   NONC

727 W. Almond — *1923 Bungalow*   NONC

737 W. Almond — *1904 Cottage Hip Roof* NONC

801 W. Almond — *1923 Mediterranean Revival*   NONC

821 W. Almond — *1924 Bungalow*   NONC

990 W. Almond @ Cambridge

SAVI: relocated into Pitcher Park from the corner.

ATCHISON STREET — NORTH
—Atchison is named for the Atchison, Topeka & Santa Fe—

Buried foundation of 1887 Depot.
On August 16, 1887, the Santa Fe Railroad Company extended their tracks south to the community of Orange, establishing a station. The depot and freight terminal were built the following year, enlarged in 1907 and replaced in 1938. Recently during renovation, the foundation of the original Depot was discovered, buried in the north end of the Depot Park.

100 N. Atchison — *1888 Parkland*   NONC
TREE: *all from 1891:*
Two Date Palms *Phoenix dactylifera* 55 feet high.
Three California Fan Palms *Washingtonia filifera*
Four Camphor *Cinnamomum camphora* 50 feet high.
The Depot Park is the second oldest parkland in Orange County and recently received a State Beautification Award.

109 N. Atchison — *1924c Mission Influenced*   NONC
This small interesting building has many tales of what it once was: from a mail-sorting house to a restaurant.

186 N. Atchison — *1938 Mediterranean Revival* NRHP:1997
Santa Fe Depot
The second Depot on this site, the new depot, dedicated on May 2, 1938, closed in 1971 and reopened as a restaurant in 1997. Although classed as a Mediterranean Revival, the building contains elements of Moderne architecture. Note the "Orange" sign at the north end is new. *The Metrolink stops here.*

This is a Mediterranean Revival style train depot, recently restored. The depot is built on a rectangular plan with three distinct wings and a loading dock. Each of the wings is in varying elevations and includes a gabled roof facing in contrasting directions. The roof is sided in adobe tiles while the facades are in stucco. The main entry features a curved canopy with mullioned transoms above.

BATAVIA STREET — SOUTH
—Batavia is named for pioneer W.M. Scott's hometown in NY—

131 S. Batavia — *1927 Craftsman Bungalow* NONC

134 S. Batavia — *1938 Craftsman* NONC

Eva Purdue and Walter Whiteman built this house as a rental, in a style that came from the previous decade.

A very late Craftsman with high side-gables and full-length porch. Wide piers support the roofline and ornamental purlins are seen in the gabled dormer. Note the transom windows.

158 S. Batavia — *Bungalow* NONC

164 S. Batavia — *Prairie* NONC

165 S. Batavia — *1924 Bungalow* NONC

173 S. Batavia — *1924 Bungalow* NONC

176 S. Batavia — *Craftsman* NONC

204 S. Batavia — *1905c Craftsman* NONC

Frank Miles, although not the first owner, bought this home in 1923. A former grocer, he began ranching before settling here. Edwin & Alma Gould paid him $5,500 for the home in 1937. Edwin managed the Anaconda Wire & Cable Co.; their son Dick went on to own Orange Camera in the Plaza District.

A large Classical Revival Box with Craftsman influence and multiple gables with wrap-around porch. A full bay front window adds style to the massive front while the upstairs front balcony gives it graceful lines. A side smaller balcony also gives interest. The carriage house in the rear with copula is the only remaining such structure in Orange.

SAVI: weir-box, located on the corner.

224 S. Batavia — *1919 Craftsman* NONC

John & Gail Young purchased four acres in 1918 and built this home. Ranching for only about 10 years they sold to John Collins by 1929. Collins stayed until his death in 1950.

A classic Craftsman with flared roofline and extended

window lintels. Curved porch piers and wide front windows with an offset roofline. A single-room second story complements the style.

286 S. Batavia —
TREE: Date Palm *Phoenix dactylifera* Oldest in Orange. Norfolk Island Pine *Araucaria heterophylla*

371 S. Batavia — *1904 Craftsman Bungalow* NONC

409 S. Batavia — *1890 Spanish Colonial Revival* NRHP:1995
The French Inn
Although constructed in 1890 as an *Italiante Victorian,* a full remodel came in 1917 when then owner John Porter and wife Carolyn changed the look to suit their entertaining lifestyle. After their deaths, David French and his wife Virginia Flippen purchased and moved in during 1937 as newlyweds. He was a Judge; she from an Orange pioneer family.

A two story framed building with a pergola on the north side, large overhang front porch and red clay tiles, stained glass windows and transom.

411 S. Batavia — *1920c Craftsman* NONC

480 S. Batavia — *1920s Mission Revival* NONC
Sister's of St. Joseph; Sanctuary, Hospital
Invited to Orange County in 1922 by then Archbishop Cantwell, the *Order of the Sisters of Saint Joseph* purchased the Burnham estate on Batavia St. and began construction of the Sanctuary and hospital. The hospital opened September 18, 1929 facing Main St.

St. Joseph's Hospital

Batavia Street — North

193 N. Batavia — *1915c Bungalow*   NONC

201 N. Batavia — *Edison Building*   NONC

250 N. Batavia — *Victorian Farm House*   NONC

273 N. Batavia — *1910c Craftsman*   NONC

290 N. Batavia — *Craftsman*   NONC

295 N. Batavia — *1919 Bungalow*   NONC

457 N. Batavia — *1920c Spanish Colonial Revival*   NONC

458 N. Batavia — *1900c Victorian Farm House*   NONC
This house can be seen *behind 456 N. Batavia*. Originally addressed to this street, the rear of the house faces Citrus St. The Parker family built this house where the eight acre grove is now committed to houses – including the one in front on Batavia. This portion of Sycamore was once known as Parker Ave. and their SAVI weir-box is located one block west. The ghost of widow Parker is supposedly still seen in the upper floors of this farm dwelling.

—Outside of Old Towne—

N. Batavia to W. Sycamore @ N. Lime
SAVI: weir-box, located in the block of Sycamore

CAMBRIDGE STREET — SOUTH
—Cambridge is named for Cambridge Massachusetts—

128 S. Cambridge — *1914 Craftsman*   NRHP:1997
Large single-story Craftsman home with clapboard siding and single side-facing gabled roof. Main roof extends forward to form a full-width porch overhang supported by classic Craftsman piers. Slatted balustrade connects these piers; large transomed picture windows adorn the front facade. A small shed dormer acts as an attic vent.

135 S. Cambridge — *1926 Mission Revival*   OTPA:1997
OWNER: Daniel Stevens
Almost always a neighborhood market; the facility now is a coffee and art shop. Several owners operated the store while living in the back portion of the house. When built, this structure marked the edge of town.

A single-story Mission Revival with central curvilinear parapet. Building is built on box plan with clapboard siding and flat roof. The facade results in an ornamental parapet across the front. Typical wood frame double doors provide the main entry.

138 S. Cambridge — *1912 Hip Roof Cottage* NRHP:1997
Single-story house with hip roof box plan and now covered by asbestos siding. A contrasting front-facing gable acts as an attic vent. Entry is via a corner recessed porch supported by wide piers.

143 S. Cambridge — *1887 Altered Victorian*   OTPA:NONC
Torrey House
Moved from the corner of Chapman in the 1920s and was batton board plastered with concrete. The front facade of this house has been modified over the years to reflect a Provincial Revival style. However the proportions in terms of height steep-pitched gable roof and the L-plan reflect the original Victorian quality. The house is now embellished with half timbering and an ornamental stone entry distinguished by an arched opening.

144 S. Cambridge — *1920 Craftsman Bungalow*   NRHP:1997
Single-story bungalow with shallow-pitched, double front-facing gables. Forwardmost gable forms, entry porch overhang supported by wide piers. Entry is beneath at center; main door is flanked by sidelights.

152 S. Cambridge — *1910 Hip Roof Cottage*   NRHP:1997
Single-story box plan house with clapboard siding and steep-pitched, hip roof. A small hipped dormer projects from the front portion of the roof. Entry is via a corner recessed porch supported by Craftsmanesque wood posts.

153 S. Cambridge — *1890c Victorian*   NRHP:1997
A large two-story Victorian house with steep-pitched multi-gable roof and shiplap siding. The house is built on a slight L-plan, with a small but ornately embellished entry porch in the apex of the ell. Each of the upper gable faces features fishscale and arched cross-ties. A multitude of shrubbery all but conceals the house.

156 S. Cambridge — *1912 Craftsman*   NRHP:1997
One and one-half story Craftsman home with rectangular plan and single side-facing gable roof. The house is sided in clapboard. Main roof extends forward to form full-width porch; overhang supported by tapered piers. A front-facing Siamese gabled dormer is located on the front portion of the roof; ornamental purlins and an ornamentally framed vent articulate this dormer.

159 S. Cambridge — *1890 Victorian Cottage*   NRHP:1997
Small single-story cottage with steep-pitched hip roof and unusual steep-pitched gable extension of roof, which forms entry porch overhang. The house incorporates a variety of influences, indicating there have been some changes over the years. The small porch overhang supported by Classical Revival piers indicates Classical Revival influences while the large picture windows, to either side, indicate Craftsman

influences. Most notable Victorian features are the original main door embellished transom in the front-facing gable and the ornamental brackets beneath the eaves.

167 S. Cambridge — *1895c Victorian*   NRHP:1997

A single-story Victorian cottage with multi-gable roof and shiplap siding. The house is characteristically Victorian particularly in the ornamental fretwork used in the brackets of the eaves and the posts on the porch overhang. Windows are framed in the classic Victorian manner.

168 S. Cambridge — *1912 Bungalow*   NRHP:1997

Single-story bungalow with clapboard siding and side-facing gable roof. A front-facing gable extends forward in the center of the front facade to form the entry porch overhang. It is supported by characteristic piers while the main entry is beneath with large windows on either side. Ornamental purlins grace the eaves throughout. The structure with low-pitched single-gabled roof and exposed rafters and beams. Porch spans the entire length of front facade and features elephantine posts and arroyo stone bases. Siding is wood shiplap with double-hung wood windows. A front shed dormer provides for attic venting and an interior brick chimney is present.

186 S. Cambridge — *1910 Hip Roof Cottage*   NRHP:1997

A hip roof cottage on a square plan with distinctive four-sloped flared hip roof with vented dormers. Molded rakeboard double-hung windows and wood clapboard siding is present. Enclosed front porch may have been open when originally constructed.

191 S. Cambridge — *1915c Craftsman*   NRHP:1997

One and one-half story Craftsman home built on a rectangular plan with clapboard siding and single side-facing gable roof. A large front-facing gabled dormer incorporates four double-hung windows and cross-ties across the front bargeboard. The main roof extends forward to form a full-width porch supported by characteristic tapered piers. Large picture windows flank the main entry at center.

203 S. Cambridge — *1923 Bungalow*   NRHP:1997
A characteristic single-story bungalow built on a rectangular plan with clapboard siding and tri-gable roof. Main house is covered by a side-facing gable roof; the front-facing gable extends forward to form the entry porch over hang, supported by Colonial-like columns. Entry is beneath at center.

204 S. Cambridge — *1909 Bungalow*   NRHP:1997
A single-story bungalow built on a rectangular plan with single side-facing gable roof. A large full-width front-facing gable originally formed entry porch but has since been enclosed giving the house a modified appearance.

218 S. Cambridge — *1925c Provincial Revival*   NRHP:1997
This single-story stucco house built on an L-plan with steep-pitched gable roof shows attempts at incorporating Provincial Revival influences. Gable roof follows the L-plan of the house with a large front-facing gable and a smaller front-facing gable which forms the entry portico.

226 S. Cambridge — *1935 Provincial Revival*   NRHP:1997
A provincial revival bungalow-type residence on a rectangular plan with gabled roof, exposed rafter tails and ridge beam extensions. Large bay window flanked by four pane lindel-type sidelights are present. Windows are wooden and siding is stucco. An arched entry portal and exterior stucco chimney are present.

231 S. Cambridge — *1919 Bungalow*   NRHP:1997
A single-story bungalow with shallow-pitched multi-gable roof and ornamental clapboard siding. Main roof is comprised of a single side-facing gable. A full-width front-facing gable forms the front facade in part and also a recessed entry porch overhang. House has been

altered through the use of brick on the front facade.

236 S. Cambridge — *1926 Provincial Revival*   NRHP:1997
A provincial revival residence on a box plan with two front facing steep pitched gables with single-paned picture window flanked by six-paned lintel-type window openings. Entry is centered between gables. Roof consists of simulated thatch with exterior brick chimney.

247 S. Cambridge — *1919 Craftsman Bungalow*   NRHP:1997
A single-story clapboard bungalow with shallow-pitched double front-facing gables. The forwardmost gable forms entry porch overhang supported by piers. Wide vertical slats adorn the upper face of each gable and are complemented by the ornamental clapboard siding.

276 S. Cambridge — *1913*   NONC

460 S. Cambridge — *1921 California Bungalow*   NONC

CAMBRIDGE STREET — NORTH

125 N. Cambridge — *1922 Bungalow*   NRHP:1997
A single-story bungalow with tri-gable roof and wide lap siding. Main portion of the house is covered by a single side-facing gable roof while a centrally located front-facing gable extends the full width of the front facade and forms an entry porch overhang. This is supported by wide tapered piers and the upper gable face is embellished with vertical slatting.

133 N. Cambridge — *1923 Mediterranean Revival*   NRHP:1997
A single-story modified box plan house with stucco siding and flat roof. The central portion of the front facade is distinguished by a projecting entry porch overhang with large arched openings and a tile hood. A large arched picture window adorns the remaining portion of the front facade. A porte cochere is to the side and is supported by round columns.

141 N. Cambridge — *1923 Bungalow*   NRHP:1997
A single-story clapboard bungalow with tri-gable roof. Main portion of the house is covered by a single gable roof with side-facing gables while a front-facing gable extends forward on the front facade to form the entry porch overhang. This is supported by wide piers connected by a low concrete porch wall. Ornamental bargeboards and rafter tails embellish the eaves.

142 N. Cambridge — *1923 Bungalow*   NRHP:1997
A single-story clapboard bungalow with a rectangular plan and multi-gable roof. The roofline takes on unusual proportions with the way the main side-facing gable extends forward to form a 3/4-width porch overhang. This is supported by piers comprised of brick bases and wood posts on top.

149 N. Cambridge — *1923 Bungalow*   NRHP:1997
A single-story tri-gable bungalow with wide lap siding on the facades. The main portion of the house is covered by a single-gable roof with side-facing gables. A large wide front-facing gable forms an entry porch

overhang. This is supported by piers with brick bases and wood posts on top. Vertical slatting adorns the upper gable face. The main door is beneath the porch and is flanked on either side by multi-pane side vents.

150 N. Cambridge — *1924 Bungalow*   NRHP:1997
A single-story clapboard bungalow with tri-gable roof. Main portion of the house is covered by a single gable roof with side-facing gables while a front-facing gable extends forward on the front facade to form the entry porch overhang. This is supported by wide piers connected by a low concrete porch wall. Ornamental bargeboards and rafter tails embellish the eaves.

157 N. Cambridge — *1923 Bungalow*   NRHP:1997
A single-story bungalow with single front-facing gable roof. The original siding on the house which was probably clapboard has since been covered over with stucco. The front entry is beneath the gable overhang and there is now a recessed arch entry to the main door.

166 N. Cambridge — *1923 Bungalow*   NRHP:1997
A single-story bungalow with wide lap siding and multi-gable roof. The front facade is distinguished by three front-facing gables. The forwardmost gable forms the entry porch overhang and is supported by piers of cast concrete. A cast concrete chimney is present on the rearmost portion of the house.

167 N. Cambridge — *1923 Bungalow*   NRHP:1997
A single-story bungalow with shallow-pitch multi-gable roof. The front facade is distinguished by a full-width recessed porch supported by piers with brick bases and wood posts on top. There is a connecting brick porch wall with half-size piers at the center near the entry stoop. Original clapboard siding is now covered by asbestos shingles.

174 N. Cambridge — *1923 Bungalow*   NRHP:1997
A single-story bungalow with shallow-pitch multi-gable roof. The main portion of the house is covered

by a single-gable roof with side-facing gables while nearly the full width of the front facade is articulated by a front-facing gable that extends forward to form the porch overhang. This is supported by piers with brick bases and wood posts on top. The original clapboard siding has since been covered by asbestos shingles.

175 N. Cambridge — *1936*   NONC

182 N. Cambridge — *1933 Provincial Revival*   NRHP:1997
A single-story stucco house with steep-pitch multi-gable roof. The house is built in the English Revival tradition with Tudor Revival influences present in the use of half-timbering on the front facade. The house is built on an L-plan with the main entry being in the apex of the ell.

183 N. Cambridge — *1923 Bungalow*   NRHP:1997
A single-story bungalow with shallow-pitch multi-gable roof and clapboard siding on the facades. The front of the house is articulated by two front-facing gables the forwardmost of which forms the entry porch overhang. This is supported by wide piers with cast concrete bases and wood posts on top. Board and batten and vertical slatting adorn the upper gable face.

192 N. Cambridge — *1939*   NONC

202 N. Cambridge — *1895 Victorian Cottage*   NRHP:1997
A single-story house with clapboard siding and steep-pitch multi-gable roof. The roofline takes on an L-plan with the frontmost leg of the ell forming a large entry porch overhang. This is supported by wood posts with classical treatment on the capitals. Ornamental turned balusters form the balustrade which connects the six porch posts. The large front-facing gable features both square butt and fish scale shingles. A high ornamental brick chimney emanates from the center of the roof.

215 N. Cambridge — *1923 Bungalow*   NRHP:1997

A single-story bungalow with ornamental lap siding and multi-gable roof. The main portion of the house is covered by a single side-facing gable roof which extends forward across three-quarters of the front facade to form the entry porch overhang. At this point the roof is supported by piers with brick bases and wood posts on top. The piers are connected by a low brick wall. There is a smaller front-facing gable which intersects the porch overhang.

222 N. Cambridge — *1925 Mediterranean Revival* NRHP:1997
A single-story bungalow with flat roof and stucco siding on the facades. The house features the typical array of pseudo-Mediterranean embellishment including use of adobe tiles along the roof edge and on the porch entry as a hood. The front facade is divided into two wings, one which extends forward of the other. The center portion of this wing has an arched entry portico. Either side of the front facade extends forward in an ornamental fashion.

231 N. Cambridge — *1923 Bungalow* NRHP:1997
A one story house with shiplap siding and low-pitched roof with two front vented gables. One-half of the original full width front porch has been enclosed, sealing off half of the front window area. The remaining porch is supported by tapered wood piers on brick bases with wood-slatted balustrade.

232 N. Cambridge — *1922 Bungalow* NRHP:1997
A single-story bungalow with ornamental lap siding and multi-gable roof. Three-quarters of the front facade is comprised of a recessed porch which is supported by tapered piers. Two smaller front-facing gables are also present on the front facade and each acts as an attic dormer.

241 N. Cambridge — *1923 Mediterranean Revival* NRHP:1997
A single-story house with stucco siding and flat roof. The house is comprised of an irregular plan with various planes jutting forward of one another. The

centermost portion of the front facade is distinguished by a tile hood and the main entry below is enclosed within an ornamental framing. Double-hung windows span all facades and the upper sashes are mullioned.

251 N. Cambridge — *1922 Bungalow*　　NRHP:1997
A single-story clapboard bungalow with multi-gable roofline comprised of a juxtaposition between a side-facing gable and a front-facing gable. The side-facing gable extends forward to form an entry porch overhang and is supported by piers with brick bases and round columns on top. The front door is the original mullioned door.

252 N. Cambridge — *1921 California Bungalow*　NRHP:1997
A single-story clapboard bungalow with multi-gable roof with side-facing gables. The centermost portion of the front facade is distinguished by a small gable entry portico supported by Colonial columns. A large 3-part window flanks either side of the main entry which is comprised of the original door.

261 N. Cambridge — *1924 Bungalow*　　NRHP:1997
A single-story tri-gable bungalow with clapboard siding on the facades. The main portion of the house is covered by a single-gable roof with side-facing gables while the front facade is distinguished by a wide front-facing gable porch overhang. This is supported by piers that incorporate ornamental brick on the bases and wood posts on top.

262 N. Cambridge — *1921 California Bungalow*　NRHP:1997
A single-story clapboard bungalow with roofline comprised of clipped gables. The main portion of the house is covered by a single gable-roof with side-facing clipped gables. To the side a small bay projection is defined also with a small clipped gable. The entry portico features a clipped gable as well and beneath it the main door is flanked on either side by fluted pilasters. The brick facing on the lower half of the front facade is a later addition.

271 N. Cambridge — *1924 Bungalow*   NRHP:1997
A single-story clapboard bungalow with double front-facing gable roof. The forwardmost gable forms the entry porch overhang and is supported by piers. To the side of the porch gable is a pergola which is also supported by an identical pier. Entry is at center and flanked on either side by a large picture window with mullioned transom.

272 N. Cambridge — *1921 Bungalow*   NRHP:1997
Rectangular plan with central door and no porch. Wide shed dormer.

281 N. Cambridge — *1923 Bungalow*   NRHP:1997
A single-story bungalow with single front-facing gable roof. What was probably original clapboard siding has since been covered with asbestos shingles. The front half of the facade is defined by a recessed corner porch which is supported by a pier comprised of a brick base and wood posts on top. There is a double door entry.

282 N. Cambridge — *1923 Bungalow*   NRHP:1997
A single-story clapboard bungalow with shallow-pitch multi-gable roofline. A large recessed corner porch which wraps around from the front to the side of the house is supported by piers composed of brick bases and wood posts on top. The house is otherwise simple and unadorned.

291 N. Cambridge — *1923 Bungalow*   NRHP:1997
A single-story clapboard bungalow with double front-facing gable roof. The forwardmost gable forms the entry porch overhang and is supported by piers with brick bases and wood posts on top.

292 N. Cambridge — *1923 Bungalow*   NRHP:1997
A single-story clapboard bungalow with shallow-pitch multi-gable roofline. The front facade is distinguished by a centrally located front-facing gable which is intersected by the main roofline. The house is built on a modified L-plan with the main entry in the apex

of the ell. There is also a simple pergola present sheltering the entry.

303 N. Cambridge — *1923 Bungalow*   NRHP:1997
A single-story clapboard house with double front-facing gable roof. The forwardmost gable forms the entry porch overhang and is supported by tapered piers with brick bases and wood posts on top.

311 N. Cambridge — *1923 Bungalow*   NRHP:1997
A single-story tri-gable bungalow with wide lap siding on the facades. The main portion of the house is covered by a single-gable roof with side-facing gables while a front-facing gable extends forward to form the entry porch overhang. This is supported by tapered piers and ornamental brick bases.

317 N. Cambridge — *1922 Bungalow*   NRHP:1997
A single-story clapboard bungalow with multi-gable roof. The center front of the house is articulated by a front-facing gable and is supported by piers with concrete bases and wood posts on top. A large arch connects these piers.

320 N. Cambridge — *1919*   NONC

325 N. Cambridge — *1937 Bungalow*   NRHP:1997
A single-story clapboard bungalow with double front-facing gable roof. The front entry is comprised of a porch recessed beneath the main facade of the two front-facing gables. A portion of the forwardmost and the pergola to the side are supported by tapered piers. Cross-ties are present in the upper gable faces.

332 N. Cambridge — *1922 Bungalow*   NRHP:1997
A single-story clapboard bungalow with double front-facing gable roof. Entry is on the center side of the frontmost gable and above it, a pergola forms an entry porch overhang.

339 N. Cambridge — *1905c Hip Roof Cottage*   NRHP:1997
A single-story house with box plan clapboard siding and steep-pitch hip roof. A small hip dormer is present

on the front portion of the roof. One-half of the front facade is defined by a recessed porch which is supported by classical columns. The original wood door is still present and on either side of the front facade there is a large picture window with mullioned transom.

340 N. Cambridge — *1917 Bungalow*   NONC
A single-story bungalow with wide lap siding and single front-facing gable roof. A smaller front-facing gable overhang forms the entry porch and is supported by wood posts. The brick work on the foundation is probably a later addition.

348 N. Cambridge — *1929 Bungalow*   NRHP:1997
A single-story clapboard bungalow with clapboard siding and double front-facing gable roof. The forwardmost gable forms the entry porch overhang and is supported by piers comprised of brick bases and tapered wood posts on top. Vertical lattice work adorns the porch gable.

349 N. Cambridge — *1901 Hip Roof Cottage*   NRHP:1997
A single-story box plan house with clapboard siding and steep pitch hip roof. A small hip dormer is present on the front portion of the roof. A small entry overhang acts as an entry porch and is now supported by wood posts. There probably has been some change in this structure.

356 N. Cambridge — *1913 Bungalow*   NRHP:1997
A single-story bungalow built on a modified L-plan with steep-pitch multi-gable roof. There is no porch present. Entry is located beneath the eaves of the main roof.

374 N. Cambridge — *1910 Hip Roof Cottage*   NRHP:1997
A single-story box plan house with steep-pitch hip roof and smaller hip dormer on the front portion of the roof. What was originally probably clapboard siding has since been covered with asbestos shingles. One-half of the front facade is defined by a recessed corner

porch supported by wood posts.

390 N. Cambridge — *1910c Transitional*   NRHP:1997

A two-story house built on an L-plan with steep-pitch multi-gable roof. The short leg of the ell forms a front-facing gable which results in an angled bay window on the first story. A smaller front-facing gable on the other half of the front facade forms the entry porch overhang. It is now supported by wrought iron posts which are a replacement for the original. Triangular bracket supports grace the eaves throughout.

—Outside Old Towne—

770 N. Cambridge —

TREE: Carrot Wood Tree *Cupania anacardioides*. Largest of this type in Orange.

890 N. Cambridge —

TREE: Crape Myrtle *Lagerstroemia indica*. Multiple trunk tree has a 15 foot spread.

The St. John's Lutheran Manse

CENTER STREET — SOUTH
—Center Street is named for the Civic Center—

121 S. Center — *1925 Spanish Colonial Revival* NRHP:1997
Women's Club
This one-story building has accommodated the Women's Club since it was built in 1925.

Built on a rectangular plan with gable roof in the rear and stucco facades the building features a modified Mission Revival entry portico; this includes an ornately arched opening below. Tile hoods are on either side of the entry parapet. Four mullioned glass doors form the entrance.

The Women's Club

141 S. Center — *1920 Craftsman Bungalow*

171 S. Center — *1921 Prairie Influenced* NRHP:1992
St. John's Lutheran Parsonage
BLDR: Orange Contracting & Milling Co.
This is the St. John's Lutheran Church Manse and has been added to the National Register along with the church building and Walker Hall in 1992.

A two story box plan with dual and wide windows; a large walk-over porch supported by large square columns. The porch railing matches the split-level roof decoration; the second level has an archway opening.

185 S. Center — *1914 Gothic Revival*   NRHP:1992
St. John's Lutheran Church
ARCT: C.B. Bradshaw
BLDR: Orange Contracting & Milling Co.
St. John's Lutheran Church is a large brick structure
fashioned in a Gothic tradition. The building is
distinguished by a large corner steeple and a second
smaller one on the opposite front corner. A gable
connects the two steeples. Each steeple is a rectilinear
formation topped with battlements, a high tent roof
and a cross. The larger steeple contains a large pointed
arch vent with a clock face. The main entry is
composed of a three-part compound pointed arched
portal with moulded archivolts and ornamental
capitals on the pilasters. The upper portion of these
and other similar doors on the building feature trefoil
and quatrefoil tracery of stained glass. A large pointed
Gothic arch window is above the main entry and
repeated again on the sides of the building. Each has
stained glass. The building is in excellent condition
and features its original architectural integrity.

St. John's Lutheran Church

206 S. Center — *1947 Moderne*   NONC

TREE: Arizona Cypress *Cupressus globra* 75 feet high.

209 S. Center — *1919 Bungalow*   NRHP:1997
A one-story bungalow built on a rectangular plan with a single gable shallow-pitched roof. Original siding is covered with asbestos shingles. The main entry is recessed beneath an entry gable articulated by vertical slatting. The original door with mullioned glass window is flanked on either side by identical sidelights.

218 S. Center — *1920c Bungalow*   NRHP:1997
A T-plan clapboard bungalow with shallow-pitched tri-gable roof. Front-facing gable forms entry wing of house. Main door is at center flanked by three high narrow vertical windows on either side.

223 S. Center — *1924 Mediterranean Revival*   NRHP:1997
A large boxy stucco house with a flat roof. Distinct Mediterranean Revival influences are derived from the raised parapet which is accented by adobe tiles in the two smaller adobe tiled hoods over the main front windows. The entry is at center beneath a small gabled portico accented with adobe tiles.

231 S. Center — *1910c Hip Roof Cottage*   NRHP:1997
This is a box plan house with pyramidal roof and clapboard siding. No porch exists but a small front-facing gable with cross-ties and attic venting is located on the front half of the house. Large picture windows flank either side of the main entry.

234 S. Center — *1913 Bungalow*   NRHP:1997
A single-story clapboard bungalow with double front-facing gables. The forwardmost gable forms the entry porch overhang supported by tapered piers.

237 S. Center — *1910c Cottage Hip Roof*

242 S. Center — *1916 Craftsman*   OTPA:1997
OWNER: John Widowson
A one and one-half story clapboard Craftsman house

with single side-facing gable roof which is contrasted by a smaller front-facing gabled dormer. The main roof extends forward to form a full-width porch supported by classic Craftsman piers. Embellishment on the dormer includes ornamentally framed transom window purlins and cross-ties at the bargeboard.

257 S. Center — *1922 Hip Roof Cottage*   OTPA:1997
OWNER: Washington Bullard
A single-story bungalow with clapboard siding and clipped gable roof. Double front-facing clipped gables are paired in an unusual way. The frontmost gable extends forward to form the entry porch overhang supported by Colonial columns. To either side of this gable a pergola is extended and also supported by round columns. Since the 1982 survey this structure has been altered with inappropriate porch posts and rail in a Victorian style.

258 S. Center — *1914*   NONC

265 S. Center — *1920c Bungalow*   NRHP:1997
A single-story clapboard bungalow with double front-facing gable roof. Forwardmost gable forms entry porch overhang supported by wide piers.

266 S. Center — *1920 Bungalow*   NRHP:1997
A clapboard rectangular plan bungalow with tri-gable roof. Main portion of house is covered by a single side-facing gable roof; front-facing gable centrally located on the front facade forms the entry porch overhang. This gable is supported by elephantine piers and is ornamented by a framed attic vent and dentils which span the full width of the gable face. Three large picture windows are located across the front facade.

274 S. Center — *1915c Craftsman*   NRHP:1997
This is a full two-story home with single front-facing gable roof. House is sheathed in clapboard. A small shed overhang forms a full-width porch beneath and is supported by tapered piers. Double door entry indicates duplex usage of house. Ornamental purlins

grace the eaves. Lattice work is located in the uppermost portion of the front gable.

327 S. Center — *1917*   NONC

328 S. Center — *1910 Hip Roof Cottage*   NRHP:1997
A single-story box plan house with a steep-pitched hip roof and clapboard siding. A smaller front-facing gable forms the attic dormer. Entry is via a corner porch recessed beneath the main portion of the house and is supported by a Classical column. Wide eaves are ornamented by brackets.

335 S. Center — *1906 Hip Roof Cottage*   NONC

343 S. Center — *1912 Bungalow*   NRHP:1997
A single-story clapboard bungalow with double front-facing gables. The frontmost gable originally formed the entry porch overhang but has been enclosed in recent years. This gable face is ornamented with dentils and a framed attic dormer.

344 S. Center — *1905 Bungalow*   NRHP:1997
A clapboard bungalow with hip roof. A separate hip roof extends forward to form the entry porch overhang, supported by slender piers. A pergola is located adjacent to the porch overhang. Since 1982 an attempt has been made toward restoration. Some details are too Victorian.

351 S. Center — *1920c Craftsman Bungalow*   NRHP:1997
This is a rectangular plan bungalow with clapboard siding and double front-facing gable roof. Forwardmost gable forms entry porch overhang supported by tapered piers. Exposed beams and triangular bracket supports adorn the front facade.

352 S. Center — *1909 Hip Roof Cottage*   NRHP:1997
A box plan clapboard house with steep-pitched hip roof. A small front-facing gable forms the attic dormer. A separate roof extension forms the porch overhang supported by three Classical columns.

357 S. Center — *1921 California Bungalow*   NRHP:1997

Although built by Harvey P. Cox he lived here only a short time. Rented out for some 18 years by several tenants. Dr. A.L. Schroeder moved here by 1939 and stayed past WWII.

This is a classic California bungalow with a rectangular plan clapboard siding and single side-facing gable roof contrasted by a centrally located front-facing gable which forms the entry porch overhang. This front-facing gable is the architectural focal point of the house and incorporates a clipped gable, return at the eaves supported by Colonial columns. A pergola is located at either side.

360 S. Center — *1912 Craftsman Bungalow*   NRHP:1997
A single-story clapboard bungalow with hip roof and gable extension to one side which forms the entry porch overhang supported by wide piers of clapboard with stucco bases. The front-facing gable is ornamented with dentils and ornamentally framed attic vent and purlins. Large picture windows with diamond pane transoms flank either side of main entry.

367 S. Center — *1909 Hip Roof Cottage*   NRHP:1997
A box plan house with steep-pitched hip roof contrasted by smaller front-facing gable which forms the attic dormer. Entry is via a recessed corner porch supported by Classical columns.

368 S. Center — *1910 Hip Roof Cottage*   NRHP:1997
A box plan house with pyramidal roof and board and batten siding. Corner recessed porch forms the entry focal porch supported by Classical columns with wide pier bases.

375 S. Center — *1912 Craftsman*   NRHP:1997
One and one-half story Craftsman house with rectangular plan and single side-facing gable roof complemented by a smaller front-facing gabled dormer. The main roof extends forward to form a full-width porch overhang. Entry is slightly off center flanked by large three-part picture windows on each

side. Front facade is board and batten and appears as if some alterations have been made to the house.

381 S. Center —*1931 Bungalow*   NRHP:1997
A single-story clapboard bungalow with double front-facing gables. Smaller forwardmost gable forms entry porch overhang supported by tapered piers.

393 S. Center — *1905 Hip Roof Cottage c* NRHP:1997
A single-story clapboard house with steep-pitched hip roof and box plan. A small front-facing gable accents the front roofline. A nearly full-width porch overhang extends from the main facade supported by Classical columns. Low porch wall connects the columns.

406 S. Center — *1909 Hip Roof Cottage*   NRHP:1997
A clapboard box plan house of one story with steep-pitched hip roof and small front-facing attic dormer gable. Entry is via a corner porch which is recessed beneath main portion of house and is supported by a single Classical column. A large single-pane picture window with leaded glass transom is on front facade.

406 S. Center — *1909 Cottage Hip Roof*   NONC

414 S. Center — *1917 Craftsman Bungalow* OTPA:1997
OWNER: Frank Pister
A single-story clapboard bungalow with shallow-pitched double front-facing gables. The forwardmost gable forms the entry porch overhang supported by piers. Wide vertical slatting ornaments each of the gable faces.

420 S. Center — 1909 Hip Roof Cottage   NRHP:1997
A single-story clapboard house with box plan and pyramidal roof. A smaller front-facing gable acts as a dormer window and is sheathed in shingles. Entry is via a corner porch recessed beneath main roof and supported by Classical columns.

436 S. Center — *1907 Hip Roof Cottage*   NRHP:1997
A single-story box plan house with clapboard siding and a steep-pitched hip roof. A small pedimented gable

sheathed in shingles with an ornamental transom vent is located to the side of the house on the front portion of the roof and is contrasted by a corner recessed porch supported by Classical columns.

438 S. Center — *1907 Cottage Hip Roof*   NONC

444 S. Center — *1919 Bungalow*   NRHP:1997
A single-story clapboard bungalow with shallow-pitched front-facing gable roof. Main entry is via a recessed corner porch supported by wide piers, also sheathed in clapboard. Wide vertical slatting accents the upper gable face. Eaves feature exposed rafters.

454 S. Center — *1907 Hip Roof Cottage*   NRHP:1997
A single-story box plan house sheathed in clapboard with a steep-pitched hip roof. A small front-facing hipped dormer is located on the front portion of the roof. A corner porch is recessed beneath the main portion of the house and is supported by Classical columns. Two picture windows each with a transom are located on the front facade.

459 S. Center — *1925* - stuccoed; note garage   NONC

460 S. Center — *1930 Bungalow*   NRHP:1997
Single-story bungalow with wide clapboard siding and shallow-pitched double front-facing gable roof. Forwardmost gable forms entry porch overhang supported by thin wood posts.

464 S. Center — *1921 Craftsman Bungalow*   NRHP:1997
A single-story bungalow with wide clapboard siding and double front-facing gables. Forwardmost gable forms entry porch overhang supported by wide concrete piers topped by wood posts. A pergola also supported by an identical pier is located to the side of the porch gable.

469 S. Center — *1890c Victorian*   NRHP:1997
A two-story house with shiplap siding and multi-gable roof. Entry is beneath the separate porch extension with a pedimented gable and turned posts with

ornamental brackets. High narrow windows are characteristic of the Victorian period. Bargeboard on gables has some ornamentation.

477 S. Center — *1899 Victorian*   NRHP:1997

A two-story house with L-plan characterized by a large front-facing gable with return at eaves of the gable. A porch covering attached to the main facade wraps around the forwardmost gable and has a slatted balcony balustrade supported by thin wood posts. This is probably a later addition.

480 S. Center — *1910c Bungalow*   NONC

481 S. Center — *1917 Craftsman Bungalow*   NRHP:1997

A single-story bungalow with rectangular plan and single side-facing gable roof. This is contrasted by a small shed dormer which acts as the attic outlet. The main house extends forward to form full-width porch overhang supported by four piers. The two outermost piers are large circular columns; the innermost piers are concrete column bases with smaller thinner columns on top.

484 S. Center — *1908 Bungalow*   NRHP:1997

A single-story clapboard bungalow with gable roof and separate adjacent portico entry consisting of a small shed roof and wood post supports.

Center Street — North

101 N. Center —
TREE: 1905c Camphor *Cinnamomum camphora.*
Herman Wyneken got the berries from S. Center St.

143 N. Center — *1912 Craftsman*   NRHP:1997
A one and one-half story house with wide lap siding and single-gable roof with side-facing gables. There is also a large front-facing gable dormer which is ornamented with cross-ties and an ornamental transom vent. The main roof extends forward to form a full-width porch and is supported by wide tapered piers with arroyo stone bases. The main entry is at center and flanked on either side by a large 3-part window.

153 N. Center — *1910 Craftsman*   NRHP:1997
A one and one-half story Craftsman house with wide lap siding and the main roof comprised of a single gable with side-facing gables. There also is present a large front-facing gable dormer ornamented with cross-ties purlins and two combination window/vent transoms. The main roof extends forward to form the full-width porch and is supported by arroyo stone piers. These piers are connected by a slatted balustrade. The original door with oval pane is still present.

158 N. Center — *1909 Craftsman Bungalow*   NRHP:1997
A single-story bungalow with wide lap siding and gable roofline. There is a small front-facing gable dormer with ornamental purlins and an attic transom. The house features a large corner wrap-around porch which is a recessed porch supported by wood posts on top of a high porch wall. The original wood door with vertical pane is still present.

163 N. Center — *1915 Bungalow*   NRHP:1997
A single-story bungalow with shingled siding and single shallow-pitch gable roof which is front-facing. There is a full-width porch recessed beneath the main roof. This porch overhang is supported by piers of cast masonry.

The original wood door and glass panes are still present.

164 N. Center — *1919 Bungalow*   NRHP:1997
A single-story house with combination lap and shingle siding and a front-facing single-gable roof. There is a full-width porch recessed beneath the main roof. This porch is supported by wide piers on top of a cast concrete masonry wall. The original door with glass pane is still present.

168 N. Center — *1925 Bungalow*   NRHP:1997
A single-story bungalow with wide lap siding and double front-facing gable roof. The format of the house is arranged a little differently than usual in that the gable projection is located on the centermost portion of the front facade and the entry is to the side of this gable projection. A large mullioned 3-part window is present on the frontmost portion of the facade.

171 N. Center — *1909 Bungalow*   NRHP:1997
A single-story bungalow with clapboard siding on the lower portion and shingles on the upper gable face. The roofline is a single-gable roof with a front-facing gable. There is a full-width porch recessed beneath the main portion of the roof. The porch is supported by wide piers with brick bases and wood posts on top. The house is distinguished by ornamental rafter tails purlins and dentils running across the lower gable face.

176 N. Center — *1912 Bungalow*   NRHP:1997
A single-story bungalow with wide lap siding and double front-facing gable roof. The forwardmost gable forms the entry porch overhang and is supported by slender wood posts. Ornamental purlins grace the eaves while the lower portion of the front facade features two large 3-part transomed windows.

181 N. Center — *1914 Bungalow*   NRHP:1997
A single-story clapboard bungalow with single-gable roof with front-facing gable. A full-width porch is present which is recessed beneath the main roof. The porch is now supported by ornamental iron piers which are certainly a replacement for the original. The house

is embellished with cross-ties in the upper gable face purlins and an ornamental transomed window. The lower portion of the house features the original front door with glass panes flanked on either side by a large transomed picture window.

190 N. Center — *1903 Gable Roof Cottage*   NRHP:1997
This house has been considerably altered although there is no mistaking the original portions of the house. What was originally a clapboard house with multi-planed roofline and dynamic wrap-around circular porch has since been modified to include an enclosure of the porch using brick facing. A portion of the clapboard facade the two gables and the original roofline are still intact.

191 N. Center — *1908 Hip Roof Cottage*   NRHP:1997
A single-story box plan house with clapboard siding and steep-pitch hip roof. There is a slender gable dormer present on the front portion of the roof. The main roof extends forward to form a full width porch overhang which is supported by classical columns atop a clapboard porch wall.

224 N. Center — *1913 Bungalow*   NRHP:1997
A single-story bungalow with clapboard siding and double front-facing gable roof. The forwardmost gable forms the entry porch overhang and is supported by tapered piers.

225 N. Center — *1924 Mediterranean Revival*   NRHP:1997
A box plan bungalow with stucco facades and a flat roof. While not totally Mediterranean this house certainly incorporates a Pueblo feel through the use of the entry porch porticos in either side of the front facade. There is a slight stepped parapet as well and the porch piers include raised pilasters.

TREE: Hong Kong White Orchid *Bauhimia blakean* 30 feet high, it is the only one in Orange.

227 N. Center — *1924 Mediterranean Revival*   NONC

231 N. Center — *1911 Bungalow*   NONC

232 N. Center — *1904 Victorian*   NRHP:1997

A two-story clapboard house with steep-pitch multi-gable roof. The front facade is comprised of two pedimented front-facing gables, the smaller and lower of which shelters the corner entry porch and is supported by classical columns. The rearmost front-facing gable is considerably ornamented through the use of transoms fashioned in a semi-Palladian manner. Ornamental jigsawn barge board is present in both gables. The wide eaves of the house are also ornamented with brackets.

240 N. Center — *1920 Mediterranean Revival*   NRHP:1997
A single-story house with modified box plan textured stuccoed siding and a flat roof. There is a half-sized porch extension which is supported by wide piers. The house may have been resided as the siding does not appear to be original.

241 N. Center — *1921 Bungalow*   NRHP:1997
A single-story clapboard bungalow with shallow-pitched gable roof. The house is built on an L-plan and the short leg of the ell results in a front-facing gable face. To the side is an open porch and the main door is sheltered by a slight gabled portico supported by ornamental brackets.

247 N. Center — *1919 Bungalow*   NRHP:1997
A single-story bungalow with ornamental lap siding and shallow-pitch gable roof. One-half of the front facade is occupied by a porch overhang which is supported by elephantine piers.

250 N. Center — *1920*   NONC

258 N. Center — *1910 Bungalow*   NRHP:1997
A single-story bungalow with wide lap siding and double front-facing gable roof. The forwardmost gable forms the entry porch overhang and is supported by tapered piers above a porch wall. The upper gable faces are ornamented with small brackets ornamental exposed beams and vertical wood slats.

264 N. Center — *1913 Bungalow*   NRHP:1997

A single-story bungalow with wide lap siding and double front-facing gable roof. The forwardmost gable forms the entry porch overhang and is supported by tapered piers above a porch wall. The original door with window panes is still present. Either side of the front facade features a large picture window with an ornamentally mullioned transom.

267 N. Center — *1938*   NONC

272 N. Center — *1923 Bungalow*   NRHP:1997
A single-story clapboard bungalow with multi-gabled shallow-pitch roof. One-half of the front facade is occupied by a large corner wrap-around porch. This porch is supported by a wide tapered pier with an ornamental brick base.

273 N. Center — *1906 Hip Roof Cottage*   NONC

279 N. Center — *1909 Bungalow*   NRHP:1997
A single-story bungalow with wide lap siding and double front-facing gable roof. The forwardmost gable forms the entry porch overhang and is supported by slender wood posts.

280 N. Center — *1915c Craftsman*   OTPA:1997
OWNER: Edward Hahn
A two-story house with single gable roof with side-facing gable faces. The facades of the house are now covered by asbestos shingles. There is a large front facing gable dormer on the front portion of the roof. The main roof extends forward to form a full-width porch and is supported by colonial-type columns.

288 N. Center — *1911 Bungalow*   NRHP:1997
A single-story clapboard bungalow with single-gable roof and side-facing gables. The roof extends forward to form a half recessed porch and is supported by slender wood posts.

289 N. Center — *1906 Hip Roof Cottage* NRHP:1997
A single-story clapboard house with steep-pitch hip roof contrasted by a gabled wing on the side. What

was once probably a·corner wrap-around porch has since been enclosed.

305 N. Center — *1905 Hip Roof Cottage*   NRHP:1997
A single-story clapboard house with box plan and steep-pitch hip roof. The roofline also features two pedimented gables which act as attic dormers which are embellished with fish scale shingles and an ornamentally framed transomed vent. A separate roof extension on the front facade once formed a full-width porch but has since been enclosed.

313 N. Center — *1915 Bungalow*   NRHP:1997
A single-story bungalow with lap siding and double front-facing gable roof. The forwardmost gable forms the entry porch overhang and is supported by tapered piers with brick bases and wood on top. Ornamental purlins grace the eaves.

323 N. Center — *1905c Hip Roof Cottage*   NRHP:1997
This is a small box-plan cottage with clapboard siding and steep-pitch hip roof. A small gabled attic dormer is present on the front portion of the roof. Just below is a nearly full-width porch with its own separate roof extension that is supported by Victorian turned posts connected with an ornamental balustrade. This small-scale house is indicative of the simplistic homes built by the early settlers and pioneers in Orange.

333 N. Center — *1922 Bungalow*   NRHP:1997
A single-story bungalow with lap siding and single-gable roof with side-facing gables. A small gabled attic dormer is present as is a small gabled entry over the main door. The portico is embellished with an arch with a large arch connecting brackets.

339 N. Center — *1920 Bungalow*   NRHP:1997
A single-story box plan bungalow with wide lap siding and double front-facing gable roof. The smaller forwardmost gable forms the entry porch overhang which is located on the center front of the house. The overhang is supported by large wood posts. Vertical

slatting in the upper gable faces act as embellishment.

345 N. Center — *1920c Bungalow*   NRHP:1997
A single-story house with double front-facing gable roof and facades now covered by asbestos shingles. The smaller forwardmost gable located on the center of the front facade forms an entry porch overhang and is supported by slender wood posts.

353 N. Center — *1915c Bungalow*   NRHP:1997
A single-story bungalow with wide lap siding and single-gable roof with side-facing gables. A small gabled attic dormer is present as is a small gabled entry portico over the main door.

363 N. Center — *1920 Bungalow*   NRHP:1997
A single-story bungalow with shallow-pitch gable roof and facades now covered by asbestos shingles. The main portion of the house is covered by a roof with side-facing gables, while a narrower front-facing gable in the center of the front facade forms an entry porch overhang. This is supported by wood posts and ornamented with vertical slatting.

373 N. Center — *1922 Normandy Eclectic*   NONC

393 N. Center — *1920 Mediterranean Revival*   NONC

413 N. Center — *1925c Mediterranean Revival*   NRHP:1997
This is a single-story box plan house with stucco facades and flat roof reminiscent of the Mediterranean Revival style. Though not really Mediterranean the house does incorporate a front-facing gable-enclosed projection flanked on either side by an entry. Large mullioned windows are present on either side of the gable projection and the gable wing itself contains two small mullioned arched windows. The raised parapet on the house is reminiscent of the Pueblo Revival influences.

423 N. Center — *1923 Bungalow*   NONC
Though the format and style of this house are intact it has been considerable altered through the use of

stucco on the facades and the changing of the windows. The house is a basic California bungalow with double front-facing gable roof of which the forwardmost gable forms an entry porch overhang supported by slender wood posts.

427 N. Center — *1923 Bungalow*   NRHP:1997
A single-story clapboard bungalow with single-gable roof with side-facing gables. The main entry is just off center and is articulated by a small gabled portico just above. A pair of large double-hung windows are on either side of the entry.

433 N. Center — *1923 Bungalow*   NRHP:1997
A small box-plan clapboard house with single-gable roof with side-facing gables. The house is simple and unadorned except for the small portico overhang above the entry door.

445 N. Center — *1920 Bungalow*   NRHP:1997
Though this house still retains its original format and style it has been altered through the use of stucco on the facades. The house is a modified box-plan with a tri-gable roof line with each of the gables front-facing. The forwardmost of these forms the entry porch overhang and is supported by tapered piers. The original hardwood door is still present.

453 N. Center — *1926 Mediterranean Revival*   NRHP:1997
A single-story box plan house with stucco facades and a flat roof. The house is simple and unadorned and harks to the Mediterranean Revival style through the use of adobe tiles at the roof ridge line. A small recessed portico shields the main entry.

463 N. Center — *1925 Bungalow*   NONC

469 N. Center — *1927 Mediterranean Revival*   NRHP:1997
A single-story stucco house with box plan and flat roof. The entry is comprised of a recessed portico with arched openings and tile hood above. The roofline is also articulated with adobe tiles.

477 N. Center — *1931 Spanish Colonial Revival* NRHP:1997
A single-story house with textured stucco siding and multi-gable roofline. The house is built on a modified L-plan with the front-facing gable, elongated to form an entry portico, which is accessed via a large arch opening. The roof is sided with adobe tiles.

485 N. Center — *1923 Bungalow* NRHP:1997
A single-story bungalow with wide lap siding and single front-facing gable roof. The house is simple and unadorned except for the small shed portico over the main entry.

489 N. Center — *1923 Bungalow* NRHP:1997
A single-story bungalow with wide lap siding and single-gable roof with side-facing gables. A small front-facing gable attic dormer is also present. The main entry is shielded by a small gable portico with ornamental bracket supports.

CHAPMAN AVENUE — EAST
—Chapman is named for one of the town founders, Alfred B. Chapman—

101 E. Chapman — *1928 Beaux Arts Commercial* NRHP:1982
First National Bank - Financial Building
ARCT: Morgan, Walls & Clements
Formed in 1906, the First National Bank of Orange
grew to consume the Bank of Orange. The original
bank building on the site, built in 1887 was razed in
1927 and the new building of 15,300 sq. ft. opened in
1928. With an original cost of $47,500, high ceilings
and a second floor add to this remarkable structure.
A step inside provides a special treat with the vaulted
ceiling's carved inlay woods.
*Note the historic plaque on the South West corner of
the building.*

102 E. Chapman — *1898 Brick Commercial* NONC
Carpenter Bank - Financial Building 11,050 sq. ft.
(with adjacent building) [10 Plaza Square]
The first location of the National Bank of Orange,
dating from 1906. Heavily modified, this building is
actually combined with the adjacent structure on E.
Chapman Ave. The bank vault & safe is still intact.

Carpenter Bank - 1934

A two story brick building, the present wood siding
hides the original brick structure, although they are

still visible from an interior garden area. Beautifully restored interior of oak woods.

108 E. Chapman — *Brick Commercial*   NONC
Now with a heavily modified facade and connected to the adjacent building to the West, this smaller two story structure has a fully enclosed, open air garden with trees in the rear.

112 E. Chapman — *1901 Brick Commercial*   NRHP:1982
Odd Fellows Hall - Pharmacy
Presently contains Watson's Drug Store, the oldest continuously operated pharmacy in Orange County and the oldest business in Orange (1898.)

Courtesy Watson's Drug

Watson's - 1930s & 1950s *

Two story brick commercial building, originally built as the Odd Fellows Hall.

202 E. Chapman — *1905 Brick Commercial*   NRHP:1982
Barger's Hall, brick commercial with cornices.

208 E. Chapman — *1915c Brick Commercial*   NRHP:1982
Business Building
Brick commercial with wood truss and basement.

211 E. Chapman — *1925 Concrete Commercial*   NRHP:1982
Elk's Building
Concrete building with second floor hall, third floor meeting room. Steel reinforced concrete structure.

Elk's Lodge Building

212 E. Chapman — *1904 Brick Commercial*   NRHP:1982
Business Building; brick commercial with wood truss
and basement. Altered facade.

214 E. Chapman — *1915c Commercial Brick*   NONC

300 E. Chapman — *1887 Victorian Fountain*   NRHP:1997
This is a three-tiered fountain constructed of sculpted
metal. Water splashes over the edges of the shallow
bowls with ruffled edges and also pours forth from the
beaks of sculpted birds beneath the lowest bowl. The
main pool has a concrete shell and a black tiled bottom.

The cannon in front of the Civic Center (Chapman at
Grand) is a captured Japanese World War II weapon,
about 50 years old.

300 E. Chapman
Cast bronze 1887 Victorian Fountain (the original
plaza fountain).

307 E. Chapman — *1905c Classical Revival*   NRHP:1997
This is a very large two-story house which dates to
just after the turn of the century. The house takes on
a particularly unusual appearance due to the fact that
the front portion was modified within the first 20
years after construction. The front portion of the

house features large two-story fluted columns with simple capitals and a second story balcony recessed below the main roof. Double French doors are featured on the upper story in the front; double hung windows are present on the lower story. The rear and sides of the house feature the typical Classical Revival elements—bay windows ornamented gables and hip roof lines.

307 E. Chapman — *1905c Vernacular*

414 E. Chapman — *1910 Queen Ann Bungalow*   NRHP:1981
OWNER: Lewis & Persis Ainsworth Cottage Feat.
BLDR: Lewis Ainsworth, Ainsworth Block Lumber
Built by Ainsworth as a retirement and entertainment home it was designed by his daughter Ina Butler. This house is the Lewis Ainsworth House which is the official restored house museum for the City of Orange.

The house features unusual proportions. It is a single-story house with a multi-gable roofline which features three front-facing gables. Recessed beneath the roof is a full curvilinear porch featuring an entrance on either side of the projecting bay in the center. Palladian transoms are present in each of the upper gable faces; a large picture window with transom is present below. Ornamental jigsawn work adorns the brackets of the porch posts.
Concrete Hitching Post.

431 E. Chapman — *1920 Craftsman*   NRHP:1997
Samuel B. & Lillian Edwards bought this home in 1922. As an insurance agent Samuel involved himself in the Chamber of Commerce and other interests. Sam died here in 1973 at age 97, Lillian sold out in 1980 passing in 1984 at age 100.

This is a two-story Craftsman house with clapboard siding and multi-gable roofline. The house is distinguished by a second story located predominantly on the rear half of the house. The lower story in front features a large front-facing gable supported by elephantine piers. The entry is beneath this porch gable. The original door with mullioned plate glass windows is still present flanked on either side by sidelights. A large three-part picture window with transom is on either side of the main entry. An ornamental brick chimney is located on the side of the house.

532 E. Chapman — *1915c Craftsman*   NRHP:1997
What was originally a Craftsman style bungalow has been modified in more recent years. The house is defined by clapboard siding and multi-gable roofline with ornamental purlins beneath the roof eaves. The major part of the house is still intact but the frontmost portion on which a porch was probably located has been modified to include brickwork and enclosure of most of the original porch.

532 E. Chapman — *1915c Craftsman Bungalow*

541 E. Chapman —
TREE: Moreton Bay Fig *Ficus macrophylla* 32" 50' 60'.

600 E. Chapman — *1930c Streamline Moderne*   NRHP:1997
This is a single-story office building constructed in the Streamline Moderne style. As is typical of this style which was popular in the thirties, the roof is flat and the facades are sided in stucco. All of the corners are curved as are the windows which round the corners. The windows are of glass-brick also very typical of the style. Horizontal banding at the cornice and across the entry is in excellent condition and very much retains its original architectural integrity.

600 E. Chapman — *1930c Moderne*

615 E. Chapman — *1914c Craftsman*   NRHP:1997
This is a large two-story house with distinct Craftsman influences, combined with several unusual features. The house has a single side-facing gable roof with each of the gables clipped. The house is sided in

elongated shingles which add an important architectural feature. The main entry is at the first story on the center beneath a roof extension, supported by very rotund columns. A double door entry with mullioned panes is present. The house features large windows which add to the architectural character. An addition on the east side has been made in recent years but does not significantly detract from the original architecture. This house has the potential for eligibility in the National Register pending development of more historic information associated with it. Since the 1982 survey this structure has had a change of use from residential to professional.

615 E. Chapman — *1914c Craftsman*

626 E. Chapman — *1912 Craftsman Bungalow*   NRHP:1997
OWNER: E. Eisenbraun, Orange Tin Shop
A one and one-half story Craftsman house with single siding and single side-facing gable roof. A front-facing dormer features ornamental exposed beams. The main roof extends forward to form a full-width porch supported by tapered piers with arroyo stone bases. The low connecting porch wall, half piers along the stoop and the chimney are also of arroyo stone. The house is an excellent Craftsman example and comes close to being as pure an example of that style as there is in Orange. Since the 1982 survey this structure has had a change of use from residential to professional.

636 E. Chapman — *1925c Mediterranean Revival*   NRHP:1997
This is a single-story box plan house with stucco facades and a flat roof. The house features the rectilinear projection common on the Mediterranean style that incorporates a slight Pueblo influence. The house was built on a symmetrical plan with entry recessed and distinguished by a large arched opening with raised pilasters. To either side of the entry is a large mullioned picture window with an adobe tile hood.

636 E. Chapman — *1925c Mediterranean Revival*

701 E. Chapman — *1915c Craftsman*

702 E. Chapman — *1926 Spanish Colonial Revival* NRHP:1997
H.F. Bartling and his wife built this elegant home for
$13,000, after living in Orange for some years. Their
daughter Mabel married Adolf Dittmer Jr., in 1923,
the son of the founder of the Mission Pharmacy, dating
from 1905.

This is a one-story house built in the Spanish Colonial
Revival style. The house design is symmetrical with
the main entry located at front center and flanked on
either side by large picture windows. The hip roof
and portico have adobe tiles; the facades have stucco
siding. The entry portico has a large arched opening
which is complemented by Roman arched picture
windows on the front facade. Wide eaves feature pairs
of ornamentally scrolled bracket. The west side of the
house includes a second entrance featuring a porch and
fountain in Hermosa tiles. The house is in excellent
condition and has been restored to its original
condition on the exterior and interior.

704 E. Chapman — *1926 Spanish Colonial Revival*

705 E. Chapman — *1908 Craftsman*   NRHP:1997
This is a large two-story house with wide lap siding
and gable roofline. The house is built on a box plan
with symmetrical front facade. The entry comprises
the architectural statement on the house featuring a
gable dormer on the upper story with an arched
opening leading to a recessed balcony. The roof
extension below is supported by ornamental brackets
with an entry door flanked by sidelights. An angled
bay is located on the south half of the front facade.

811 E. Chapman — *1922c Spanish Colonial Revival* NRHP:1997
This is a large two-story house with a box plan stucco
facades and a flat roof. The center portion of the house
is distinguished by a rectangular projection which

houses a recessed entry beneath. The arched opening of this entry is accented by two rotund columns. On either side of the entry are mullioned French doors with adobe tile hoods. Adobe tiled hoods are also located on the cornice around the entire circumference of the upper portion of the house. The windows on the second story have been modified over the years.

811 E. Chapman — *1923c Spanish Colonial Revival*

820 E. Chapman — *1924 Spanish Colonial Revival*   NRHP:1997
Immanual Lutheran Church
Built from a group separated from St. Johns on Center St., this congregation formed younger members.
Church This is a Spanish Colonial Revival church built during the mid-20's when this style was at the height of its popularity. Typical to the style the church features stucco facades and adobe tiling coupled with a Mission oriented cupola and bell tower.

Immanuel Lutheran Church

The main front entry of the church features a large gabled face with three arched entry openings incorporating floral relief work around the recessed portion of these openings. A large rosette stained glass window is featured just above. The cupola which is to the side features arched openings and a domed tower crowned with a cross on top.

Immanuel Lutheran - Inside & out

820 E. Chapman — *1924 Spanish Colonial Revival*

910 E. Chapman — *1925c Spanish Colonial Revival* NRHP:1997
Fred A. Loescher's retirement home after years as a millwright and later in Orange a citrus grower.

This is a large two-story house with adobe tiled hip roof and stucco facades. The house occupies a corner lot and plays a prominent role as a distinguished house along East Chapman. The house features a second story balcony defined by a balcony wall with raised pilasters. A mullioned door with mullioned sidelights forms the entry to this balcony and are flanked on either side by a large three-part window. The entry below is slightly recessed and accessed via a stoop. The entry is articulated with ornamental pilasters on either side of the main door. A large fixed-pane window is also present on either side of the main entry. A porte cochere with piers modeled after the pilasters of the main entry is featured on the side of the house.

924 E. Chapman — *1921 Craftsman*

932 E. Chapman — *1924 Spanish Colonial Revival* NRHP:1997
This is a small single-story Spanish Colonial Revival bungalow with stucco facades and an adobe tiled gable roof. The roofline profile of the house is fashioned in

an L-plan with the short leg resulting in a front-facing gable adorned with a large mullioned picture window. The entry is recessed beneath a small projection, with an arched opening. The remaining half of the front facade is articulated by a projection with raised pilasters which is carried through in the porte cochere on the side of the house.

940 E. Chapman — *1913 Craftsman*   NRHP:1997

A one and one-half story Craftsman house with single side-facing gable roof and clapboard siding. A large front-facing gable dormer is present and features mullioned windows. The main roof originally extended forward to form a full-width porch which was supported by arroyo stone piers. This porch has since been enclosed although the piers are still present.

—Outside of Old Towne—

1006 E. Chapman — *1937 Spanish Colonial Revival* NRHP:1997

This is another of the large stately Spanish Colonial Revival homes that were built by the wealthier businessmen along East Chapman. This is a two-story house with stucco facades and an adobe tiled hip roof. The entry is at center via a small recessed opening. For the most part the house is simple and unadorned with the primary architectural focus being on the many mullioned windows. A three-tiered fountain is located in front of the entry.

1015 E. Chapman — *1924 Spanish Colonial Revival* NRHP:1997

This is a small single-story Spanish Colonial Revival bungalow with stucco facades and a flat roof complemented by adobe tiled hoods. The house is built on a symmetrical rectangular plan with the entry at center which is contrasted by two raised projections on either side. The entry is recessed beneath the main roof and is enclosed by a low patio wall.

1025 E. Chapman — *1936*   NRHP:1997

An L-shaped stucco commercial building with no

special ornamentation.

1440 E. Chapman — *1929 Mediterranean*
Charles C. Reed, Merle Ramsey 3,500 sq. ft. $20,000
Built for Reed of Orange the pretentious home came
with large dimensions and illustrious features.
Covered in adobe-like plaster this large
Mediterranean came with 10 room four bathrooms a
central court a billiard room and 23 foot high ceilings.
The two-story structure also came with electronic
speakers in every room.

Chapman Avenue — West

100 W. Chapman — *1888 Brick Commercial*   NONC
Ainsworth Block Mercantile [48 Plaza Square]
Lewis Ainsworth settled in Orange during 1901 and
with his sons, operated the Ainsworth Lumber
Company. Purchasing the Armor building of 1888, he
enlarged the structure to 11,250 sq. ft., by adding a
second floor in 1907.

Brick veneer, wire glass skylighting and a second floor.
[see Ainsworth House, 414 E. Chapman]
*Note the iron support post stamped: 1888 Baker Iron
Works - Los Angeles.*

105 W. Chapman — *1912 Brick Commercial*   NRHP:1982
Jorn Building Mercantile
ARCT: C.B. Bradshaw [55 Plaza Square] 15,300 sq. ft.
(with adjacent building]
Insurance Salesman Carl Jorn, built this building and
had his offices on the second floor. E.H. Smith's
Jewelry store started on the first level.

Yellow brick veneer with stone cornices & skylight.
The 1920 adjacent addition on W. Chapman follows the
same style architecture.

109 W. Chapman — *1920 Brick Commercial*   NRHP:1982
Jorn Addition

131 W. Chapman — *1922 Brick Commercial*   NRHP:1982

118 W. Chapman — *1922 Brick Commercial*   NRHP:1982
Brick single story with wood trusses and concrete
floor, wire glass skylight and drive through. Originally
a gas station.

201 W. Chapman — *1912 Brick Commercial*   NRHP:1982

204 W. Chapman — *1916 Brick Commercial*   NONC

207 W. Chapman — *1910 Brick Commercial*   NONC
Extensive remodeling.

223 W. Chapman — *1935 Brick Commercial*   NRHP:1982

W.O. Hart Post Office
The first Postmaster in 1873 was Dr. George Beach. Later, W. O. Hart as Postmaster, used this structure for the cities mail. Hart ran the Orange Daily News; Hart park (originally Orange City Park) was re-named for him.

Brick single story with decorative front.

234 W. Chapman — *1920 Brick Commercial*

238 W. Chapman — *1885 Victorian Hotel* NRHP:1997
Dr. W. F. Bailey built a large addition to his residence as a hotel. It contained 14 rooms fully furnished and was named Vineland, prior to the grape blight of 1888.

A two-story building with a hip roof and regularly spaced sash windows. Ornamental brackets embellish the chimney but other than this the building is simple and unadorned. Originally built on the rear of a one-story L-plan Victorian cottage, today that house is replaced by a stucco store-front commercial building which renders the original hotel building nearly invisible from the street. The hotel building remains in its architectural state however, and always was barely visible from the street due to the presence of the house in front.

Vineland Home

235 W. Chapman — *1925 Moderne*   NRHP:1997
Originally a small gas station and in fact, one of the first in Orange. This structure consists of two projecting bays, each supported by columns. The roof of each of these bays is in the curvilinear style with banding typical of Moderne structures.

308 W. Chapman — *1935 Spanish Colonial Revival* NRHP:1997
This is a single-story post office building comprised of a rectangular plan with stucco facades and adobe tile roof. The building features a slightly recessed entry with transom window and wrought iron balustrades ascending stoop to the entry. Windows include large mullioned sash windows. The building was built to serve as a post office and still has that function.

308 W. Chapman — *1935 Spanish Colonial Revival*
The first federal building in Orange, this WPA structure cost $65,000 and was dedicated August 26, 1935. Vera Wetlin was then installed as Postmistress. In-town delivery had previously begun in 1912, with only three letter carriers.
Note the historic scenes painted inside by Howard Huizing.

321 W. Chapman — *1922 Brick Commercial*

401 W. Chapman — *1920c Brick Commercial*   NRHP:1997
As typical with commercial buildings of this era the lower portion of the store front is devoted almost exclusively to showcase windows. The double door entry features wood doors with a single plate glass window and transom above. Transom windows were located across all of the windows on the lower portion of the building but signs have since been placed in these transoms. Horizontal banding distinguishes the cornice.

424 W. Chapman — *1921 Brick Commercial*   NRHP:1997
This is a single-story commercial building with flat roof and combined brick and stucco siding. The

building sits on the curbside lot line and includes wide showcase window bays separated by brick pilasters. The parapet is raised at each of the main entries and receives unusual detailing on the main corner of the building. Here the brick pilasters rise above the parapet and flank two modified Mission style raised parapets. An ornamental arrangement of contrasting brick is placed along the parapet walls and along the cornice line of the building. A narrow tile hood just below the cornice extends along the upper portion. The building is in good condition and retains its original architectural integrity down to the original entry doors and transom windows.

424 W. Chapman — *1923 Commercial Brick*

525 W. Chapman — *1919c Western False front*

535 W. Chapman — *1900 Victorian*

611 W. Chapman — *1900c Victorian*

616 W. Chapman — *1915c Craftsman Bungalow*

711 W. Chapman — *1915c Craftsman*

727 W. Chapman — *1910 Bungalow*

737 W. Chapman — *1904 Cottage Hip Roof*

—Outside of Old Towne—

1111 W. Chapman — *1919 Craftsman*
Cal Lester House

CLARK STREET — SOUTH
—Clark is named for pioneer A. B. Clark—

122 S. Clark — *1915 Bungalow*   NONC

123 S. Clark — *1924 Vernacular*   NONC

133 S. Clark — *1917 Cottage Hip Roof*   NONC

132 S. Clark — *1913 Craftsman Bungalow*   NONC

140 S. Clark — *1924 Bungalow*   NONC

141 S. Clark — *1909 Vernacular*   NONC

148 S. Clark — *1929 Bungalow*   NONC

149 S. Clark — *1915c Craftsman*   NONC

156 S. Clark — *1910 Bungalow*   NONC

161 S. Clark — *1904 Cottage Hip Roof*   NONC

165 S. Clark — *1904 Cottage Hip Roof*   NONC

339 S. Clark — *1927 Mediterranean Revival*   NRHP:1997
Rectangular plan with flat roof and ornamental tile ridges. Characteristic stucco siding with arched porte cochere. Gabled entry portico has arched opening and small arched window to the side.

353 S. Clark — *1925 Bungalow*   NRHP:1997
Modified L-plan clapboard siding and shallow pitched gable roof. Frontmost gable face includes a large multi-paned, three-part window. Two pairs of large multi-paned windows flank either side of main entry door.

375 S. Clark — *1927 Mediterranean Revival*   NRHP:1997
Box plan flat roof and stucco siding. Roof edges are highlighted with adobe tiles. Frontmost entry is through projecting vertical portico with arched openings. Small tile hoods adorn windows on front facade.

CLEVELAND STREET — NORTH
—Cleveland is named for the 22nd & 24th President Grover Cleveland—

125 N. Cleveland — *1920c Bungalow*   NRHP:1997
Owner: Miss Emily & Ernestina Gollin
BLDR: Orange Contracting & Milling Co.
A single-story clapboard bungalow with multi-gable roof. The majority of the front facade is comprised of a large front-facing gable with a smaller front-facing gable which forms the entry porch overhang. This is supported by wide ornamental, concrete piers and also features ornamental purlins and an ornamentally framed attic vent.

Emily & Ernestina Gollin Home

132 N. Cleveland — *1931 Bungalow*   NRHP:1997
A single-story clapboard bungalow with double front-facing, gable roof. The forwardmost gable forms the entry porch overhang and is supported by tapered piers. Exposed beams grace the eaves of the house.

135 N. Cleveland — *1920 Bungalow*   NRHP:1997
A single-story bungalow with ornamental lap siding and shallow-pitched, gable roof. The main portion of the house is covered by a single-gable roof with side-facing gable which extends forward along three-quarters of the front facade to form an entry porch overhang. It is supported by large triangular supports. Just above is a small front-facing, attic

dormer with exposed beams and ornamental attic vent.

140 N. Cleveland — *1921c Bungalow*   NRHP:1997
A single-story bungalow with wide lap siding and single-gable roof with side-facing gables. A small entry portico is articulated with a small front-facing gable, supported by an ornamental arrangement of exposed beams.

145 N. Cleveland — *1910 Craftsman*   NRHP:1997
A one and one-half story Craftsman house with clapboard siding and single-gable roof with side-facing gables. There is also a front-facing gable dormer ornamented with cross-ties and purlins. One-half of the front facade is distinguished by a recessed porch which is supported by ornamental wood posts. Large picture windows adorn the front facade and each features beveled glass transoms.

148 N. Cleveland — *1920 Bungalow*   NRHP:1997
A single-story bungalow with shallow-pitch multi-gable roof. Facade is now covered with asbestos siding. The house is distinguished by a large corner wrap-around porch formed by an extension of the main side-facing gable roof. This porch overhang is supported by piers comprised of brick bases and wood posts on top. There is a smaller front-facing gable whose facade is adorned with a large transomed picture window. The original front door with three vertical panes is still present and is flanked on either side by sidelights.

155 N. Cleveland — *1921 Prairie*   NRHP:1997
OWNER: Alfred & Sophie Huhn
ARCT: 'DOC' Miller
BLDR: Orange Contracting & Milling Co.
Huhn worked in the Ehlen & Grote store marrying the daughter of Henry Grote (Grote St. is now Cleveland) eventually making president of the firm.

A two-story box plan house with stucco facade and

flat roof. The house incorporates features of the prairie style pioneered by architect Frank Lloyd Wright. The wide overhanging eaves and horizontal banding between the first and second story are typical of the style. There is a large projecting entry porch which is supported by wide ornamental concrete piers and connected by a large arch opening.

The Alfred Huhn Home

The Alfred Huhn Home Interior

156 N. Cleveland — *1932 Bungalow*   NRHP:1997

A single-story clapboard bungalow with multi-gable roof which includes double front-facing gable roof on the front facade. The forwardmost gable here forms the entry porch overhang and is supported by tapered piers.

162 N. Cleveland — *1922 Spanish Colonial*   NRHP:1997
A Spanish colonial residence on a rectangular plan with red-tiled low-pitched roof and double-hung multipaned wooden windows. The front porch fronts half of the front facade and features a flat roof with single pole posts. An exterior brick chimney stucco siding and single-board window sills are present.

165 N. Cleveland — *1922 California Bungalow*   NRHP:1997
A single-story bungalow with single side-facing gable roof and a front-facing gable entry porch overhang centrally located along the front facade. This overhang is supported by ornamental wood posts. All the roof gables are clipped. Large combination of three casement windows is present on the front facade.

172 N. Cleveland — *1922 California Bungalow*   NONC

216 N. Cleveland — *1920c Bungalow*   NRHP:1997
A single-story bungalow with double front-facing gable roof and facade, snow covered by asbestos shingles. The forwardmost gable forms the entry porch overhang and is supported by tapered piers with brick bases. Ornamental slatting adorns the upper portion of each gable face.

224 N. Cleveland — *1914 Bungalow*   NRHP:1997
A single-story bungalow with single front-facing gable roof and facade s now covered by asbestos shingles. What was probably originally a recessed porch has since been enclosed. The brickwork on the front foundation is not original.

227 N. Cleveland — *1914 Bungalow*   NRHP:1997
A single-story bungalow with single front-facing gable roof and facade snow covered by asbestos shingles. Entry is via a small recessed porch. The house is simple and unembellished except for the ornamental purlins beneath the eaves.

232 N. Cleveland — *1909*   ·   NONC

233 N. Cleveland — *1915 Bungalow*   NRHP:1997
This bungalow incorporates both Victorian and Classical influences in a most unusual way. The house is a basic box plan bungalow with wide lap siding and double front-facing gable roof. The forwardmost gable acts as the entry porch overhang and is supported by fluted classical columns. The upper gable faces have the Victorian type embellishment comprised of spindle work.

241 N. Cleveland — *1920 Bungalow*   NRHP:1997
A single-story bungalow with ornamental lap siding and double front-facing gable roof. The main portion of the house is covered by a single front-facing gable while attached to the front facade is a smaller front-facing gable which forms a full-width entry porch overhang. This is supported by tapered piers. Vertical slatting in the upper gable faces create an ornamental feel. Since the 1982 survey this structure has been altered with inappropriate porch rail and removal of porch pier.

247 N. Cleveland — *1919 Bungalow*   NRHP:1997
A single-story bungalow with wide lap siding and double front-facing gable roof. The forwardmost gable forms the entry porch overhang and is supported by tapered piers. Vertical slatting in the gable faces creates ornamentation .

248 N. Cleveland — *1919 Bungalow*   NRHP:1997
A single-story bungalow with ornamental lap siding and shallow pitched multi-gable roof. The main portion of the house is covered by a single-gable roof with side-facing gables. A third gable which faces the front of the house extends forward to form the entry porch overhang. It is supported by wood posts and connected by a slatted balustrade.

250 N. Cleveland — *1919 Bungalow*   NONC

255 N. Cleveland — *1912 Bungalow*   NRHP:1997
A single-story bungalow with wide lap siding and double front-facing gable roof. The forwardmost gable forms the entry porch overhang and is supported by wood posts. Cross-ties and triangular bracket supports ornament the upper gable faces.

256 N. Cleveland — *1920*

264 N. Cleveland — *1914 Craftsman*   NRHP:1997
A single-story house with wide lap siding and single side-facing gable roof which is contrasted by a smaller front-facing gable dormer. What was originally a full-width porch has since been enclosed. Since the 1982 survey this structure has been altered with appropriate reopening of porch and appropriate porch rail.

272 N. Cleveland — *1912 Vernacular Bungalow* OTPA:1997
TREE: Red Flowering Gum *Eucalyptus ficifolia*
A James Purviance home. A two-story house with wide lap siding and multi-gable roof. The front facade is distinguished by a large front-facing gable with flared eaves. What was originally a corner recessed porch has since been enclosed but the original pier is still present. Cross-ties adorn the upper gable face as do triangular bracket supports.

273 N. Cleveland — *1911*   NONC

280 N. Cleveland — *1914 Bungalow*   NRHP:1997
A single-story bungalow with ornamental lap siding and steep-pitched multi-gable roof. The main portion of the house is covered by a single-gable roof with side-facing gables. A full-width front-facing gable forms the entry porch overhang. This is supported by wood piers with concrete bases and wood posts on top. The original wood door is still present and features three window panes. This door is flanked on either side by large transomed picture windows.

288 N. Cleveland — *1923c Mediterranean Revival* NRHP:1997

A single-story box plan house with stucco facades and flat roof. The house features an entry porch projection on the front facade also of stucco. This is supported by large piers. The stepped parapet around the roofline creates the only embellishment on the house.

310 N. Cleveland — *1914*   NRHP:1997
Box-shaped church with small square popped out entry which was likely a steeple. Siding is clapboard material.

317 N. Cleveland — *1922 Bungalow*   NRHP:1997
A single-story bungalow with wide lap siding and shallow-pitched multi-gable roof. The main portion of the house is covered by a single gable roof with side-facing gables. A nearly full-width front-facing gable forms the entry porch overhang. This is supported by tapered piers and features slatted wood in the upper gable face.

324 N. Cleveland — *1923 Bungalow*   NRHP:1997
A single-story bungalow with ornamental lap siding and multi-gable roof with all gables being clipped at the peak. The main portion of the house is covered by a single gable roof with side-facing gables. A large front-facing gable extends forward to form the entry porch overhang. This is supported by tapered piers. This gable is embellished with dentils and an ornamental transom vent.

325 N. Cleveland — *1909 Bungalow*   NRHP:1997
A single-story clapboard bungalow with double front-facing gable roof. The forwardmost gable originally formed an entry porch overhang but has since been enclosed. The original tapered piers are still present.

332 N. Cleveland — *1890 Hip Roof Cottage*   NRHP:1997
This is a small single-story box plan house with shiplap siding and modified hip roof. The front facade features a separate roofed extension which forms the entry porch overhang. This is supported by slim wood posts. High narrow windows indicate the Victorian period.

343 N. Cleveland — *1922 Bungalow*   NRHP:1997
A single-story clapboard bungalow with rectangular
plan and shallow pitched multi-gable roof. The main
portion of the house is covered by a single gable roof
with side-facing gables. A centrally located front-
facing gable forms the entry porch overhang. This is
supported by tapered piers. The original mullioned
door is still present. On either side of the porch is
located a large 3-part transomed window.

348 N. Cleveland — *1909 Hip Roof Cottage*   NRHP:1997
A single-story box plan house with wide lap siding and
steep-pitched hip roof. The front facade is adorned
with a small pedimented gable which is embellished
with fish scale shingles. Attached to the front facade
is a separate roofed overhang which forms the entry
porch and is now supported by wrought iron piers a
replacement for the original.

355 N. Cleveland — *1921 Bungalow*   NRHP:1997
A single-story bungalow with wide lap siding and
clipped gable roof. The front facade features an
unusual clipped gable with a return at the eaves which
extends on either side to form what was probably
originally a full-width porch. It has since been
enclosed.

356 N. Cleveland — *1922 Bungalow*   NRHP:1997
A single-story bungalow with wide lap siding and
double front-facing gable roof. The forwardmost gable
forms the entry porch overhang and is supported by
wide piers with concrete bases and wood posts on top.

365 N. Cleveland — *1922c Cottage Gable Roof*   NONC

372 N. Cleveland — *1924*   NONC

CULVER AVENUE — EAST
—Culver is named for pioneer Charles Z. Culver—

115 E. Culver — *1920 California Bungalow*   NRHP:1997
Single-story bungalow with lap siding and single side-facing gable roof. There is a double entry indicating duplex usage. Each entry is covered by a small portico gable with diagonal braces.

231 E. Culver — *1915c Craftsman Bungalow*   NRHP:1997
Small single-story bungalow with single front-facing gable roof. The main roof extends forward to form a full-width porch overhang supported by tapered piers. Ornamental purlin and slatted venting adorn the upper gable face.

333 E. Culver — *1919 Craftsman Bungalow*   NRHP:1997
Small single-story tri-gable clapboard bungalow with main roof comprised of side-facing gables and a front-facing gable on the central portion of the facade supported by wide piers. Entry is beneath at center.

337 E. Culver — *1905c Hip Roof Cottage*   NRHP:1997
TREE: Jacaranda *Jacaranda acutifolia* and Bottle *Brachychiton populneu.*
Single-story house with lap siding and a steep-pitched hip roof. The house features a large wrap-around corner porch and a front-facing bay window gable. The gable on the bay window is pedimented while the porch and columns a retreated in the usual Classical manner.

354 E. Culver — *1910*   NONC

407 E. Culver — *1905c Hip Roof Cottage* NRHP:1997
A single-story house with hip roof and box plan. A small pedimented gable adorns the front of the roof; just offset from center is an attached porch supported by Classical columns.

415 E. Culver — *1905c Hip Roof Cottage* NRHP:1997
A single-story house with both a gable and a steep-pitched hip roof. The house has symmetrical

proportions with a nearly full-width front porch extending from the main roof and supported by Classical columns. There is a smaller hipped dormer on the front side of the roof.

504 E. Culver — *1909 Hip Roof Cottage*   NRHP:1997
A single-story hip roof cottage with combination hip and gable roof. A full-width front porch is recessed beneath the main roof and is supported by wood posts. Entry is at center beneath porch and is flanked on either side by large picture windows with transoms.

511 E. Culver — *1922 Craftsman Bungalow*   NRHP:1997
A single-story clapboard bungalow with double front-facing gables. The forwardmost gable forms the entry porch overhang supported by tapered piers with brick bases.

512 E. Culver — *1909 Hip Roof Cottage*   NRHP:1997
A single-story box plan house with steep-pitched hip roof contrasted by a smaller front-facing pedimented gable. Entry is via a recessed corner porch supported by Classical columns.

519 E. Culver — *1921 California Bungalow*   NRHP:1997
A single-story clapboard bungalow with single side-facing gable roof contrasted by both a front-facing attic gable vent dormer vent and a smaller entry portico gable. Entry is beneath at center flanked on either side by a pair of windows.

526 E. Culver — *1912 Craftsman*   NRHP:1997
TREE: Crape Myrtle *Lagerstroemia indica* 14" 30' 20'. Oldest Crape Myrtle in Orange-pink color.
This is an unusual house both for its proportion and styling. Primarily it has a large rectangular plan gable structure with clapboard siding. A smaller front-facing gable at the first story defines the porch overhang and attached is a full wrap-around porch. The porch is supported in five places by tapered piers with brick bases. Since the 1982 survey this structure has been altered with appropriate rear addition

sufficiently compatible and not intrusive.

527 E. Culver — *1924 Bungalow*   NRHP:1997
OWNER: Leo A. & Virga Pyeatt
BLDR: Orange Contracting & Milling Co.

The Leo & Virga Pyeatt Home

A single-story tri-gable bungalow with symmetrical proportions derived from a front-facing gable porch overhang in the center front facade. Porch gable is supported by tapered piers and entry is via either side of the porch.

535 E. Culver — *1921*   NONC

536 E. Culver — *1906 Hip Roof Cottage*   NRHP:1997
A single-story box plan and clapboard house with a steep-pitched hip roof. A small dormer with hip roof is on the front portion. Entry is via recessed corner porch supported by Classical columns.

543 E. Culver — *1914 Craftsman Bungalow*   NRHP:1997
A single-story bungalow with lap siding and double front-facing gables . The smaller forwardmost gable forms the entry porch overhang supported by tapered piers with brick bases. Ornamental purlins grace the eaves.

546 E. Culver — *1908 Hip Roof Cottage*   OTPA:1997

OWNER: Charles Rundall
A single-story house with clapboard siding and pyramidal roof. The main roof is contrasted by a smaller front-facing gable with cross-ties and ornamental bargeboard. Probably the original entry was beneath the corner porch which has since been enclosed.

555 E. Culver — *1915 Craftsman*   NRHP:1997
One and one-half story Craftsman house with main roof comprised of side-facing gable contrasted by front-facing dormer gable. The main roof extends forward to form what was originally a porch overhang but has since been enclosed with large multi-pane windows. Porch overhang is supported by tapered piers. The house has lap siding.

556 E. Culver — *1915 Craftsman*   NRHP:1997
A one and on-half story Craftsman house built on a rectangular plan with single side-facing gable roof contrasted by a small shed dormer on the front portion. The main roof extends forward to form a full-width porch supported by tapered elephantine piers. Entry is beneath at center flanked on either side by large three-part windows.

569 E. Culver — *1915c Craftsman*   NRHP:1997
A one and one-half story Craftsman house with rectangular plan clapboard siding and a single side-facing gable roof contrasted by a front-facing dormer gable. There is a full-width porch recessed beneath the main porch supported by wide piers with lap siding. Two smaller half-size piers define the front stoop entry and are connected to the other piers by slatted balustrade.

577 E. Culver — *1915 Craftsman Bungalow* NRHP:1997
A single-story bungalow with lap siding and tri-gable roof. Front portion of house is defined by a large front-facing gable which forms the full-width entry porch. This gable is adorned by a three-part window with

transom.

585 E. Culver — *1924 Mediterranean Revival*   NRHP:1997
A single-story bungalow scale house with a box plan stucco siding and a flat roof. The front facade is defined by raised pilasters at the corners. Roof ridges are articulated with adobe tiles.

595 E. Culver — *1914 Craftsman*   NRHP:1997
A one and one-half story Craftsman house with clapboard siding and primary roof comprised of side-facing gables. This roof is contrasted by a front-facing dormer gable ornamented with a pair of multi-pane transoms and cross-ties between the bargeboards. The main roof extends forward to form a full-width porch supported by wide tapered piers connected to a low porch wall.

618 E. Culver — *1917 Bungalow*   OTPA:1997
BLDR: Boaz Atherton-Rancher
Atherton built the home in 1917 and initially planted plum trees. He later changed over to citrus and ran these until his death in 1923. His daughter Ella Mae was married in the home in 1922 to Thomas Jefferson Hight.

A single-story clapboard bungalow with double front-facing gables. The forwardmost gable forms the entry porch overhang supported by piers with clapboard bases and woodposts atop.

630 E. Culver — *1910c Hip Roof Cottage*   NRHP:1997
A single-story clapboard house with steep-pitched hip roof contrasted by a smaller pedimented front-facing gable defining the front facade and a large corner wrap-around porch, supported by Classical columns.

632 E. Culver — *1908 Hip Roof Cottage*   NRHP:1997
A single-story clapboard house with pyramidal roof extending forward to form a large wrap-around porch supported by Classical columns. This is contrasted and offset by a pedimented gable defining the remainder

of the front facade.

638 E. Culver — *1915c Craftsman*   NRHP:1997
A one and one-half story Craftsman home built on a rectangular plan with clapboard siding. The main roof has a large side-facing gable contrasted by a front-facing dormer gable with vented transom and ornamental purlins. The main roof extends forward to form a full-width porch supported by very wide tapered piers.

652 E. Culver — *1911 Craftsman*   NRHP:1997
A one and one-half story Craftsman house with clapboard siding. The main roof has side-facing gables. A front-facing dormer gable has multi-pane windows in a modified Palladian fashion and ornamental purlins beneath the dormer eaves. The main roof extends forward to form a full-width porch overhang, supported by wide tapered piers with arroyo stone bases.

720 E. Culver — *1926 Provincial Revival*   NRHP:1997
A provincial revival rectangular plan residence with side gabled roof and arched gabled entry portal. Siding is stucco with double-hung wood windows and lintel type openings (4/1 paned). Exposed rafter tails are present.
Orange grove remnant.

742 E. Culver — *1925 Craftsman Bungalow*   NRHP:1997
A single-story bungalow with double front-facing gables. The larger gable forms the main roof while the lower gable is located exactly parallel to the larger gable. This has a full-width porch overhang supported by tapered pier s with brick bases.

804 E. Culver — *1912 Bungalow*   NRHP:1997
A single-story clapboard bungalow with gable roof and square shingles in the upper front-facing gable face. Multi-pane windows are across the front facade; a smaller square gabled bay is on the side.

816 E. Culver — *1905c Hip Roof Cottage* NRHP:1997

A single-story house with box plan lap siding and pyramidal roof. The pyramidal roof is contrasted by a smaller gable defining one-half of the front facade. What was originally a corner porch has since been enclosed.

Culver Avenue — West

215 W. Culver — *1920c Gable Roof Cottage*   NONC
Since the 1982 survey this building no longer is considered to be of historic architectural significance.

215 W. Culver — *1920 Cottage Gable Roof*   NONC

218 W. Culver — *1923 Bungalow*   NONC

222 W. Culver — *1915c Craftsman Bungalow*   NONC

225 W. Culver — *1920 Bungalow*   NRHP:1997
Tri-gabled bungalow with each of the three gables facing front. Center most gable is largest. Two smaller gables at either end form entry porch porticos . Each is supported by piers with wood posts. Slatting adorns upper gable faces.

225 W. Culver — *1920c California Bungalow*   NONC

226 W. Culver — *1920c California Bungalow*   NONC

228 W. Culver — *1923 California Bungalow*   NONC

504 W. Culver *1926 Bungalow*   NRHP:1997
Low to the ground clapboard bungalow with single-gable roof.

512 W. Culver — *1925 Bungalow*   NRHP:1997
Double front-facing clapboard bungalow with frontmost gable forming entry porch overhang. This gable is supported by slim tapered posts. Entry is at center and flanked on either side by double-hung windows.

518 W. Culver — *1895c Victorian Cottage* NRHP:1997
Vertical emphasis common to Victorian era homes. Steep pitched gable roof with L-plan to gable and corresponding plan on shiplap siding on facades. Special roof overhang in apex of ell forms porch overhang. Entry is just beneath this.

525 W. Culver — *1924 Bungalow*   NRHP:1997
Small double-gable bungalow with two front-facing gables and clapboard siding. Frontmost gable forms

entry porch overhang and is supported by wood posts. Entry is just beneath.

527 W. Culver — *1924 Bungalow*   NONC
Low to the ground clapboard bungalow with double front-facing gables. Foremost gable forms entry porch overhang and is supported by wood posts. Vertical slatting adorns uppermost portion of gable face. Since the 1982 survey this structure has been severely altered by inappropriate aluminum windows and stucco siding.

528 W. Culver — *1925 Bungalow*   NRHP:1997
Small bungalow home with single-gable roof and clapboard siding. Smaller gabled portico forms entry and is supported by wood posts.

539 W. Culver — *1928 Provincial Revival*   NRHP:1997
A single-story stucco rectangular plan provincial revival residence with multi-gabled shingled roof. Entry contains multi-arched portico. Large arched mullioned window on front facade. Large matching arched windows also exist on west facing facade.

603 W. Culver — *1923 Craftsman Bungalow*   NRHP:1997
Bungalow home with double front-facing gables and clapboard siding on facades below. Frontmost gable forms entry porch overhang and is adorned with dentils in upper gable face. Since the 1982 survey this structure has been altered with inappropriate stucco siding.

611 W. Culver — *1925 Mediterranean Revival*   NRHP:1997
Small low-to-the-ground Mediterranean Revival bungalow with flat roof and stucco siding. Interesting character to this house is derived from the wall extensions both at the roof and on the sides. Double arched porte cochere forms driveway entry. Low wall screens stoop which forms main entry to house. Awnings span full width of front facade.

618 W. Culver — *1924 California Bungalow*   NRHP:1997

Double-gable clapboard bungalow with smaller gable symmetrically placed at center of front facade and forming entry porch overhang. This gabled portico is supported by tapered piers. Entry is beneath at center.

619 W. Culver — *1924 Spanish Colonial Revival* NRHP:1997
Flat roof stucco sided L-plan Spanish Colonial Revival bungalow. Special arched entry is located in apex of ell. Roof of this entry porch is tiled .

626 W. Culver — *1923 Bungalow*   NONC

627 W. Culver — *1930c Provincial Revival*   NONC

629 W. Culver — *1926 Provincial Revival*   NRHP:1997
A single-story provincial revival stucco box residence with simple gable over front entry.

638 W. Culver — *1926 Commercial*   NONC

643 W. Culver — *1924 Mediterranean Revival*   NRHP:1997
Flat roof with adobe tiled ridges stucco facades on rectangular plan. Entry is at center and flanked by picture windows on either side. What appears to be a slightly later gabled porch overhang is located across front facade.

703 W. Culver — *1930 Spanish Colonial Revival* NRHP:1997
U-facing gables on either end of front. Roof is of adobe tiles while siding is in stucco. Large arched picture window adorns front of larger gable face. Entry is in center of U.

711 W. Culver — *1928 Gable Roof Cottage*   NRHP:1997
Small simple box with single-gable roof and clapboard siding. Entry is at center.

719 W. Culver — *1926 California Bungalow*   NRHP:1997
Multi-gable bungalow with clapboard siding. Front-facing gable forms entry porch overhang and is supported by round columns. Entry is at center beneath.

727 W. Culver — *1924 Spanish Colonial Revival* NRHP:1997

Multi-gable roof stucco siding large arched windows and arched opening to entry.

743 W. Culver — *1929 Provincial Revival*   NRHP:1997
Multi-gable roof with steep pitch and rolled eaves. Stucco siding. Main entry has separate smaller gabled overhang. Since the 1982 survey this structure has been altered with inappropriate window replacements.

Cypress Street — South
—Cypress is named for one of the horticultural grove trees—

100 S. Cypress —
TREE: Camphor *Cinnamomum camphora* 65 foot spread.

128 S. Cypress — *1909c Industrial*   NRHP:1997
Red Fox Orchards
This former packing house is a most pragmatic industrial building exhibiting no particular style. The long, boxy structure has a flat roof and shiplap siding. The building follows the contour of the railroad tracks on the west side and even has its own spurline which connects with the loading docks of the packing house. The main street-facing facade has a stepped parapet with a remnant of the old sign, Sunkist Consolidated Orange Growers. The building is in a deteriorated state and unused at this time.

145 S. Cypress — *1910c Hip Roof Cottage*   NRHP:1997
Box plan house with pyramidal roof and facades now covered by asbestos shingles. Separate pedimented gable forms entry portico and is supported by slender columns typical of the Classical Revival homes. Decorative shingles on the gabled portico and broad eaves with decorative brackets further distinguish the house.

153 S. Cypress — *1910c Hip Roof Cottage* NRHP:1997
Steep pitched, gable roof, shiplap siding and front-facing gable form the entry porch overhang. This gable is supported by Classical Revival columns. Windows are framed typical of the period.

160 S. Cypress — *1930 Industrial*   NRHP:1997
A concrete structure supported by metal piers and roofed with metal material.

163 S. Cypress — *1889 Victorian Eastlake*   NRHP:1997
Parker House
This is a large, two-story Victorian house with the typical Victorian massing and detailing. Though

simpler than the Victorians located in more urban areas, this is quite detailed for a rural Victorian which was once surrounded by some farmland. The two-story house has shiplap siding and a combined gable and mansard roof. A larger wrap-around porch is supported by ornate turned columns. Each of the upper gable faces and the gabled dormer in front are embellished with jigsawn bargeboard with an inner arch and a drop spindle as well as combined fish-scale and saw-toothed shingling. Wide eaves are embellished with ornamental brackets like those on each of the window hoods. The house is in good condition, though in need of painting, and retains its original architectural integrity to an excellent degree. This residence was added to the National Register of Historic Places in 1989.

173 S. Cypress — *1915c Craftsman Bungalow*   NRHP:1997
Single, front-facing gable roof with lap siding on facades. A porch spans full width of the front of the house beneath main roof extension. Entry is at center with large picture windows flanked on either side.

191 S. Cypress — *1920c Craftsman Bungalow*   NRHP:1997
Double, front-facing gables above an L-plan house. Lap siding is used on all facades. Entry is beneath a separate porch overhang in apex of ell. Ornamental cross-ties and purlins adorn upper gable faces. Frontmost gable has a large, three-part picture window.

193 S. Cypress — *1921 Vernacular*   NRHP:1997
This is a small, single-story clapboard church with a single gable roof. The corner entry is articulated by a rectilinear entry tower with a pyramidal roof. Casement windows around the building are arranged in pairs, and each is crowned with a large, stained glass transom. These arched windows are repeated in the entry tower. Triangular bracket supports are located beneath the eaves on the front gable face. The

church was built adjacent to a small, Classical Revival style house which still forms part of the church. These two are connected in such a way that together they appear as one building. The church shows slight Craftsman influence but is more a vernacular adaptation, incorporating structural and economic pragmatics. The arched windows and entry tower are characteristic of small rural churches. The building is well-maintained and exhibits its original architectural integrity.

200 S. Cypress — *1924 Industrial*   NRHP:1997
A single-story industrial building with a flat roof and facades built to the lot line. Brick is used along the lower foundation wall and in the pilasters; plaster is used above. Entry is defined by a double door (not original) with side lights. Brick pilasters are on either side with a large arched connecting transom.

243 S. Cypress — *1905c Hip Roof Cottage*   NRHP:1997
A single-story, box plan house with clapboard siding and steep-pitched, hip roof. Entry is via a recessed corner porch supported by a Classical column.

246 S. Cypress — *1923 Mediterranean Revival*   NRHP:1997
A boxy house with flat roof and flush stucco sides. Entry is at corner recessed beneath main portion of house. Paired, double-hung windows are located across front and sides.

255 S. Cypress — *1923 California Bungalow*   NRHP:1997
A irregular plan bungalow residence with multi-gables and clapboard siding. The entry is formed by a suspended gable with ornamental brackets. The front door is flanked by 2 sets of paired multi-mullioned (10-light) windows. A similar set windows is present on the facade of a front facing gable. Brick piers and a brick chimney are present.

263 S. Cypress — *1923 Craftsman Bungalow*   NRHP:1997
Low to.the ground, single-story bungalow with very shallow pitched roof. Main portion of house is covered

by side-facing gable, while a smaller, front-facing gable extension forms entry porch overhang. This overhang is supported by wide tapered columns. Entry is beneath and flanked on either side by large transomed, picture windows. Vertical slatting adorns front gable entry.

280 S. Cypress — *1930c Commercial*   NONC

284 S. Cypress — *1900c Victorian*   NONC

294 S. Cypress — *1926 Spanish Colonial Revival* NRHP:1997
Small bungalow-scale house, but multi-faceted due to varying elevations and extensions. Main roof is flat with parapet with tiled ridges. A gable extension and smaller, rectangular porch extension is dressed with arched openings. Both have tiled roofs.

Cypress Street — North

142 N. Cypress — *1937 Brick Commercial*   NRHP:1997
A brick commercial building with low-pitched roof and wooden facade on a rectangular plan. No windows are present. A industrial wooden sliding door is present on each end of the building.

153 N. Cypress — *1923 Brick Commercial*   NRHP:1997
A large warehouse style brick commercial building on a rectangular plan. Large industrial sliding doors in center of building are flanked by street-level double-hung single-paned wooden windows.

171 N. Cypress — *1905c Hip Roof Cottage*   NRHP:1997
A single-story house with box plan and truncated hip roof. The original siding has since been covered with asbestos shingles. A full-width front porch extends across the front facade and is supported by wood posts. Entry is at center and is flanked on either side by a sash window.

177 N. Cypress — *1905c Hip Roof Cottage*   NRHP:1997
A single-story box plan house with clapboard siding and truncated hip roof. The house has a nearly full-width front porch supported by 2 x 4's. This house has the same symmetrical and simple appearance as others on this block. Since the 1982 survey, this structure has deteriorated.

185 N. Cypress — *1905c Hip Roof Cottage*   NRHP:1997
This house is identical to the one next door at 177

200 N. Cypress — *1924 Industrial*   NRHP:1997
California Wire & Cable Co. (1921-1930)
Anaconda Wire & Cable Co.
California Wire & Cable started in 1921 and was bought out by Anaconda Wire & Cable in 1930.
This building complex consists of a full block on both sides which have always been put to industrial use. The building complex is one-story with brick facade. The roofline is alternately flat and domed, but always

screened by a raised parapet. The building is built up to the sidewalk. Large multi-paned windows are spaced across the facades. A small row of accent brick highlights the cornice.

California Wire & Cable Co.

296 N. Cypress — *1929 Industrial*   NONC

337 N. Cypress — *1917*   NONC

343 N. Cypress — *1895c Victorian Cottage*   NRHP:1997
A single-story house built on an L-plan with shiplap siding and steep-pitched gabled roof. There is a double entry in the apex of the ell which also forms the entry porch and is covered by a separate shed roof overhang supported by 2 x 4's. The high, narrow, double hung windows and centrally located chimney indicate the house was built prior to 1900.

350 N. Cypress — *1933 Industrial*   NRHP:1997
This is the Villa Park Orchard's Association Packing House which was originally the Santiago Orange Grower's Association Packing House. The original portion of the packing house built in 1919 is still present on the site but is much obscured by the more recent building. The building is still in use as a packing house today. It is constructed in a warehouse style and has been adapted to the needs of the building owners.

It's a simple boxy building with a flat roof and stucco facades.

365 N. Cypress — *1920c Gable Roof Cottage*   NONC
A single-story box plan house with clapboard siding and single-gabled roof. Entry is sheltered by its own separate, simple portico.

369 N. Cypress — *1920 Bungalow*   NONC

373 N. Cypress — *1920c Bungalow*   NRHP:1997
A single-story clapboard bungalow with L-plan and multi-gable roof. The house is simple and unadorned.

379 N. Cypress — *1920c Bungalow*   NRHP:1997
A small, single-story clapboard bungalow with shallow-pitched multi-gable roof with vertical slats in the gable vent. The house is built on the symmetrical plan with a centrally located, front-facing gable forming the entry porch. Double-entry indicates the house was intended for duplex usage.

413 N. Cypress — *1919 Vernacular*   NRHP:1997
This is a simple, small and probably hand-constructed house. It is built of board and batten with a single gabled roof which extends forward to form a nearly full-width porch overhang.

417 N. Cypress — *1919 Gable Roof Cottage*   NRHP:1997
A single-story bungalow with single front-facing gabled roof. A full-width porch is formed by a separate roof extension and is supported by 2 x 4's. The original siding has since been covered with asbestos shingles. Double doors indicate that the house was originally intended for duplex usage.

421 N. Cypress — *1923*   NONC

435 N. Cypress — *1920*   NONC

424 N. Cypress — *1924 Mission Revival*   NONC
Rev. M. L. Pearson Church
The Orange Community Mens Bible Class
Originally built as a neighborhood church, the building now houses a local community center. Essentially the

center of the highest density Hispanic district in Orange, the building has always served for community use.

A flat roof and glass-brick windows show the styling of this Mission Revival architecture.

445 N. Cypress — *1920 Bungalow*   NRHP:1997
This is a single-story clapboard bungalow built on an L-plan with multi-gabled roof. Entry is near the apex of the ell and the main roof extends forward at this point to form the entry porch overhang. It is supported by simple 2 x 4's with a connecting slatted balustrade.

455 N. Cypress — *1922*

465 N. Cypress — *1913 Vernacular Bungalow*   NRHP:1997
A small box plan house with single-gabled roof. The main roof extends forward to form a full-width porch overhang which is supported by 2 x 4's. The house is very simple and very basic.

473 N. Cypress — *1890c Vernacular Victorian*   NONC

GLASSELL STREET — SOUTH
—Glassell is named for founder Andrew Glassell—

100 S. Glassell —1905 Brick Commercial   NRHP:1982
see 36 Plaza

107 S. Glassell — *1902 Brick Commercial* NRHP:1982
see 26 Plaza

108 S. Glassell — *1907 Brick Commercial* NRHP:1982
see 42 Plaza
Ehlen and Grote Building 51,250 sq. ft.
The largest commercial building in Old Towne Orange,
the 'Big White Store' with three floors, is built from
white glazed brick, giving it the name. William Boyd
"Hopalong Cassidy" made horse-and-wagon deliveries
in the early years.

Courtesy Smith & Ebert

The Big White Store - front & rear

109 S. Glassell — *1910 Brick Commercial* NRHP:1982
3,600 sq. ft.

119 S. Glassell — *Brick Commercial*   NONC
Once a historic building, fire gutted this facility,
leaving only a facade.

131 S. Glassell — *1906 Brick Commercial* NONC
Gunther Building 8,100 sq. ft.
A new building and addition were added and now
partially surrounds original building. The total facade
change is now out of character with the District

although the top of the structure can still be seen above the new front.

Courtesy Army Navy Store

Gunther Building - 1950s *

132 S. Glassell — *1914 Brick Commercial*   NRHP:1982
Friedman Hall 13,600 sq. ft.
A Brick commercial with a second floor hall and wire glass skylights. This building once held a movie theatre.

135 S. Glassell — *1924 Brick Commercial*   NONC
3,000 sq. ft.

141 S. Glassell — *1923 Brick Commercial*   NONC
J.P. Boring Block Addition 2,000 sq. ft.

142 S. Glassell — *1887 Brick Commercial*   NRHP:1982
M. Dobner Building 1,650 sq. ft.
Veneered brick single story with rear addition.

155 S. Glassell — *1910 Brick Commercial*   NONC
J. P. Boring Block 20,000 sq. ft.

185 S. Glassell — *1922 Commercial Brick/Concrete*   NONC
Apartments 3,300 sq. ft.

195 S. Glassell — *1922 Mediterranean*   NRHP:1982 $10,000
Orange County Fruit Exchange 2,700 sq. ft.
Formed in 1893, the Orange County Fruit Exchange became a cooperative system for marketing citrus products throughout the U.S. Sunkist became the link

between the citrus grower and the nation. Under construction for two years, the Mediterranean Revival structure opened on December 12, 1922.

The new office building cost $20,000 to erect. Hollow brick with frame cornice and tile roof. There is a similar Exchange Building for Riverside in Arlington Heights.

Orange County Fruit Exchange - from a sketch & in the 1930s

205 S. Glassell — *1905 Hip Roof Cottage*   NRHP:1997

A classic hip roof box plan cottage with wood-shingled siding and double-hung windows. Three such windows ornament the front facade. A canopied kneebrace is present over the front door.

221 S. Glassell — *1903 Victorian Helen Arnim*   OTPA:1997

This is a two-story, turn-of-the-century house in the style sometimes known as Princess Anne. The Princess Anne style is a derivative of the larger Queen Anne style but incorporates more simplified detailing and design which was popular after the turn-of-the-century. The two-story clapboard house features a complex roofline with steep-pitched gables. The house is built on a modified L-plan with the apex of the ell resulting in a porch overhang supported by Classical columns. Turned balusters are on the ornamental balustrade connecting the porch posts. The largest, front-facing gable features an ornamental window in somewhat of a reverse Palladian style.

239 S. Glassell — *1905c Victórian*   NRHP:1997
OWNER: William Henry Harrison Clayton
In 1917 Ora Clayton moved from Chapman & Lemon
during the construction of the Pacific Red Car Station
by Clayton in 1917, mules moved the structure by
windlass with Ora sitting quietly on the porch the
whole time. Like the house next door at 221 South
Glassell, this one is also fashioned in what was
sometimes called the Princess Anne style.

This too is a large, two-story house with multi-gable
roofline and built on an L-plan. A large, wrap-a round
porch is present and the porch overhang is supported
by columns with Corinthian capitals. The short leg of
the ell results in a front-facing, gable wing with
exposed beam ornamentation, a small vented transom
and a large, three-part picture window with transom
on the first story. The original wood door with plate
glass window is still present.

244 S. Glassell — *1905c Hip Roof Cottage* NRHP:1997
A two-story house with steep-pitched, hip roof and
wide lap siding. What was probably originally
clapboard was maybe later covered with the present
lap siding. Also what was originally probably a corner
porch supported by Classical columns has since been
enclosed. All of the windows and remaining format of
the house remain original. Since the 1982 survey, the
front porch has been reopened but an extra, not
entirely appropriate, porch added.

254 S. Glassell — *1894 Victorian*   NRHP:1997
A small, one and one-half story house built on an L-
plan with steep-pitched, gable roof and shiplap siding.
The house features two front-facing, gable dormers
each with arched transoms and the rearmost with
elaborate transom sash window. The apex of the ell is
characterized by an entry porch overhang supported
by wood posts. The house is an excellent, unaltered
example of a pre-1900 cotta ge-scale house in Orange.

257 S. Glassell — *1910c Hip Roof Vernacular*   NRHP:1997
This is an unusually designed house in that it incorporates the format and massing of the Classical Revival period but is coupled with more bungalow architectural detailing. It is a box plan which features a complex, hip roofline and clapboard siding on the facades. The entry is recessed and features a double door entry, indicating the house was originally intended to be used as a duplex.

262 S. Glassell — *1898 Victorian Cottage*   OTPA:1997
OWNER: Mary Roberts
A small, cottage-scale, pioneer dwelling with multi-gable roofline and shingle siding which probably replaces the original shiplap siding. The house is built on a modified rectangular plan and features a single, front-facing gable projection. To the side of this an extra roof overhang forms the entry porch supported by a single wood post. The house is basic and unadorned, reflecting the fact that a very modest budget and limited resources were used to build the house . Since the 1982 survey, this structure has been altered with acceptable Victorian ornamentation.

265 S. Glassell — *1920c Bungalow*   NRHP:1997
A single-story clapboard bungalow with double, front-facing gable roof. Forwardmost gable forms the entry porch overhang and is supported by tapered piers. Vertical slatting adorns the upper portions of the gable. Large picture windows are present on the lower portion of the front facade.

272 S. Glassell — *1900 Altered Victorian*   NONC
This house has been modified over the years, but its origins in the turn-of-the-century period are clear. The house features typical steep-pitched, gabled roof and simple embellishment which characterizes early houses in Orange. The house has since been stuccoed, and all the windows, doors and entry have been substantially modified.

281 S. Glassell — *1904 Hip Roof Cottage* NRHP:1997
A single-story house with combination hip and gable roof and clapboard siding which has since been covered by asbestos shingles. The house has a squatty, boxy quality typical of the period, but this is enhanced by a large, wrap-a round, corner porch supported by wide columns with Corinthian capitals. An important element of the house is the large, boxy picture windows with diamond pane transoms. Near the porch entrance is a small, transomed window with stained glass and an ornamental frame.

291 S. Glassell — *1904 Hip Roof Cottage* NRHP:1997
A single-story, box plan house with clapboard siding and steep-pitched, hip roof. Hip dormers are also present along the roofline. Entry is via a corner recessed porch supported by Classical columns. Windows are framed in the manner typical of the period.

292 S. Glassell — *1915c Craftsman* NRHP:1997
A two-story house with shallow-pitched, multi-gable roofline and wide lap siding on the facades. The house features the second story portion located predominantly on the rear half of the house while the front, lower story is characterized by several gables. One-half of the front facade is devoted to a large entry porch which is supported by wood posts. A brick chimney with special detailing rises up the front of the house. The house features many windows typical of the Craftsman period.

330 S. Glassell — *1923 Mediterranean Revival Apts.* nrhp:1997
This is a small apartment complex built on a rectangular plan with a flat roof and stucco facades. Each of the entries is articulated by a small portico with adobe tile hoods and ornamental braces. In addition, this same hood arrangement is located on the front facade over the windows.

334 S. Glassell — *1900c Victorian* NRHP:1997

This is an unusual turn-of-the-century house for Orange which features a steep-pitched, gable roof in combination with a corner turret with a conical roof. Juxtaposed opposite to the turret is a large entry porch supported by Classical Columns. An ornamental brick chimney is also present. The add-on on the north side of the house is a later addition and does detract from the original architectural appearance.

335 S. Glassell — *1915c Craftsman Bungalow*   NRHP:1997
A single-story bungalow with lap siding and double, front-facing gable roof. The forwardmost gable forms the entry porch overhang and is supported by brick piers. These piers are connected by a low, brick porch wall.

345 S. Glassell — *1915c Craftsman Bungalow*   NRHP:1997
A single-story bungalow with lap siding and double, front-facing gable roof. The forwardmost gable forms the entry porch overhang and is supported by brick piers. The original entry door is still present and features six small, plate glass windows. On either side are large picture windows with transoms. Ornamental purlins grace the eaves.

350 S. Glassell — *1915c Craftsman*   NRHP:1997
TREE: CAMPHOR *Cinnamomum camphora*
BLDR: Nelson Edwards - Edwards Block
Edwards began work as a butcher after his father but eventually went in to banking and built (also with his father) the Edwards Block in the Plaza district. Going into local politics, he pursued this career until the 1920s.

This is a large, two-story Craftsman house designed in much the same manner as many of the Greene & Greene houses in Pasadena. The multi-gable roofline is repeated in the roof overhang of the large, wrap-around porch. This overhang is supported by wood posts on brick bases. The vertical slatting on the upper porch gable faces is also present on the main gables.

The original entry door is still present; its extra large width is particularly notable as are the vertical glass panes and the flanking sidelights. The house is in excellent condition and retains its original architectural character. The most outstanding Craftsman style home in Orange, this house was built for Edwards, a state senator and a local banker in 1915.

353 S. Glassell — *1926 Mediterranean Revival*   NRHP:1997
This is a small, single-story, box plan Mediterranean Revival house built with simplistic architectural detailing. The house features a flat roof coupled with stuccoed facades. As typical of the period, there are several projecting wings with the entry formed by a special enclosed portico with large openings and a tile hood.

360 S. Glassell — *1925 Eastlake*   NRHP:1997
A two-story residential structure with features of Victorian and Italianate style. Front facade appears to identify with Victorian and features a tower. Siding is wood shiplap and facade also features single-light double-hung wood windows. The original structure is of rectangular plan.

361 S. Glassell — *1914 Altered Hip Roof Cottage*   NRHP:1997
A single-story, clapboard bungalow with multi-hip roof. The house appears to have undergone some modification over the years, of which the prominent bay window and stoop are probably the primary examples. The house is basically simple and unadorned.

368 S. Glassell — *1915c Craftsman Bungalow*   NRHP:1997
A single-story bungalow with wide lap siding and double, front-facing gable roof. The forwardmost gable forms the entry porch overhang and is supported by tapered piers on molded cast concrete bases. A low porch wall connects these piers. The original entry door with plate glass windows is still present and is

flanked on either side by a large, three-part picture window with leaded glass transom. Cross-ties and purlins adorn the upper gable faces.

369 S. Glassell — *1925 Mediterranean Revival*   NRHP:1997
This is a small, box plan bungalow designed with Mediterranean Revival and some Mission Revival influences. The house is characteristically designed with a flat roof and stucco facades. It is built on a modified L-plan with one-half of the front facade devoted to a large, entry porch arcade with arched openings. Two Mission style parapets are also located on the front facade. Double entry doors on the remaining half of the front facade are sheltered by a tile hood.

374 S. Glassell — *1898 Victorian*   NRHP:1997
BLDR: A.J. Harding Although built by Harding the home has a variety of residents in its history, mostly as renters. William Hagthrop, co-owned the Orange Star, previously known as the Orange Post and Orange Tribune.

A one and one-half story Victorian house with combination clapboard and ornamental siding. The roof is comprised of several steep-pitched gables. The smaller of the two, front-facing, pedimented gables defines the angled bay window of the front facade. This bay window features sash windows on either side with ornamental frames and a fixed-glass pane on the frontmost portion with a leaded glass transom. Both of the upper gable faces feature sawtooth shingles and ornamentally framed windows and attic transom. The house is a good Victorian example, though some question remains as to whether the house was remodeled just after the turn-of-the-century. Since the 1982 survey, this structure has had a change of use from residential to professional.

377 S. Glassell — *1915c Craftsman Bungalow*   NRHP:1997
A single-story bungalow with ornamental lap siding

and shallow-pitched, multi-gable roof. The house is predominantly covered by a single, side-facing gable, while two, front-facing gables are juxtaposed to this for contrast. The original door with mullioned glass panes is still present. Large windows with mullioned headers are also present on the front facade. Since the 1982 survey, the original front door has been removed.

391 S. Glassell — *1923*

392 S. Glassell — *1905c Hip Roof Cottage* NONC
Since the 1982 survey, this structure has been replaced with a 2-story office/professional building.

406 S. Glassell — *1903 Victorian Cottage* NRHP:1997
A single-story clapboard house with combination steep-pitched and gabled roof. The house is built on an L-plan with the short leg of the ell resulting in a front-facing gabled projection which forms an angled bay window on the lower half. These windows are distinguished by ornamental brackets. This upper gable face is distinguished by a sunray embellishment. A large corner, wrap-around porch is present and is supported by Classical columns.

413 S. Glassell — *1904 Hip Roof Cottage* NRHP:1997
A single-story clapboard house with box plan and steep-pitched, hip roof. A small gabled dormer is present on the front portion of the roof and features an ornamentally framed transom vent and fish scale shingles. Entry is via a corner recessed porch supported by Classical columns.

416 S. Glassell — *1903 Victorian Cottage* NRHP:1997
A two-story clapboard house with steep-pitched, multi-gabled roofline. The entry is distinguished by a pedimented gabled entry portico supported by wood posts with ornamental jigsawn brackets. The inner portion of the pediment is adorned with fish scale shingles. To the side a special roof extension forms an enclosed sun porch. The original screen door with

jigsawn wood is still present. The upper front, gable face is adorned with ornamental brackets and a half-moon transomed vent.

419 S. Glassell — *1904 Hip Roof Cottage*   NRHP:1997
A single-story house with combination steep-pitched, hip and gabled roof. The house is unusual in that its siding is formed of cast concrete blocks. Entry is via the corner recessed porch supported by Classical columns. The front-facing gable features a return at the eaves and also a half-moon, sunray embellishment. An angled bay window is located on the side of the house.

437 S. Glassell — *1908 Hip Roof Cottage*   NRHP:1997
A single-story, box plan house with clapboard siding and combination steep-pitched, hip and gabled roof. A small entry portico is distinguished by a pedimented gable supported by Classical columns.

445 S. Glassell — *1915c Bungalow*   NRHP:1997
A single-story bungalow with wide lap siding and multi-gabled roof. The house is predominantly covered by a single-gabled roof with side-facing gables, but this is juxtaposed by two smaller, front-facing gables. One-half of the front facade is devoted to a porch which is supported by wide, tapered piers. The front facade features two three-part windows with ornamental transoms.

453 S. Glassell — *1904 Post Victorian Vernacular* OTPA:1997
OWNER: R.J. Fyffe
This is a modified, two-story house with clapboard siding and single, front-facing gabled roof. A separate porch roof extension across the full width of the front facade is supported by slender wood posts. The original door with plate glass windows is still present. Since the 1982 survey, this structure has been altered with turned baluster rail and panel door.

454 S. Glassell — *1922 Mediterranean Revival*   NRHP:1997

A single-story, box plan house with stucco facades and a flat roof. As is characteristic of the style, there are several different projecting wings. In this case, the entry portico projects forward and is characterized by a large, arched opening. A small ornamental opening is present above the door, and the curvilinear pattern of this opening is echoed in the main entry door below. To either side are French windows with mullioned panes. Above each of these windows is an adobe tile hood.

458 S. Glassell — *1916 Craftsman Bungalow*   NRHP:1997
A single-story bungalow with wide lap siding and multi-gabled roof. Two front-facing gables characterize the front facade, and the forwardmost of these gabled forms the entry porch overhang. It is supported by tapered piers. Each of the upper gable faces features an ornamental transomed window with ornamental purlins. The original entry door is still present, flanked on either side by large windows with transoms.

461 S. Glassell — *1921 Bungalow*   NRHP:1997
A simple, single-story bungalow with wide lap siding and single, front-facing gabled roof. The entry was originally via a corner recessed porch supported by brick piers, but it appears that this was later enclosed. The entry is still on the side, covered by a shed roof extension.

469 S. Glassell — *1920c Bungalow*   NONC

472 S. Glassell — *1896 Queen Anne Victorian*   NRHP:1997
OWNER: Henry & Marie Dierker
BLDR: Park Grower Built by Park, the home sold first in 1900 to the Woodhouse family and then in 1901 to the Dierkers. Originally with a barn, the land extended to Olive St. Dierker Grew walnuts and kept bees.

This is a very large, two and one-half story house with shiplap siding and combination steep-pitched, hip and gabled roof. The most predominant and distinguishing feature of the house is the corner turret with conical roof. This is juxtaposed by a projecting wing on the other side of the front facade which is defined by a pedimented gable on the uppermost portion and ornamentally framed windows below. What was originally a wide front porch has since been enclosed and modified somewhat. The entry is now recessed. All the windows are the high, narrow variety common to the Victorian period. They feature mullioned panes unusual for the period and ornamental molding around the windows.

488 S. Glassell — *1912 Craftsman Bungalow*   NRHP:1997
TREE: Australian Tea *Leptospermum lacoigatum* 28" 25' 30' *Note the old twisted trunk.*

A one and one-half story bungalow with wide lap siding and multi-gabled roof. The front facade is characterized by a large, front-facing gable which originally formed a porch overhang but was later enclosed. The original piers are still present. The upper gable face is adorned with cross-ties, a louvered transom and ornamental purlins. Two sculpted lions adorn the half piers on the side of the stoop.

525 S. Glassell — *1936 Gothic Revival*   NRHP:1997
BLDR: Ray Welch Contractor Built by and for Welch, his father and brother both operated in Orange in the contracting business.

A Gothic revival rectangular plan residence with Richardsonian brick arch on front large window and features a gabled portal entry. Roof features multiple high-pitched gables with high ridge beam. Siding is stucco with wood windows present.

566 S. Glassell —
TREE: 1875 Moreton Bay Fig *Ficus macrophylla* 140" 108' 160'. Planted by grower Henri Gardner to honor his wife on the birth of his son. *(See 700 S. Grand)*

655 S. Glassell — *1941 Prairie*   NONC
     Kellar & Vi Watson Home
     Kellar Watson Watson ran his fathers store - Watson's
     dating from 1899 and bought this remnant of land from
     the Orange Park development of 1935.

     Two story, box-like structure with ship-lap siding and
     wide windows typical of the Prairie style.

701 S. Glassell — *1936 Mediterranean Revival*
     The Orange Horse Shoe Club

GLASSELL STREET — NORTH

101 N. Glassell — *1905 Brick Commercial* NRHP:1982
N.T. Edwards Block *see 77 Plaza*

102 N. Glassell — *1912 Brick Commercial* NRHP:1982
D.F. Campbell's Opera House Theater *see 75 Plaza*

114 N. Glassell — *1886 Brick Commercial* NONC
G. Schirm Bakery 4,400 sq. ft.
Wire glass skylight, the original facade has been
extensively remodeled.

122 N. Glassell — *1886 Brick Commercial* NONC
D.C. Pixley Building, Funiture Store 10,800 sq. ft.
Second floor in rear, extensive remodeling.

Pixley Furniture Store - 1910c

129 N. Glassell — *Brick Commercial* NONC
Kogler Addition 3,600 sq. ft.
Single story addition has extended the front tile but
is inconsistent with the remainder of the building.

131 N. Glassell — *1916 Brick Commercial* NRHP:1982
Kogler Hardware Building 13,200 sq. ft.

138 N. Glassell — *1931 Brick Commercial* NONC
Facade has been extensively remodeled.

149 N. Glassell — *1919 Brick Commercial* NONC
2,700 sq. ft.
The current building appears to be newer and out of

character with the District.

150 N. Glassell — *1885 Commercial, Brick*   NONC
C. M. Woodruff Building 2,250 sq. ft.
The first brick building in Orange is the oldest existing business structure. Extensive facade remodeling.

153 N. Glassell — *1915 Brick Commercial*   NONC
3,000 sq. ft.
The facade has been extensively remodeled.

154 N. Glassell — *1914 Brick Commercial*   NRHP:1982
Santa Ana Valley Irrigation Co 3,600 sq. ft.
Classic brick commercial with rear garage.

161 N. Glassell — *1911 Brick Commercial*   NRHP:1982
M. Eltistie Building 8,000 sq. ft.

162 N. Glassell — *1920 Brick Commercial*   NRHP:1982

172 N. Glassell — *1925 Concrete Theater*   NRHP:1982
Orange Theater
Reinforced concrete with wood trusses, includes a balcony, a stage and considerable ornamentation with a plastered interior.

177 N. Glassell — *1912 Brick Commercial*   NRHP:1982
M. Eltistie Addition 2,025 sq. ft.

205 N. Glassell — *1921 Period Apt. Building*   NRHP:1997
Apartments
This is a two-tiered apartment building outfitted with a flat roof and wide lap siding on the facades. This building has a boxy format and is simple and unadorned.

224 N. Glassell — *1905 Altered Victorian* NRHP:1997
This is a two-story clapboard house with steep-pitched, gable roof including two large, front-facing gables with a return at their eaves. Entry is via a corner recessed porch now supported by wood posts but which probably originally had Classical column supports. Windows are framed in the Period manner,

and the larger of the two front-facing gables features ornamental exposed beams and a small ornamental vent.

229 N. Glassell — *1915 Craftsman Bungalow*   NRHP:1997
A single-story bungalow with wide lap siding and double, front-facing gable roof. The forwardmost gable forms the entry porch overhang and is supported by tapered piers. Each of the upper gable faces is distinguished by ornamental purlins, cross-ties and a vented transom. The original door is still present and features four vertical panes.

234 N. Glassell — *1910c Hip Roof Cottage* NRHP:1997
This is a single-story house with modified L-plan and steep-pitched hip roof. The short leg of the ell results in a small, front-facing gable projection which features a large, three-part with diamond pane header, window. The main roof extends forward on one side to form a large, wrap-around corner porch. This porch is supported by Classical columns. The original door is still present and features a single paned window with dentils.

237 N. Glassell — *1920c Bungalow*   NRHP:1997
A single-story bungalow with wide lap siding and steep-pitched, multi-gable roof. Entry is via a recessed portico articulated with Classical pilasters. A brick chimney rises up the front face of the house.

244 N. Glassell — *1906 Hip Roof Cottage* NRHP:1997
A single-story box plan house with clapboard siding and steep-pitched hip roof. A small gable attic dormer is present and features a Palladian transom. Entry is via a corner recessed porch supported by wood posts.

245 N. Glassell — *1938*

253 N. Glassell — *1927*

260 N. Glassell — *1920c Bungalow*   NRHP:1997
A single-story bungalow with wide lap siding and multi-gable roof. Front-facing gable extends forward

to form a half-entry porch and is supported by an ornamental turned post which is probably a replacement of the original. The original entry door is still present and features four plate glass windows.

261 N. Glassell — *1905c Classic Box*   NRHP:1997
This is a large, two-story house which was originally built in the Classical Revival style but has been altered through the addition of a storefront on the lower level. As was typical of the house of this period, this one originally featured a box plan with steep-pitched, hip roof and small, hip dormer. The house has wide lap siding. A recessed corner porch probably was present originally but was removed when the storefront addition was made. Since the 1982 survey, the inappropriate storefront addition has been improved.

264 N. Glassell — *1910 Craftsman (altered)*

269 N. Glassell — *1905 Hip Roof Cottage* NRHP:1997
A single-story clapboard house with steep-pitched, hip and gable roof. The house is built in a modified L-plan with the short leg of the ell resulting in a front-facing gable with a modified Palladian transom. The remaining half of the house is devoted to a large circular, wrap-around porch supported by Classical columns. The original door with plate glass window is still present. Accompanying this door on the side is a large, three-part window with transom.

274 N. Glassell — *1913 Craftsman*   NRHP:1997
This is a large, two-story Craftsman house with single, side-facing gable roof and combination shingle and lap siding. A large, front-facing gable dormer is present and features a balcony with slatted balustrade and a recessed entry comprised of an ornamental door with diamond pane side vents on either side. The main roof extends forward to form a full-width porch which is supported by tapered piers atop an arroyo stone porch wall. Large picture windows with transoms flank

either side of the main entry. Since the 1982 survey, this structure has undergone restoration and has been altered with appropriate balcony remodel.

277 N. Glassell — *1905 Hip Roof Cottage* NRHP:1997
This is a single-story clapboard structure with hip roof and double front entry. The right entry is immediately via a stoop. On the left side is a small hip dormer with shingle siding and ornamental exposed rafter tails. On the left side is a cut-away porch supported by Classical columns. The original door is still in place and features a single plate glass window flanked on either side by narrow sash windows. This is complemented by a three-part window to the side. All are ornamentally framed.

284 N. Glassell — *1921 Dutch Colonial Revival* NRHP:1997
OWNER: Mason & Mabel Fishback
Built for his new bride, Fishback began in Orange as a history teacher in 1906 at OUHS. Mabel as well taught at the old school on Glassell.

This is a large, two-story house with a gambrel roof fashioned after the Dutch tradition. The entry is articulated by a large pedimented portico supported by Classical columns. The original door is still in place and flanked on either side by mullioned sidelights. Two large, picture windows with transoms adorn the lower half of the front facade. Groupings of sash windows with eight-over-one pane arrangements adorn the upper facade.

285 N. Glassell — *1910c Bungalow* NRHP:1997
A single-story bungalow with steep-pitched, hip and gabled roof with wide lap siding. The house combines elements of both the Classical Revival and the Bungalow styles. The house is built in a modified L fashion with the short leg of the ell resulting in a small, pedimented gable dormer with sawtooth shingles and a louvered vent.

287 N. Glassell — *1910 Bungalow*

291 N. Glassell — *1912 Bungalow*   NRHP:1997
A single-story house with wide lap siding and multi-gable roof with wide overhangs and knee braces. The front porch is enclosed with ribbon windows.

304 N. Glassell — *1909 Craftsman*   NRHP:1997
This is a two-story Craftsman house with single, side-facing gable roof and wide lap siding. A large, front-facing gable dormer with ornamental purlins is present also. One-half of the front facade is devoted to a recessed porch which is supported by wood posts. Large, three-part windows are present on the lower story of the front facade.

312 N. Glassell — *1915 Altered Craftsman*   NRHP:1997
This is a classic, single-story Orange bungalow but has been significantly modified on the front of the property through the addition of a boxy stucco storefront. The original lap siding, gable roof, windows and door are still present on the sides and rear of the house.

320 N. Glassell — *1917 Craftsman*   NRHP:1997
A one and one-half story house with clapboard siding and single, side-facing gable roof. A large, front-facing gable dormer is present, ornamented with purlins and an ornamental transom window. What was originally a full-width porch was later enclosed, but the original porch piers with brick bases are still present. Since the 1982 survey, this structure has been altered with appropriate partial front porch restoration.

328 N. Glassell — *1914 Craftsman*   NRHP:1997
A single-story box plan bungalow with single, front-facing gable roof with wide eave overhangs and knee braces. One-half of the front facade is devoted to a recessed porch supported by a slender wood pier. The house is simple and unadorned. Since the 1982 survey, this structure has been altered by a porch remodeling.

333 N. Glassell — *1904-1928 Neo-Classicism*   NRHP:1975
Orange Union High School

Orange Union High School, as it was in 1919

Now occupied by Chapman University, the original Neo-classicism buildings stand symmetrically arranged as the former Orange Union High School.

Five Chapman University buildings of Neo-classic Architecture are on the National Register of Historic Places. *Wilkinson Hall* is the oldest, dating from 1904, and was moved 300 ft. off Glassell in 1920. *Smith & Reeves Halls* are 1913 twins, and *Memorial Hall,* built in 1921, holds the 999 seat auditorium. Built in 1928 as Founders Hall, *Roosevelt Hall* recently went through major renovation.

OUSD Memorial Hall - 1924

TREE: Bristlecone Pine *Pinus aristata* 56" 76' 75', also called a Hickory Bristlecone is located near Orange St. at Palm Ave.

338 N. Glassell — *1920c Bungalow*   NRHP:1997
A single-story clapboard bungalow with multi-gable roof. The front-facing gable which extends forward originally formed the porch overhang but was later enclosed. The original tapered piers on cast masonry bases are still present.

344 N. Glassell — *1910c Hip Roof Cottage* NRHP:1997
A single-story clapboard house with box plan and steep-pitched, hip roof. A small gable dormer is also present on the front portion of the roof and features a small slatted balustrade balcony. The main roof extends forward in an attached fashion to form a nearly full-width porch which is supported by Classical columns.

370 N. Glassell — *1914c Mediterranean Revival*   NRHP:1992
Central Grammar School
The large, two-story building with strong Renaissance influence is based upon the 4th Century Basilica dei Santi Vitale e Agricola, in Bologna Italy. Built on a rectilinear plan with tile roof and stucco facades, a monumental fashion common to institutional buildings of the period.

Central Grammar School - only the central facade remains

401 N. Glassell — *1930c Moderne*

402 N. Glassell — *1920*

410 N. Glassell — *1920c California Bungalow*   NONC
A single-story bungalow with multi-gable roof and

wide lap siding. Most of the house is covered by a single-gable roof with side-facing, clipped gables. Two parallel, front-facing gable dormers, each with clipped gables, adorn the upper front portion of the roof and define the main entry which is below. This entry is recessed and distinguished by the original wood door with mullioned sidelights. Since the 1982 survey, this structure has been severely altered by remodeling for office use, the door eliminated and windows c hanged.

418 N. Glassell — *1929 Provincial Revival*   NRHP:1997
A provincial revival residence on a rectangular plan with lintel-type window openings with six-pane wood windows. Exterior brick chimney features dual chimney pots. Roof consists of simulated thatch. Entry is gabled with wooden diagonal braces over stucco.

428 N. Glassell — *1907 Hip Roof Cottage*   NONC
A single-story, box plan house with clapboard siding and steep-pitched, hip roof. A small, gable dormer with a keystone transom is present on the front portion of the roof. What was originally a corner recessed porch has since been screened in, but the original Classical columns are still present. It looks as though the porch was enclosed early, given the presence of the older style screen door. Since the 1982 survey, this structure has been severely altered by remodeling for office use—all fenestrations changed.

434 N. Glassell — *1902 Hip Roof Cottage* NRHP:1997
A single-story, box plan house with steep-pitched, hip roof. What was originally clapboard siding has since been stuccoed. At the same time, modifications were made to the recessed porch which would have originally been supported by Classical columns but is now characterized by a large, arched opening. Despite the porch modifications and stuccoing, everything else about the house retains the original design.

446 N. Glassell — *1902 Hip Roof Cottage* NRHP:1997
A hip roof cottage (Richardson Romanesque Revival)

with distinctive flared roof eaves on a box plan. Diamond-paned transomed windows are scattered in a linear pattern with a large single-paned bay window topped with similar diamond shaped windows present on the front facade. A multi-arched porch is present with rounded corners. Decorative molded fascia boards are also featured.

452 N. Glassell — *1903 Hip Roof Cottage* NRHP:1997
A single-story, box plan house with steep-pitched, hip roof and a sloping roofline which results in exceptionally wide eaves. A petite gable dormer i s present on the front portion of the roof. Entry is via a corner recessed porch supported by Classical columns. The remaining front half of the facade is defined by an angled bay window of which each plane has its own window pane.

462 N. Glassell — *1918 Craftsman Bungalow* NRHP:1997
This is a single-story bungalow with multi-gable roof and siding which is now covered by asbestos shingles. The roof is fashioned in an L-plan with the short leg resulting in a projecting, front-facing gable extension which acts as the entry porch overhang. This is supported by tapered piers on brick bases. The original wood door with plate glass windows is still present. It is flanked on either side by large picture windows with beveled glass transoms.

474 N. Glassell — *1921*

576 N. Glassell — *1910*   OTPA
OWNER: Charles & Bertha Lawonn

GRAND STREET—SOUTH
—Grand was renamed from Grape St. after the grape blight in 1888—

204 S. Grand — *1920c Craftsman Bungalow*   NRHP:1997
A low, single-story clapboard bungalow with shallow-pitched, multi-gable roof. The front façade is distinguished by a centrally located gable which extends forward to form the entry porch overhang. Cross-ties in the upper gable face provide ornamentation; a pergola is located to either side. The porch overhang is supported by wide piers with brick bases and wood posts on top.

212 S. Grand — *1905c Hip Roof Cottage*   OTPA:1997
OWNER: George Cosart
A single-story clapboard house with box plan and pyramidal roof. What was once an open corner porch recessed beneath the roof has since been enclosed. The large boxy window with diamond paned transom is typical of the period. Since the 1982 survey, this structure has been altered with appropriate side wing enlargement which complements the original.

224 S. Grand — *1910 Victorian Cottage*   NONC
A single-story box plan house with clapboard siding and multi-planed roof. The front portion of the house features a small dormer attic gable embellished with fish scale shingles and jigsaw bargeboard. Also located on the front is an attached porch which was originally a full-width porch, but one-half has been enclosed. The original remaining portion of the porch includes ornamental turned posts and spindle work beneath the roof of the porch. Windows are vertical, characteristic of the Victorian period and are framed in the Victorian manner.

225 S. Grand — *1924 Mediterranean Revival*   NRHP:1997
A single-story box plan house with stucco siding and flat roof. Most notable feature of the house is the front facade which includes a circular entry portico supported by Classical columns with an ornamental

balcony balustrade above. Flanked on either side of this porch are large picture windows with tile hoods.

230 S. Grand — *1913 Craftsman*   NRHP:1997
OWNER: Henry Dahnke
BLDR: Orange Contracting & Milling Co.
A one and one-half story Craftsman home with a rectangular plan, clapboard siding and a single-gable roof with side-facing gables. Also located on the upper portion of the house is a front-facing dormer gable with cross-ties and ornamental purlins. Entry is via a corner porch recessed beneath the main portion of the house. The porch is supported by fluted, tapered piers connected by a low, clapboard porch wall.

Henry Dahnke Home

240 S. Grand — *1915c Craftsman*   NRHP:1997
A one and one-half story Craftsman home with rectangular plan, clapboard siding and single-gable roof with side-facing gables. There is also a large, front-facing dormer gable which includes a small, ornamentally framed transom window with beveled glass and four pairs of casement windows. The main roof extends to form a full-width porch supported by elephantine piers which are fluted and have Classical caps.

271 S. Grand — *1904 Hip Roof Cottage*   NRHP:1997

A single-story house with clapboard siding and pyramidal roof. There is a smaller dormer gable projection on the front portion of the roof which includes saw-tooth shingles and a framed attic vent. Main entry is beneath a recessed corner porch supported by wood posts.

272 S. Grand — *1919 Gable Roof Cottage* NRHP:1997
A very small, bungalow cottage with multi-gable roof and facades now covered by asbestos shingles. A centrally located shallow-pitched, front-facing gable covers the entry on the center front facade, flanked on either side by a double-hung window.

320 S. Grand — *1923 California Bungalow* NRHP:1997
A single-story bungalow with wide lap siding and shallow-pitched, multi-gable roof. The front facade is distinguished by a centrally located entry porch gable supported by wood posts.

329 S. Grand — *1910c Hip Roof Cottage* NRHP:1997
A single-story, clapboard house with steep-pitched, hip roof. The main entry is via a recessed corner porch supported by slim Classical columns.

335 S. Grand — *1908 Hip Roof Cottage* NRHP:1997
A single-story, box plan, clapboard house with steep-pitched, hip roof contrasted by a small hipped dormer. Entry is via corner recessed porch supported by posts sheathed in clapboard. The two most ornamental features are the dormer and large, four-part, double-hung windows on the front facade.

340 S. Grand — *1915c Craftsman* NRHP:1997
A one and one-half story Craftsman house with lap siding and single-gable roof contrasted by a front-facing gabled dormer. The main roof extends forward to form entry porch overhang supported by elephantine piers.

343 S. Grand — *1909 Hip Roof Cottage* NRHP:1997
A single-story, clapboard house with steep-pitched, hip roof and a contrasting smaller pediment gable over

one-half of the front facade. Beneath is a large diamond-paned picture window. Entry is at center via a recessed porch supported by a single Classical column with a Corinthian capital.

348 S. Grand — *1908 Hip Roof Cottage*   NRHP:1997
A single-story, clapboard house with box plan and steep-pitched, hip roof. A hip roof dormer, with wide eaves, is on the front portion of the roof. Main entry is via a corner recessed porch supported by a Classical column.

351 S. Grand — *1909 Hip Roof Cottage*   NRHP:1997
A single-story, clapboard house with double-hip roof and large, circular wrap-around porch. The main roof extends forward to form the porch overhang supported by Classical columns with Corinthian capitals. The frontmost portion of the facade, with its own separate hip roof, features a three-part window with diamond-paned transom.

354 S. Grand — *1915 Craftsman Bungalow*   NRHP:1997
A single-story house with lap siding and single-gable roof with side-facing gables. There is also a smaller shed dormer which is the attic vent. The main entry is via a corner recessed porch supported by an elephantine pier with brick base and wood top.

359 S. Grand — *1913 Craftsman Bungalow* OTPA:1997
OWNER: Emil Weiss

Emile K. Weiss Home

BLDR: Orange Contracting & Milling Co.
A one and one-half story Craftsman house with wide lap siding and a single-gable roof with side-facing gables. There is also a front-facing dormer gable projection ornamented with purlins, cross-ties between the bargeboard and a framed attic vent. The main roof extends forward to form a full-width porch supported by tapered piers of arroyo stone with wood tops. The arroyo stone piers are connected by a slatted balustrade.

365 S. Grand — *1907 Hip Roof Cottage* NRHP:1997
A single-story house with box plan and steep-pitched, hip roof contrasted by a hip roof dormer on the front portion. Main entry is via a corner recessed porch supported by wood posts which are probably a later addition. Wide eaves on the house feature ornamental rafter tails.

368 S. Grand — *1904 Hip Roof Cottage* NRHP:1997
A one-story, box plan, clapboard house with steep-pitched hip roof and a small hip roof dormer. Entry is via a recessed corner porch supported by three classical columns. An angled bay window is on the north side.

373 S. Grand — *1910 Bungalow* NRHP:1997
A single-story, bungalow-scale home with rectangular plan, lap siding and a single, front-facing gable roof. Main entry is via a corner recessed porch supported by a group of three Classical columns. Triangular bracket supports grace the eaves on the front facade.

374 S. Grand — *1920c Craftsman Bungalow* NRHP:1997
A single-story, bungalow house with lap siding and single, front-facing gable roof. The main roof extends forward to form a full-width porch overhang supported by tapered piers. Ornamental embellishments on the house include purlins beneath the eaves, an ornamentally framed attic vent and a

slatted balustrade on the porch.

383 S. Grand — *1913 Craftsman Bungalow*   NRHP:1997
A single-story bungalow with rectangular plan and double, front-facing gables. The forwardmost gable extends forward to form the entry porch overhang supported by tapered piers. There is a connecting, slatted balustrade between the piers. Ornamental purlins grace the eaves.

384 S. Grand — *1915c Craftsman*   NRHP:1997
A one and one-half story house with wide lap siding and a single, side-facing gable roof and front-facing dormer gable with cross-ties and three-part transom window. One-half of the front facade is devoted to a recessed corner porch supported by a tapered wood pier.

391 S. Grand — *1915 Craftsman Bungalow*   NRHP:1997
A single-story bungalow with double, front-facing gables. The forwardmost gable forms the entry porch overhang supported by fluted, tapered piers. Embellishments on the base include ornamental purlins and dentils on the front gable faces. Adjacent to the porch is a pergola.

394 S. Grand — *1910 Craftsman Bungalow*   NRHP:1997
A single-story house with single-gable roof with side-facing gables. There is a small, shed dormer with diamond-paned transom also. Entry is via a corner, recessed porch supported by a single pier with wood base and wood posts on top. All windows on the front facade include upper panes with diamond-paned windows.

404 S. Grand — *1906 Bungalow*   NRHP:1997
A single-story, clapboard bungalow with rectangular plan and single, front-facing gable roof. A smaller, front-facing gable runs parallel to the main roof across the full width of the house, forming an entry porch overhang supported by Classical columns. Triangular brackets grace the eaves.

405 S. Grand — *1909 Craftsman*   NRHP:1997
A two-story house with single, front-facing gable roof and lap siding on the first floor and square shingle siding on the second story. The porch is formed by a separate attached roof at the single story which includes a gable definition of the entry supported by wood posts treated in the Classical manner. Another notable feature of the house is the ornamental purlins and rafter tails beneath the eaves.

413 S. Grand — *1916 Craftsman Bungalow*   NRHP:1997
A single-story bungalow with lap siding and multi-gable roof. Front facade is composed of two front-facing gables, the smaller of which forms the entry porch overhang supported by wide piers. Exposed beams with ornamental tails and latticed attic venting further ornament the house. A large, picture window with transom is centered beneath the entry gable.

414 S. Grand — *1916 Craftsman*   NRHP:1997
A one and one-half story Craftsman house with rectangular plan, clapboard siding and single, side-facing gable roof. There is a smaller, front-facing dormer gable ornamented by triangular bracket supports and a leaded glass, transom window. The main roof extends forward to form a full-width porch supported by piers with brick bases.

421 S. Grand — *1921 Craftsman Bungalow*   NRHP:1997
A low, single-story bungalow with clapboard siding and multi-gable roof comprised of shallow-pitched, clipped gables. The principal part of the front facade has a gable roof over the porch supported by piers with concrete bases and wood posts atop.

424 S. Grand — *1906 Hip Roof Cottage*   OTPA:1997
OWNER: Theodore Loescher
A single-story cottage with a box plan, wide lap siding and pyramidal roof. Victorian ornamentation is present in the smaller, front-facing attic dormer, ornamented with fish scale shingles and decorative

bargeboard. The front window is also framed in an ornamental Victorian manner. The recessed corner is supported by ornamental posts with decorative spindle work at the brackets.

429 S. Grand — *1920 Bungalow*   NRHP:1997
A single-story bungalow with lap siding and double, front-facing gable roof. The forwardmost gable originally formed the entry porch overhang but has since been enclosed.

430 S. Grand — *1916 Craftsman*   NRHP:1997
A one and one-half story Craftsman house with rectangular plan, lap siding and a single, side-facing gable roof. There is a front-facing dormer gable on the front portion of the roof ornamented by decorative purlins and a 3-part transom window fashioned in the Palladian manner. The main roof extends forward to form a full-width porch supported by tapered piers with brick bases.

438 S. Grand — *1904 Hip Roof Cottage*   OTPA:1997
OWNER: George & Carrie Black
A single-story, box plan clapboard house with a steep-pitched, hip roof contrasted by a smaller, hip gable on front portion. Entry is via a corner recessed porch supported by Classical columns. Wide eaves are ornamented by decorative brackets.

439 S. Grand — *1904 Craftsman Bungalow*   NRHP:1997
BLDR: Schoenbergs
The unusual molded-concrete-block form hides some of the Craftsman look. A single-story bungalow with double, front-facing gable roof and slump stone siding on the lower portion and square shingles on the upper gable faces. The forwardmost gable forms the entry porch overhang supported by slump stone piers in the low slump stone connecting wall. Cross-ties are in the upper gable faces.

446 S. Grand — *1916 Craftsman Bungalow*   NRHP:1997
Single-story bungalow with double, front-facing

gables. The forwardmost gable forms the entry porch overhang supported by tapered piers with brick bases. The house is now covered by asbestos siding. Ornamental purlins and wood ornamentation around the upper portions of the piers provide embellishment.

447 S. Grand — *1910*

453 S. Grand — *1909 Hip Roof Cottage*   NRHP:1997
Single-story, clapboard house with box plan and a steep-pitched hip roof. There is a small hip-roof dormer with louvered attic venting on the front portion of the roof. Entry is via a corner recessed porch supported by Classical columns. The original door with single, square pane, is also present. Two large, picture windows with multi-paned transoms are on the front facades.

454 S. Grand — *1909 Craftsman Bungalow*   NRHP:1997
A low, single-story bungalow with multi-gable roof and elongated, square butt, shingle siding. The lower foundation of the house is sided in ornamental lap siding. A single-gable main roof with side-facing gables is contrasted by two smaller, front-facing gables, one of which is the attic vent and the other defines half of the front facade. A half-sized porch is recessed beneath the main roof supported by elephantine piers of concrete.

458 S. Grand — *1913 Craftsman Bungalow*   NRHP:1997
A single-story, tri-gable bungalow now covered with asbestos siding. The house is built on a rectangular plan, the main portion of which is covered by a single-gable roof with side-facing gables. The center front facade is defined by a large, front-facing gable which forms the entry porch overhang supported by tapered piers with arroyo stone bases.

461 S. Grand — *1915 Craftsman Bungalow*   NRHP:1997
A single-story bungalow with rectangular plan, tri-gable roof and asbestos siding. The main portion of the house is covered by a single-gable roof which is

contrasted by a smaller, front-facing gable entry porch in the center of the front facade. The porch is supported by elephantine piers with brick bases. Ornamental purlins and louvered venting further distinguish the front gable .

469 S. Grand — *1909 Hip Roof Cottage*   NRHP:1997
A single-story, clapboard house with box plan and a steep-pitched, hip roof. There is a small dormer with hip roof on the front portion. Main entry is via a recessed corner porch supported by Classical columns.

470 S. Grand — *1912 Craftsman Bungalow*   NRHP:1997
Single-story, clapboard bungalow with double, front-facing gable roof. The forwardmost gable forms the entry porch overhang and is supported by tapered piers. Ornamental purlins provide embellishment.

475 S. Grand — *1920 California Bungalow*   NRHP:1997
A single-story clapboard bungalow with a single-gable roof with side-facing gables. A centrally located, front-facing gable forms the entry porch overhang and is supported by a paired combination, one each square and Colonial-type column. Double French doors provide the entry at center, flanked on either side by tri-part casement windows.

478 S. Grand — *1904 Hip Roof Cottage*   NRHP:1997
A single-story clapboard house with box plan and hip roof. A smaller, hip roof dormer is included. What was the original porch has since been enclosed, and the original Classical columns are no longer present. The house features exceptionally wide eaves with ornamental brackets below.

484 S. Grand — *1923 Mediterranean Revival* OTPA:1997
OWNER: Frank Maroney
A low, single-story box plan house with stucco siding and flat roof. The front half of the facade is defined by a recessed entry porch with a large arch opening.

487 S. Grand — *1915c Craftsman*   NRHP:1997

TREE: Fern Pine *Podocarpus elongatus* 24" 55' 50'.
A two-story house with a steep-pitched, multi-gable roof and lap siding now covered by asbestos shingles. The front facade is characterized by a front-facing gable with cross-ties and a recessed porch below supported by tapered piers. Entry door is at center with a large, picture window with transom on either side.

492 S. Grand — *1920c California Bungalow*   NRHP:1997
A single-story bungalow with tri-gable roof and siding now covered by asbestos. The main portion of the house is covered by a single-gable roof with side-facing gables, contrasted by a centrally located, front-facing gable over a porch overhang supported by wood posts.

493 S. Grand — *1922 Bungalow*   NRHP:1997
A single-story, clapboard bungalow with single, front-facing gable roof contrasted by a smaller, front-facing gable porch overhang supported by ornamental posts. The original door with three small, rectangular panes is still present.

504 S. Grand — *1922 Bungalow*   NRHP:1997
A single-story clapboard bungalow with single-gabled roof with side-facing, clipped gables. Entry is via a projecting portico supported by ornamental wood posts. The house is otherwise simple and unadorned. Nutwood Place 1906 Arroyo Stone Marker

505 S. Grand — *1901 Victorian*   NRHP:1997
OWNER: John Henry, Lawyer
Part of the exclusive Nutwood Tract (1909) this early home represents the early farmland of the area. Later owned by Fred Klahn, carpenter.

This is a large, two-story, rural Victorian house with steep-pitched, multi-gabled roof and asbestos shingles covering the original shiplap siding. The house is build on a modified L-plan and features a full-width front porch with a separate roof overhang supported by ornamental turned columns. The primary entry is distinguished by a pedimented gable with jigsawn brackets. An angled bay window is present adjacent to the front door on the lower story. The same jigsawn brackets which adorn the porch portico are also located beneath the eaves around the house. The original front door is still in place and features flashed glass in both the door and transom window above. This house is a good Victorian example, but the presence of the asbestos shingles and other slight modifications make it slightly different from the average. Nutwood Place 1906 Arroyo Stone Marker

515 S. Grand — *1919 Craftsman Bungalow*   NRHP:1997
A one and one-half story clapboard house with single, side-facing gabled roof. A large, front-facing gabled dormer is present with four, single-pane windows. The main roof extends forward to form a full-width porch overhang and is supported by wide, square piers. On either side of the main entry is located a large, three-part transomed window.

520 S. Grand — *1914 Craftsman Bungalow*   NRHP:1997
A one and one-half story Craftsman house with wide lap siding and single, side-facing gabled roof. The main roof extends forward to form a full-width porch which is supported by tapered piers. The original door with plate glass windows is present, flanked on either side by large, transomed picture windows. A front-facing, gabled dormer with combination louvered and glass transom is also present.

528 S. Grand — *1919*

529 S. Grand — *1916 Craftsman Bungalow*   NRHP:1997
OWNER: Carl G. & Bertha Jorn (Jorn Building)
BLDR: Orange Contracting & Milling Co.
A single-story bungalow with clapboard siding and shallow-pitched, multi-gabled roof. The full width of the front facade is articulated by a large, front-facing gable which extends forward to form a full-width

porch. This gable is supported by ornamental concrete piers on the outer edges and half piers with wood posts on top on the inner portion near the entry. Ornamental exposed beams characterize the eaves around the house.

Carl G. & Bertha Jorn Home

536 S. Grand — *1934 Bungalow*   NRHP:1997

A single-story clapboard bungalow with single, front-facing gabled roof. What was originally a full-width porch was later enclosed, but the porch posts are still present.

545 S. Grand — *1913 Craftsman*   OTPA:1997

OWNERS: William E. & Nora Clement
BLDR: W.E. Clement Lumber Co.

Clement a widower already with two children, married Nora Miller in 1907. Three more children prompted him to build this large up-scale home by 1913. Clement owned the Clement Lumber Co. and was involved in the community.

This is a large, two-story Craftsman house with clapboard siding and a multi-gabled roofline. The house has dynamic and complex proportions and is distinguished by a gabled projection on the lower story which forms the entry porch overhang. This overhang is supported by wide piers with concrete bases and wood posts on top. Half-timbering embellishes the upper porch gable. Ornamental purlins and latticed work embellish the remaining gables around the house.

552 S. Grand — *1920c Bungalow*   NRHP:1997
TREE: Monterey Pine
A single-story bungalow with ornamental lap siding and double, front-facing gabled roof. The forwardmost gable forms the entry porch overhang and is supported by piers comprised of brick bases with wood posts on top. Vertical slatting, exposed beams and triangular bracket supports distinguish each of the upper gable faces. This property is distinguished by the presence of a very large and old Monterey Pine tree.

604 S. Grand — *1911 Hip Roof Cottage*   NRHP:1997
A small, single-story cottage with wide lap siding and hip roof. A separate roof extension defines a small entry porch which is supported by wood posts . Entry is at center and flanked on either side by a double-hung window. Since the 1982 survey, this structure has been altered with appropriate porch railings.

610 S. Grand — *1920 Craftsman Bungalow*   NRHP:1997
A single-story bungalow with ornamental lap siding and shallow-pitched, gabled roof. The house features two entries, indicating the intention for duplex usage originally. Each entry is articulated by a shallow-pitched, gabled portico supported by piers with wide concrete bases and wood posts on top. A small shed dormer is located in the center portion of the front roof. The central portion of the front facade features two large, sash windows with mullioned upper sashes.

615 S. Grand — *1920c Bungalow*

625 S. Grand — *1920c Bungalow*

636 S. Grand — *1916 Craftsman Bungalow*

644 S. Grand — *1910 Craftsman*

651 S. Grand — *1921 Bungalow*

667 S. Grand — *1915c Craftsman*   NRHP:1997
A large, two-story Craftsman house characterized by a single-gabled roof with side-facing gables. This is in contrast to a large, front-facing gabled dormer with a balustrade and shingle embellishment in the upper gable face. The main roof extends forward to form a half porch which is supported by concrete piers and connecting, slatted balustrade. A large entry features the original door flanked on either side by sidelights.

700 S. Grand — *1936 Spanish Colonial Plunge*
BLDR: WPA
Constructed from 1935 to 1936, the Plunge offered the first structure built in the new City Park. The Victorian fountain was once here as well (1936-1950s)

Luann & Fred in the 1940s

700 S. Grand — *Hart Park*
TREE: Moreton Bay Fig *ficus marcurphylls* 1875c.
The large Moreton Bay planted by Henri Gardner, is the twin of a similar tree at 500 S. Glassell St.
Twisted Juniper *Juniperus chinesis torulosa*
Pine *Pinus*.

GRAND STREET — NORTH

127 N. Grand — *1915c Bungalow*   NRHP:1997

A single-story shingled bungalow with double front-facing, gable roof. The forwardmost gable forms the entry porch overhang and is supported by wide piers with brick bases. Shingling on the house is composed of elongated, staggered butt shingles which is unusual for Orange. A large 3-part transomed window adorns the front facade.

133 N. Grand — *1915 Craftsman*   NRHP:1997

A one and one-half story house with gable roof and wide lap siding. The main roof extends forward to form a full-width and wrap-around porch; this overhang is supported by large, fluted elephantine piers. Cross-ties embellish the upper gable faces.

143 N. Grand — *1905 Victorian*   NRHP:1997

A two-story house with shiplap siding and steep-pitched, multi-gable roof . The main portion of the roof is fashioned in an L-plan with the short leg of the ell forming the front gable face. The remaining half of the front facade is devoted to a porch and the overhang is supported by wide wood posts. The porch connecting wall is faced with ornamental shingles. A small hipped dormer is present just above the porch.

183 N. Grand — *1905 Transitional*   NRHP:1997

A two-story house with shiplap siding on the first story and clapboard siding on the second story. The roofline is composed of a single-gable, front-facing roof. A full-width porch is present and extends from the first story of the house and is supported by wood posts. Wide eaves throughout feature exposed rafters. Ornamental purlins and vertical slatting embellish the upper gable face.

191 N. Grand — *1900c Victorian*   NRHP:1997

A high two-story house with a single front-facing, steep-pitched gable roof. One-half of the front facade is devoted to a recessed entry porch supported by a classical column. The original siding has been covered by asbestos shingles. A smaller gabled dormer is present on the side facing Maple Street.

205 N. Grand
TREE: Deodor Cedar *Cedrus deodora*. Only 3 or 4 in Orange @ Maple.

215 N. Grand — *1909 Gothic Brown Shingle*   NRHP:1997
Trinity Episcopal Church
The congregation formed in 1876 and hired Phillip H. Frohman as architect. This was his first church design and he went on to design the National Cathedral in Washington, DC. The manse is next door.

Having the characteristics of the typical Victorian rural church with Gothic influence, it incorporates the style with the then popular (1910c) shingle and Craftsman styles. Built on a rectangular plan, featuring a single gabled roof with a rectilinear bell tower.

222 N. Grand — *1912 Craftsman*   NRHP:1997
A single-story house with wide lap siding and single-gable roof with side-facing gables. A low shed attic dormer is present on the front portion of the roof. The main roof extends forward to form a full-width porch overhang and is supported by elephantine piers. The original hardwood door with plate glass windows is still present.

225 N. Grand — *1915c Craftsman*   NRHP:1997
TREE: Aleppo Pine *Pinus halepensis*.
A one and one-half story house with single-gable roof of which the gables are side facing. The original siding has been recovered with asbestos shingles. A low shed dormer window is present on the front portion of the roof. The main roof extends forward to form a full-width porch overhang and is supported by elephantine piers. Large 3-part transomed windows flank either side of the main entry.

230 N. Grand — *1909 Hip Roof Cottage*   NRHP:1997
A single-story clapboard cottage with steep-pitched, hip roof. A small pedimented gable attic dormer is present on the front portion of the roof. Just below, covering one-half of the front facade, is a wide gabled porch overhang supported by classical columns atop ornamental brick piers.

231 N. Grand — *1912 Craftsman*   NRHP:1997
A one and one-half story clapboard house with single, side-facing gable roof. There is a large front-facing gable dormer on the front portion of the roof which is ornamented with purlins and a louvered transom. One-half of the front facade is devoted to a recessed porch supported by a tapered pier. There is a double entry. The original hardwood doors are still present. Large 3-part transomed windows are present on the front facade.

238 N. Grand — *1900 Victorian*   NRHP:1997
A two-story clapboard house with combination steep-pitched, hip and gable roof. The house is built on a modified L-plan with one corner devoted to a large wrap-around porch supported by classical columns. The front-facing gable features an ornamental attic vent. Exceptionally wide eaves on the house are embellished with ornamental brackets.

243 N. Grand — *1921c Gable Roof cottage*   NRHP:1997
A single-story clapboard cottage with steep-pitched, multi-gable roof. The front facing gabled porch overhang is located at the center of the front facade and is supported with Colonial columns connected by an ornamental balustrade. An ornamental transom vent is located in the front of this gable face.

246 N. Grand — *1920 Bungalow*   NRHP:1997
A single-story bungalow with ornamental lap siding and shallow-pitched, multi-gable roof. There are two front-facing gables to the roofline, the forwardmost is the entry porch overhang supported by wood posts.

247 N. Grand — *1913 Bungalow* NRHP:1997
A single-story bungalow with lap siding and multi-gable roof. The roofline takes on an L format. The frontmost leg of the ell results in a front-facing gable, the entry porch overhang. This is supported by tapered piers atop brick bases connected with a low brick porch wall. The original front door with plate glass windows is still present. The upper portion of the porch gable has an unusually shaped attic vent.

254 N. Grand — *1920c Bungalow* NRHP:1997
A single-story clapboard bungalow with roofline which follows a T-plan. The roof is gabled with each of the gable peaks being clipped. The front-facing gable in the center of the front facade acts as the entry porch overhang. It is supported by wood posts and flanked on either side by an ornamental pergola which is also supported by wood posts.

257 N. Grand — *1912 Bungalow* NRHP:1997
A single-story bungalow with single-gable roof with side-facing gables. A low shed dormer is present on the front portion of the roof. The original siding has been covered by asbestos shingles. What was originally a full-width porch overhang has since been enclosed, but the original piers are still present.

265 N. Grand — *1915c Bungalow* NRHP:1997
A single-story bungalow with single-gable roof comprised of side-facing gables. A low shed dormer is present on the front portion of the roof. The original siding has since been covered with asbestos shingles. One-half of the front facade is recessed beneath the main roof to form an entry porch. Large 3-part transomed windows are present on the front facade.

268 N. Grand — *1904 Hip Roof Cottage* NRHP:1997
A single-story box plan house with clapboard siding and steep-pitched, hip roof. A small gabled attic dormer is present on the front portion of the roof. Main entry is via a recessed corner porch supported by

classical columns.

275 N. Grand — *1921 Bungalow*   NRHP:1997
A single-story bungalow based on an L-plan with ornamental lap siding and a shallow-pitched, multi-gable roof. One-half of the front facade is devoted to a porch which is supported by colonial-like columns. Multi-paned casement windows are present on either side of the main door.

276 N. Grand — *1919 Craftsman*   NRHP:1997
A single-story bungalow with double front-facing, gable roof. The original lap siding has since been covered by asbestos shingles. The forwardmost gable forms the entry porch overhang which is supported by piers with wood posts on top. Ornamental brackets and purlins are present on the porch gable. The original hardwood door and screen door are still present and are flanked on either side of the front facade by large 3-part transomed windows.

281 N. Grand — *1905 Hip Roof Cottage*   NRHP:1997
A single-story box plan house with clapboard siding and steep-pitched, hip roof. The house features a full wrap-around porch across the front and side facades. The porch has its own separate overhang which is supported by slim wood posts connected by a slatted balustrade. Since the 1982 survey, this structure has been altered by removal of porch and change in windows and siding.

284 N. Grand — *1915c Craftsman*   NRHP:1997
A two-story house with clapboard siding and multi-gable roofline. The frontmost portion of the house features a wide front-facing gable which extends for ward to form a full-width porch. This is supported by wood posts connected by a slatted ballustrade.

287 N. Grand — *1910 Bungalow*   NRHP:1997
A single-story bungalow with single-gable roof with side-facing gables. A low shed dormer is present on the front portion of the roof. The original siding of the

house has since been covered with asbestos shingles. The main roof extends forward to form a full-width porch which is supported by piers with brick bases and wood posts on top. An ornamental brick chimney is visible on the roof.

292 N. Grand — *1915c Bungalow*   NRHP:1997
A single-story bungalow with wide lap siding and double front-facing, gable roof. The forwardmost gable forms the entry porch overhang and is supported by tapered piers. The front facade contains two large picture windows with single-paned transoms.

HARWOOD STREET — SOUTH
—Harwood is named for pioneer Nathan D. Harwood 2nd Postmaster—

135 S. Harwood — *1915c Craftsman Bungalow* NRHP:1997
A single-story bungalow with wide lap siding and single-gable roof with a front-facing gable. A full-width porch is recessed beneath the main portion of the and is supported by tapered piers with brick bases. The upper gable face features a three-part window, including a large, fixed pane window in the center with double transom and multi-paned, double-hung windows on either side. Ornamental purlins grace the eaves.

140 S. Harwood — *1915 Craftsman Bungalow* NRHP:1997
A small Craftsman bungalow with two super-imposed front-facing gables with vertical slat vents and knee braces. The front gable covers a front porch and is supported by wood posts on plastered piers. A large, cottage-style window faces onto the porch. There is a large addition in the rear.

141 S. Harwood — *1905 Hip Roof Cottage* NRHP:1997
A small, single-story clapboard house with hip roof and small, recessed entry porch on the corner.

146 S. Harwood — *1915 Craftsman Bungalow* NRHP:1997
A low, single-story bungalow with shallow-pitched, double, front-facing gables and now covered by asbestos siding. The smaller forwardmost gable forms the entry porch overhang supported by tapered piers.

151 S. Harwood — *1906 Hip Roof Cottage* NRHP:1997
A small, one-story cottage built on a box plan with a steep-pitched hip roof. What was originally a full-width front porch, probably supported by Classical columns, was enclosed early on; this enclosure features several mullioned, casement windows. Original siding has since been covered with replacement lap siding.

158 S. Harwood — *1922 Bungalow* NRHP:1997
A single-story bungalow with shallow-pitched and

double, front-facing gable roof. Siding is now covered by asbestos shingles. The forwardmost gable originally must have formed the entry porch overhang but has since been enclosed.

161 S. Harwood — *1919 Bungalow*   NRHP:1997
A single-story house with single gable roof with front-facing gables and wide lap siding. A recessed corner porch is supported by wood posts.

168 S. Harwood — *1923 Bungalow*   NRHP:1997
A single-story clapboard bungalow with multi-gable roof and front-facing gable which forms entry porch overhang. This is supported by tapered piers.

169 S. Harwood — *1909 Hip Roof Cottage*   NRHP:1997
A single-story clapboard house with modified box plan and multi-planed roof. Entry is via a corner recessed porch supported by Classical columns. Two smaller gables are present, one on the front and one on the side. Each is embellished with ornamental shingles.

191 S. Harwood — *1910 Victorian*   NRHP:1997
A single-story clapboard house with hip roof. A full-width porch is attached to the front of the house and is supported by ornamental, turned posts. Located above the center front facade is an ornamental gable which serves as an attic vent. It is embellished with ornamental shingles and an ornamental bargeboard.

215 S. Harwood — *1904*

268 S. Harwood — *1935 Bungalow*   NRHP:1997
A single-story L-plan bungalow with clapboard siding and multi-gable roof. Entry is at apex of ell. House is simple and unembellished.

HARWOOD STREET — NORTH

121 N. Harwood — *1915c Bungalow*   NRHP:1997
A two-story house on a rectangular plan with a steep-pitched, gable roof. A complementary gable dormer is present. Entry door is on side, though no entry porch is present.

130 N. Harwood — *1915c Bungalow*   NRHP:1997
A single-story bungalow with wide lap siding and a double front-facing, gable roof. The forwardmost gable forms entry porch overhang and is supported by taper piers atop a lap-sided porch wall with connecting slatted balustrade. Original door with plate glass windows is present; also on the inner porch facade are three mullioned casement windows.

131 N. Harwood — *1890 Board & Batten Cottage* NRHP:1997
This is a single-story board and batten house representative of the early, hand-built, settlement houses in Orange. The roof is both gabled and with a saltbox slope. The house is built on a modified L-plan with the entry being in the apex of the ell. A small attached roof, supported by slender bracketed posts, acts as the entry porch overhang. The house is basic, simple and unadorned, reflecting the attention to economy and lack of resources available at the time the house was constructed in 1890. Considering the age and construction method, the house is in excellent condition and retains its original architectural appearance.

138 N. Harwood — *1911 Bungalow*   NRHP:1997
A single-story house with combination hip and gable roof. The original siding has since been covered by asbestos shingles. A front-facing gable forms the entry porch overhang which is supported by tapered piers. A pergola is located to the side. Dentils and an ornamental transom are present in the front porch gable. The front facade is adorned by an angled bay window which features a large picture with mullioned

transom, which is identical to the one on the other half of the front facade.

139 N. Harwood — *1920 Bungalow*   NRHP:1997
A single-story bungalow with wide lap siding and double front-facing, gable roof. The rearmost gable actually forms the entry porch overhang which is supported by a tapered pier. The house is simple and basically unembellished.

145 N. Harwood — *1919 Bungalow*   NRHP:1997
Orange Tin Shop
OWNER: Walter J. & Ruth Leichtfuss
BLDR: Orange Contracting & Milling Co.
A single-story bungalow with ornamental lap siding and multi-gable, shallow-pitched roof. Two front-facing gables distinguish the front facade. The entry has its own small overhang and is comprised of the original door with diamond-pane glass plate.

Walter J. & Ruth Leichtfuss Home

146 N. Harwood — *1913 Bungalow*   NRHP:1997
A single-story bungalow with wide lap siding and double, front-facing gable roof. The entry is on the side of the forwardmost gable. Ornamental purlins grace the eaves. Since the 1982 survey, this structure has been altered with in appropriate shutters.

154 N. Harwood — *1913 Spanish Colonial Revival* NRHP:1997

A small single-story Spanish Colonial Revival bungalow with stucco facades and multi-gabled roof with adobe tiles. The house was built in a modified L-plan with the short leg of the ell resulting in an elongated front-facing gable. A small arch opening shelters the main entry. A recessed arch window and arch gateway entrance are present on the front portion of the house.

159 N. Harwood — *1920 Bungalow*   NRHP:1997
A single-story bungalow with ornamental lap siding and multi-gable roof. Centrally located, front-facing gable forms the entry porch overhang and is supported by wood posts.

162 N. Harwood — *1927 Spanish Colonial Revival* NRHP:1997
A single-story, rectangular plan house with stucco siding and single-gable, adobe tile roof. Entry is via a recessed porch which is supported by a large arch opening.

169 N. Harwood — *1922c Spanish Colonial Revival* NRHP:1997
A two-story house with textured stucco siding and flat roof. Three large arched openings articulate a recessed porch, while an adobe tile hood defines the upper front of the house.

205 N. Harwood — *1922 Bungalow*   NRHP:1997
A single-story clapboard bungalow with shallow-pitched, multi-gable roof. A front-facing gable and side-facing gable intersect to form a half-sized recessed porch which is supported by piers with concrete bases and wood posts on top. A large transomed picture window is located on the frontmost facade.

213 N. Harwood — *1924 Mediterranean Revival* NRHP:1997
A single-story box plan house with stucco siding and a flat roof with raised parapets. The small projection on the front facade forms an entry portico with arched openings. Adobe tile hoods adorn the front windows.

225 N. Harwood — *1920c Bungalow*   NRHP:1997
A single-story clapboard bungalow with shallow-pitched, multi-gable roof. The main portion of the house is covered by a single-gable roof with side-facing gables. A centrally located, front-facing gable forms the entry porch overhang. It is supported by tapered piers with brick bases. There is a double entry. Both have original doors indicating duplex usage of the house.

232 N. Harwood — *1914 Gable Roof Cottage*   NRHP:1997
This is a small box-plan clapboard house with single-gable roof with side-facing gables. The main roof extends forward to form a full-width porch overhang, supported by slim wood posts. The house is very small, simple and unembellished, indicating that it was probably hand built with no architect or contractor involved.

237 N. Harwood — *1921 Bungalow*   NRHP:1997
A single-story clapboard bungalow with shallow-pitched, multi-gable roof. A centrally located, front-facing gable forms a porch overhang and is supported by colonial columns. The main roof extends forward on either side and is also supported by the same type of columns. The original, multi-paned glass door and screen door are still present and are flanked by sidelights.

240 N. Harwood — *1909 Bungalow*   NRHP:1997
This is a small, single-story bungalow with a single, front-facing gable roof. The original clapboard siding has been covered by asbestos shingles. There is a small roof overhang above the front door and window which acts as a full-width entry porch and is supported by wood posts.

245 N. Harwood — *1922 Mediterranean Revival* NRHP:1997
This is a single-story box plan house with stucco siding and flat roof. A centrally located, projecting entry portico is articulated by a large arched opening. To

either side of the entry is a large 3-part window. The masonry work on the lower portion of the house is probably a later addition.

252 N. Harwood — *1931 Spanish Colonial Revival* NRHP:1997
A single-story house with rectangular plan, textured stucco siding and double, front-facing, gable roof. The roof is of adobe tiles. Entry is on the side of the frontmost gable and is comprised of a small recessed porch with a wide pier support. A large 3-part window on the front facade is set within an embossed arched embellishment.

253 N. Harwood — *1922 Mediterranean Revival* NRHP:1997
A single-story house with stucco facades and flat roof. The house is built on a modified L-plan with a small entry portico porch in the apex of the ell. The entry portico is comprised of a large, half-sized arch opening and a tile hood.

256 N. Harwood — *1931 Spanish Colonial* NRHP:1997
This house is identical to that at 252 N. Harwood.

263 N. Harwood — *1920c Bungalow*

264 N. Harwood — *1922 Bungalow* · NRHP:1997
A single-story clapboard bungalow with single, front-facing, gable roof . Entry is via a corner recessed porch which is supported by a slim wood post. A small octagonal transom window is present on the front facade.

269 N. Harwood — *1924c Spanish Colonial Revival* NRHP:1997
This single-story house combines Mediterranean and Provincial Revival influences. The house is built on a L-plan and includes stucco facades with steep-pitched, gable roof. The entry is at the center of the front-facing gable facade and is comprised of a multi-paned, arched door beneath a recessed arched entry portico. The main entry is flanked on either side by large arched windows. The pitch of the roof and the stucco facades indicate the Provincial influences. The arches indicate the Mediterranean influences.

273 N. Harwood — *1925 Mediterranean Revival* NRHP:1997
A single-story box plan house with textured stucco
siding and a flat roof with raised parapets. The front
facade is distinguished by a projecting entry portico
with three large arched openings and a gabled tile
roof. The two front windows are 3-part transomed
windows with an arched embellishment above.

276 N. Harwood — *1930c Spanish Colonial Revival* NRHP:1997
This is a single-story house with modified rectangular
plan and single, front-facing, gable roof. The roof
features adobe tiles. Entry is via a corner recessed
porch supported by a wide stucco-sided pier. The
house is otherwise simple and unembellished.

278 N. Harwood — *1930 Spanish Colonial Revival* NRHP:1997
This house is identical to that at 276.

283 N. Harwood — *1921 Bungalow* NRHP:1997
A single-story bungalow with wide lap siding and
multi-gable roof. The main portion of the house is
covered by a single-gable roof with side-facing gables.
There is also a small front-facing, gabled attic dormer
and a front-facing, gable porch overhang supported
by wide wood posts. The main door is beneath at
center and flanked on either side by a double-hung
window.

291 N. Harwood — *1928 Provincial Revival* NRHP:1997
This house incorporates a Provincial Revival influence
through the use of the steep-pitched, gable roof. The
house is built on a modified L-plan and has wide lap
siding. A narrow, front-facing gable forms the entry
porch portico which is accessed through a large arched
opening.

315 N. Harwood — *1914 Bungalow* NRHP:1997
A small, single-story bungalow with wide lap siding
and single-gable roof with side-facing gables. The main
roof extends forward to form a full-width porch which
is supported by narrow wood posts connected by a
slatted balustrade.

316 N. Harwood — *1903 Victorian*   NRHP:1997
A single-story house built on an L-plan with steep-pitched, gable roof and shiplap siding. The short leg of the ell results in a large front-facing gable which is embellished in its upper face with sawtooth shingles. Just below are a pair of high, narrow, double-hung windows. Entry is in the apex of the ell and is sheltered by a small roof overhang.

324 N. Harwood — *1915c Bungalow*   NRHP:1997
A single-story bungalow with wide lap siding and single, front-facing, gable roof. A small gabled portico is present on the center of the front facade and is supported by piers comprised of concrete bases and narrow wood posts. Vertical slatting and cross-ties adorn the gables.

325 N. Harwood — *1910 Bungalow*   NRHP:1997
A small, single-story bungalow with clapboard siding and double, front-facing gable roof. The smaller, forwardmost gable forms an entry porch overhang and is supported by tapered wood posts.

335 N. Harwood — *1920c Bungalow*   NRHP:1997
A single-story bungalow with wide lap siding and double, front-facing gable roof. The smaller forwardmost gable forms the entry porch overhang and is supported by tapered wood posts. Triangular bracket supports and vertical slatting in the porch gable ornament the house.

336 N. Harwood — *1909 Hip Roof Cottage*   NRHP:1997
A one and one-half story box plan house with modified hip roof which results in a small gabled dormer at the peak. The main roof extends forward to form a full-width porch supported by slender wood posts. The original siding has been covered with asbestos shingles.

341 N. Harwood — *1905c Victorian Cottage*   NRHP:1997
Moved here in 1905. A single-story clapboard house with steep-pitched, multi-gable roof. The two parallel,

front-facing gables are present on the front facade, and each is embellished with ornamental shingles. Entry is via a corner recessed porch supported by wood posts with a row of connecting jigsawn ornament at the top portion of the porch.

345 N. Harwood — *1920 Bungalow*   NRHP:1997
A single-story bungalow with wide lap siding and multi-gable roof. The front facade is articulated by a front-facing, gabled porch overhang supported by wood posts. The house is rather simple and unembellished.

350 N. Harwood — *1930c Spanish Colonial Revival* OTPA:1997
OWNER: Della Prince
A single-story house built on an L-plan with textured stucco siding and a multi-gable, adobe tile roof. Entry is at the apex of the ell, and there is no porch or portico of any kind. The windows on this house have been modified from the original. Since the 1982 survey, this structure has been altered with appropriate windows and features closer to its original design.

359 N. Harwood — *1925 Bungalow*   NRHP:1997
A single-story clapboard bungalow with single, front-facing, gable roof. A full-width porch is recessed beneath the main roof overhang and is supported by tapered piers with brick bases.

374 N. Harwood — *1912 Bungalow*   NRHP:1997
A single-story clapboard house with single-gable roof with side-facing gables. A small, centrally located, pedimented gable portico is present on the front facade and is supported by slender wood posts.

375 N. Harwood — *1903 Gable Roof Cottage*   NRHP:1997
A single-story house built on an L-plan with shiplap siding and steep-pitched, multi-gable roof. Entry is at the apex of the ell beneath a corner porch supported by wood posts. An angled bay window is present on the side of the house.

384 N. Harwood — *1906 Hip Roof Cottage* NRHP:1997
A single-story box plan house with clapboard siding and steep-pitched, hip roof. The corner of the house features a large, wrap-around porch which is supported by classical columns atop a clapboard porch wall.

393 N. Harwood — *1920*

523 N. Harwood — *1924 Dutch Gabled Provincial* NRHP:1997
A rectangular plan house with multi-gabled roof and tongue and groove wide siding. The roof has 2 side facing gables articulated with clipped gables. A very steep gable forms an entry. The stucco chimney is set in a second front facing gable. The door and windows are arched.

533 N. Harwood — *1924 Provincial Revival* NRHP:1997
A stucco house built on an irregular rectangular plan. The roof consist of two gables facing side to side and the other front to back. The front to back gable meets the other at its center and is several feet higher. The street side of the side to side gable frames the shed roof of the entry portico. The entry portico and the side wall extending over the driveway have arched openings.

JEFFERSON AVENUE — EAST
-Jefferson is named for the 3rd US President, Thomas Jefferson-

533 E. Jefferson — *1920c Bungalow*   NRHP:1997
A single-story clapboard bungalow with multi-gable roof. The center of the front facade is adorned with a front-facing gabled porch overhang supported by tapered piers with ornamental brick bases and wood posts on top. The original hardwood door with plate glass windows is still present.

541 E. Jefferson — *1920c Bungalow*   NRHP:1997
A single-story clapboard bungalow with double, front-facing gable roof. The forwardmost gable forms the entry porch overhang and is supported by piers comprised of ornamental brick bases and wood posts on top. To either side of the main entry door is a large 3-part window with a transom over the center window.

545 E. Jefferson — *1920c Provincial Revival*   NRHP:1997
A single-story clapboard house built on an L-plan with a steep-pitched, multi-gable bonnie roof. Entry is at the apex of the ell via a small entry portico. The house incorporates Provincial Revival influences through its massing and refined profile with steep-pitched gables.

557 E. Jefferson — *1915c Bungalow Modified*
The original bungalow with flagstone siding was replaced with a new bungalow style residence.

603 E. Jefferson — *1905c Mediterranean Revival* NRHP:1997
A single-story box plan house with stucco facade and flat roof with slightly raised parapets at the corners. The front facade is articulated by an entry portico with a high arched opening and gable roof with adobe tiles.

611 E. Jefferson — *1925c Mediterranean Revival* NRHP:1997
A single-story box plan house with stucco facades and flat roof. A large recessed entry portico is supported by wide stucco piers. Adobe tiles highlight the roof ridges.

615 E. Jefferson — *1936 Classical Revival*   NRHP:1997
A classical revival residence on a rectangular plan with single-pane 4/1 bay windows with matching sidelights, detailed cornice molding, and rake board. The roof contains a single high-pitched gable. A complimentary porch addition with Greco/Roman columns appears to have been added.

631 E. Jefferson — *1920c Bungalow*   NRHP:1997
A single-story clapboard bungalow with three, front-facing gables. The forwardmost gable forms an entry porch overhang and is supported by tapered piers. These piers have brick bases which extend along the foundation wall of the house. It may not be original. The gable on the left side is an addition.

La Veta Avenue — East
—La Veta is named for an agricultural grape variety—

222 E. La Veta — *1921 Craftsman Bungalow*   NRHP:1997
A single-story bungalow with multi-gable roof and wide lap siding. Roof gables form an L arrangement with the main entry being at the apex of the ell. A pergola flanks the side of the house and is supported by wide concrete piers with wood tops.

226 E. La Veta — *1917 Craftsman Bungalow*   NRHP:1997
A single-story bungalow with double, front-facing gables and a combination clapboard siding along the foundation wall and wide lap siding on the upper portions of the house. The forwardmost gable forms the entry porch overhang supported by wide tapered piers connected by a slatted balustrade.

330 E. La Veta — *1920 Craftsman Bungalow*   NRHP:1997
A single-story, tri-gable bungalow with ornamental lap siding. Main portion of the house is covered by a single-gable roof with side-facing gables. A centrally located, front-facing gable forms the entry porch overhang supported by tapered piers.

336 E. La Veta — *1917 Craftsman Bungalow*   NRHP:1997
A low, single-story bungalow with shallow-pitched, multi-gable roof and wide lap siding. Roof gables form an L-plan, and the entry is via a corner porch beneath the main roof extension. This portion of the roof is supported by piers with wood posts on top.

344 E. La Veta — *1920 Bungalow*   NRHP:1997
Single-story clapboard bungalow with double, front-facing gables. A small shed roof attached to the front facade forms the entry porch overhang and is supported by tapered piers with concrete bases and wood tops. Each of the planes of the front facade has a large picture window with diamond-paned transom.

352 E. La Veta — *1912 Craftsman*   NRHP:1997
A one and one-half story Craftsman house with single-

gable roof with side-facing gables and wide lap siding. A dormer with smaller gable is on the front portion of the roof, embellished with a three-part window, cross-ties between the bargeboard and ornamental purlins. Entry is via a corner recessed porch supported by a tapered pier atop a low connecting porch wall. Ornamental purlins grace the remaining eaves of the house.

360 E. La Veta — *1921 Craftsman Bungalow*   NRHP:1997
A single-story bungalow with shallow-pitched, double, front-facing gables. Siding is now covered by asbestos shingles on the facades. The smaller, forwardmost gable forms the entry porch overhang supported by elephantine piers with concrete bases and wood posts on top.

420 E. La Veta — *1923 Mediterranean Revival*   NRHP:1997
A single-story box plan house with flat roof and stucco facades. An entry portico is formed by an extension of the main facade with three large, arched openings and a tile hood roof. The ridges of the main roof are ornamented with adobe tiles.

433 E. La Veta — *1922 Bungalow*   NRHP:1997
A single-story, simple unadorned bungalow with single, front-facing gable roof and small gable entry portico.

437 E. La Veta — *1919 Craftsman Bungalow*   NRHP:1997
A single-story clapboard bungalow with shallow-pitched, double, front-facing gables. The forwardmost gable forms the entry porch overhang supported by tapered piers with concrete bases and wooden posts on top. Notable feature of the house is two large picture windows with ornamentally paned transoms.

445 E. La Veta — *1919 Craftsman Bungalow*   NRHP:1997
A single-story clapboard bungalow with shallow-pitched, double, front-facing gables. The forwardmost gable forms the entry porch overhang supported by

tapered piers with concrete bases and wood posts on top. Vertical slatting ornaments the upper gable face of the porch; narrow slatting defines the connecting balustrade below.

LA VETA AVENUE — WEST

505 W. La Veta — *1926 Western*
False front pressed tin.

513 W. La Veta — *1926 Mediterranean Revival*   NRHP:1997
A small, one-story house with stucco facades and a flat roof. Entry is defined by a portico extension with rectilinear openings.

517 W. La Veta — *1924 Craftsman Bungalow* NRHP:1997
Double, front-facing gables with shallow pitch and clapboard siding on facades. Forwardmost gable is smaller and forms entry porch overhang. It is supported by tapered piers. Entry is beneath.

525 W. La Veta — *1932*   NRHP:1997
A small clapboard residence located in rear of deep lot. Contains recessed front entry on a modified box plan.

527 W. La Veta — *1920c Cottage*

533 W. La Veta — *1923 Craftsman Bungalow* NRHP:1997
Double, front-facing gables with shallow pitch and foremost gable forming entry porch overhang. This gable is supported by tapered piers. Entry is beneath. House is sided in lap siding.

541 W. La Veta — *1924*

617 W. La Veta — *1924 Bungalow*

625 W. La Veta — *1923 Bungalow*

637 W. La Veta — *1923 Bungalow*

810 W. La Veta — *1905 Picturesque*
OWNER: J.W. Morrison
Grower Morrison kept 10 acres of Mediterranean Sweets (later Navels,) along with two acres of mixed fruit trees. He built this house from stones on the ranch. An arroyo stone house built without reinforcement and three foot thick walls at the base.

LEMON STREET — SOUTH
—Lemon is named for one of the agricultural trees—

143 S. Lemon — *1928 Mediterranean Revival*   NRHP:1997
American Legion Hall
Built as one of many American Legion Halls throughout the US, this building still has the photographs of every man & woman in Orange to go to war during WWI.

American Legion Hall - 1935

This is a Mediterranean Revival influenced building constructed for an institutional purpose. This is a large, two-story, rectangular plan building with a single gable roof covered in adobe tiles. The facades are sided in textured stucco. The fenestration includes regularly spaced, multi-paned windows at the second story and two large mullioned windows on the first story flanking either side of the main entry. The entry is reached via a stoop and is composed of a large arched entry of rusticated stone. A small gabled parapet on the front further emphasizes the entry. The building is in well-maintained condition and exhibits its original architectural integrity.

146 S. Lemon — *1910c Hip Roof Cottage*   NRHP:1997
Box plan house with a steep-pitched, hip roof and wide overhanging eaves. House is now sided in asbestos

shingles. Entry is beneath a separate, symmetrically placed, porch overhang supported by Classical columns. Either side of the main entry is flanked by large transomed, picture windows.

156 S. Lemon — *1910c Vernacular*   NRHP:1997
Rectangular plan house with single, front-facing gable roof with steep pitch to gable. House is sided in clapboard. Main entry is at front center beneath separate tilt-up porch overhang. Large transomed, picture windows flank either side of entry.

166 S. Lemon — *1916 California Bungalow*

173 S. Lemon — *1923 Mediterranean Revival*   NRHP:1997
Bungalow Court
This U-plan Bungalow Court is comprised of a boxy formatted building with flat roof and tiled ridges. Siding is in stucco. This is one of two Bungalow Courts located in Old Towne Orange and is part of a very popular movement in the early 20's for consolidating families under one roof. At the rear of this structure is a small cottage facing the alley. It has a gable roof and weatherboard siding and simple, multi-pane wood sash windows.

176 S. Lemon — *1915c Craftsman*   NRHP:1997
TREE: Black Oak
Adolph Dittmer brought the acorns for this tree from Camp Nelson in the southern Sierra. (Rear)
A one and one-half story house with side-facing, gable roof and single, front-facing gable to dormer. House is sided in clapboard. Main entry is beneath corner porch which is recessed beneath main roof. Porch wall and support piers are of brick. Craftsman slatting and transomed windows adorn the front gabled dormer.

186 S. Lemon — *1924 California Bungalow*   NRHP:1997
This is a small, low-to-the-ground, bungalow cottage with shallow-pitched, gable roof. Front-facing gable forms entry porch overhang and is supported by wood posts. Main entry is at center beneath and is flanked

by sidelights.

206 S. Lemon — *1910c Hip Roof Cottage* NRHP:1997
Modified L-plan house with a steep-pitched, hip roof contrasted by front-facing gable with return at the eaves. Roof extends forward in apex of ell to form entry porch overhang and is supported by Modified Classical columns. Ornamental vent on front-facing gable is complemented by a pair of double-hung windows below.

210 S. Lemon — *1920c Craftsman Bungalow* NRHP:1997
A duplex bungalow with box plan and single main, front-facing gable roof. Just below is a secondary, front-facing gable which forms entry porch overhang and is supported by tapered piers. A pair of doors is just beneath and flanked on either side by a large transomed picture window. Ornamental purlins are located beneath the eaves on front portion of house.

223 S. Lemon — *1915c Bungalow* NRHP:1997
Low-to-the-ground bungalow with very shallow pitched roof comprised of a single, front-facing gable. House is sided in clapboard. A secondary roof extension forms entry porch overhang and is supported by piers comprised of concrete bases and wood posts on top. Two pairs of windows flank either side of main entry.

228 S. Lemon — *1921 Bungalow* NRHP:1997
A tri-gable roof with each gable front-facing. Two forwardmost gables are supported by tapered piers comprised of concrete bases and wood tops. Arrangement of gables is in a symmetrical fashion. House is sided in clapboard. Gable venting and slatting adorn gable faces.

253 S. Lemon — *1924*

262 S. Lemon — *1921 Bungalow* NRHP:1997
Small, low-to-the-ground bungalow with double, front-facing gables. Smaller gable symmetrically placed

beneath main gable and forms entry porch overhang. It is supported by wood posts. Entry is at center and flanked by double-hung window on either side.

272 S. Lemon — *1920c Bungalow*   NRHP:1997
Low-to-the-ground bungalow cottage with shallow pitched, multi-gable roof. Single, front-facing gable forms entry porch overhang and is supported by wood piers. House is sided in clapboard.

290 S. Lemon — *1910c Hip Roof Cottage*   NRHP:1997
Clapboard siding and hip roof with small, pedimented gable on center front of roof. Roof extension forms entry porch overhang and is supported by Classical columns.

305 S. Lemon —
TREE: Arizona Cypress *Cupressus globra*.

357 S. Lemon — *1922*   NRHP:1997
A single story structure with high-pitched, single gabled roof and crown molding. Siding is wood with double-hung wood windows and large facia board and clover detail embellishment.

429 S. Lemon — *1923 Bungalow*

445 S. Lemon — *1930 Bungalow*

Lemon Street — North

121 N. Lemon — *1940c Western False-Front*   NRHP:1997
This is a very small, single-story commercial building with a rectangular plan, a single-gabled roof and a western false front parapet. The building has been stuccoed and modified on the front facade.

145 N. Lemon — *1922 Western False-Front*   NRHP:1997
This is a large industrial building with combination wood-lap siding and ornamental pressed tin. The building features the typical rectangular plan with single-gabled roof falsified by a large stepped parapet which disguises the true smallness of the building. The ornamental pressed tin on the upper portion of the parapet was common to the period and is a rare remaining architectural complement.

149 N. Lemon — *1930c Mediterranean Revival*

155 N. Lemon — *1914 Bungalow*   NRHP:1997
A single-story bungalow with double front-facing gabled roof. The forwardmost gable, while not covered by a porch, forms the entry portion of the building.

163 N. Lemon — *1914 Bungalow*   NRHP:1997
A single-story box plan house with wide-lap siding and single front-facing gabled roof. No porch is present at this time. The house is simple and unadorned.

171 N. Lemon — *1905c Hip Roof Cottage* NRHP:1997
A single-story box plan house with clapboard siding and steep-pitched hip roof. A small, hipped dormer is present on the front portion of the roof. Entry is via a corner recessed porch supported by a classical column.

189 N. Lemon — *1906 Hip Roof Cottage*   NRHP:1997
A single-story box plan house with clapboard siding and steep-pitched roof. A small pedimented gable with ornamental shingles is present on the front portion of the roof. Just beneath, in a central location, is a separate porch overhang supported by classical columns. Entry is beneath at center. Since the 1982

survey, this structure has undergone restoration.

193 N. Lemon — *1905c Hip Roof Cottage* NRHP:1997

A single-story box plan house with combination hip and gable roof. The house is built on a box plan and incorporates clapboard siding. What was originally a nearly full-width front porch has since been enclosed. Brick chimneys with ornamental cornices emerge from the center of the roof.

233 N. Lemon — *1914 Industrial* NRHP:1997

Hammond Lumber Co. &
Orange Contracting & Milling Co.
BLDR: Orange Contracting & Milling Co.

What were originally two separate, industrial Western, False front style industrial buildings were joined together in later years. The two buildings have similar descriptions in that both are built on a basic rectangular plan and feature a single-gable roof obscured by the large stepped Western False front. The front facades of the building are in rolled tin.

Orange Contracting & Milling Co.

253 N. Lemon — *1920c Bungalow* NRHP:1997

A single-story house with multi-gabled shallow pitched roof. The original clapboard siding has since been covered by asbestos shingles. A front-facing gable forms the entry porch overhang and is located along the center of the front facade. This is supported by slender tapered piers. Vertical venting distinguishes this gable face. The entry door is at center and is flanked on either side by sidelights.

269 N. Lemon — *1920c Bungalow*   NRHP:1997
A single-story clapboard bungalow with shallow-pitched multi-gable roof. Three-fourths of the front facade is covered by a front-facing gable overhang which forms the entry porch. Entry is beneath and is flanked on either side by half-size sidelights.

311 N. Lemon — *1909 Bungalow*   NRHP:1997
A single-story house with wide-lap siding and steep-pitch gable roof. Entry is via a corner recessed porch supported by Classical columns.

321 N. Lemon — *1906 Bungalow*   NRHP:1997
A single-story clapboard house with single front-facing gable roof. Entry is located beneath a small gabled entry portico supported by 2 x 4's.

327 N. Lemon — *1905 Victorian*   NRHP:1997
A two-story house built on an L-plan with shiplap siding and steep-pitched gable roof. The house is a classic rural farm house built prior to 1900 particularly in the Midwest. Entry is in the apex of the ell beneath a separate roofed extension which forms an entry porch. This porch overhang is supported by ornamentally trimmed posts characteristic of the Victorian Period.

328 N. Lemon — *1922 Bungalow*   NRHP:1997
A single-story clapboard bungalow with shallow-pitch, multi-gable roof. A front-facing gable is located in the centermost portion of the front facade and forms an entry porch overhang. Entry is beneath at center and flanked on either side by large three-part picture windows with mullioned sections.

336 N. Lemon — *1925 Bungalow*   NRHP:1997

A single-story clapboard bungalow with rectangular plan and shallow-pitch, multi-gable roof. The main portion of the house is covered by a single side-facing gable roof while a centrally located front-facing gable forms the entry porch overhang. This is supported by elephantine piers with ornamental brick bases.

337 N. Lemon — *1904 Double Hip Roof Cottage*   NONC
Since the 1982 survey, this structure appears to have been replaced.

345 N. Lemon — *1937*

356 N. Lemon — *1928*

360 N. Lemon — *1923 Bungalow*   NRHP:1997
A single-story bungalow with shallow-pitch, multi-gable roof. The original siding has been covered with asbestos shingles. A centrally located front-facing gable forms the entry porch overhang and is supported by tapered piers. It appears as though the original screen door is still present on the house and is particularly notable for its ornamentation. Since the 1982 survey, the structure's original screen door has been removed.

388 N. Lemon — *1905 Hip Roof Cottage*   NRHP:1997
A single-story box plan house with steep-pitch, hip roof. A hitched dormer is present on the front portion of the roof. One-half of the front facade is devoted to a recessed entry porch supported by wood posts.

402 N. Lemon — *1905 Hip Roof Cottage*   NRHP:1997
A small, single-story box plan house with truncated hip roof. The original siding has been covered with asbestos shingles. A full-width porch is present on the front facade and has its own separate roof extension supported by wood posts. These posts are connected by a slotted balustrade.

405 N. Lemon — *1913 Bungalow*   NRHP:1997
A single-story house with single side-facing gable roof. The main roof extends forward to form a full-

width porch supported in four places by tapered piers.

412 N. Lemon — *1913 Bungalow*   NRHP:1997
A single-story house with wide-lap siding and single-front facing gable roof. One-half of the front facade is devoted to a recessed porch which forms the entry. This porch has since been screened. Since the 1982 survey, this structure has been altered by stucco siding.

415 N. Lemon — *1900c Hip Roof Cottage* NRHP:1997
A single-story box plan house with clapboard siding and steep-pitch, hip roof which results in an unusual small gable attic dormer. Nearly full-length porch is present and is defined by a separate roof extension supported by wood posts.

419 N. Lemon — *1915 Bungalow*   NRHP:1997
A single-story house with wide-lap siding and single side-facing gable roof. A shed dormer is present on the front portion of the roof. A large angled bay window is present beneath the roof, the side of which is the main entry. Since the 1982 survey, this structure has deteriorated.

420 N. Lemon — *1913 Bungalow*   NRHP:1997
A single-story bungalow with wide-lap siding and double front-facing gable roof. The forwardmost gable forms the entry porch overhang which is now supported by ornamental iron posts. Cross-ties on the upper gable faces ornament the appearance of the house.

426 N. Lemon — *1914 Bungalow*   NRHP:1997
A single-story bungalow with wide-lap siding and intersecting gable roof. The front-facing gable in combination with the separate roof extension form the entry porch which is supported by wood posts on a solid rail.

428 N. Lemon — *1911 Bungalow*   NRHP:1997
A single-story house with wide-lap siding and single

side-facing gable roof. An unusual appearance is derived from the two small front-facing gabled dormers.

429 N. Lemon — *1914 Bungalow*   NRHP:1997
A single-story bungalow with double front-facing gable roof. The forwardmost gable forms the entry porch overhang which is supported by wood posts. The original siding has since been covered with asbestos shingles.

437 N. Lemon — *1914 Bungalow*   NRHP:1997
A single-story bungalow with wide-lap siding and single front-facing gable roof. An additional front-facing gable, smaller than the main one, forms the entry porch overhang and is supported by tapered wood piers. Since the 1982 survey, this structure has deteriorated.

442 N. Lemon — *1911 Bungalow*   NRHP:1997
A single-story house built on an L-plan with steep-pitch, gable roof. The house has been considerably altered through the use of stucco and ornamental iron porch piers. The return of the eaves on the gable and windows clearly indicates the true age and style of the house.

450 N. Lemon — *1910 Bungalow*   NRHP:1997
A single-story house with rectangular plan and single side-facing gable roof. A centrally located front-facing gable forms the entry porch overhang and is supported by wood posts. The house is typical of the bungalow period but has been modified through the use of stucco on the facades.

460 N. Lemon — *1917 Vernacular*   NONC
A two-story boxy house with single front-facing gable roof where there is a return of the eaves. Entry is via a corner recessed porch supported by wood posts. The house is very simple and unadorned. Since the 1982 survey, this structure has been severely altered by

totally remodeling.

469 N. Lemon — *1919 Bungalow*   NONC
Modified Style
A single-story clapboard bungalow with single front-facing gable roof. Entry is via a corner recessed porch supported by wood posts. Since the 1982 survey, this structure has been severely altered by totally remodeling.

470 N. Lemon — *1920c Bungalow*   NRHP:1997
A single-story bungalow cottage with wide lap siding and single front-facing gable roof. Smaller centrally located front-facing gable extends forward to form the entry porch overhang. It is supported by wood posts with a connecting slatted balustrade.

477 N. Lemon — *1920c Bungalow*   NRHP:1997
A single-story bungalow with wide lap siding and double front-facing gable roof. The forwardmost gable forms the entry porch overhang and is supported by wood posts.

480 N. Lemon — *1906 Bungalow*   NRHP:1997
A single-story bungalow with wide lap siding and steep-pitch, multi-gable roof. The roof is fashioned in an L-plan with the short leg of the ell resulting in a front-facing gable which originally formed a recessed porch but has since been enclosed.

484 N. Lemon — *1910 Bungalow*   NRHP:1997
A single story house with wide lap siding and single front-facing gable roof. One-half of the front facade is defined by a recessed porch supported by ornamental wood posts.

493 N. Lemon — *1905c Cottage, Hip Roof*

504 N. Lemon — *1923 Hip Roof Cottage*   NRHP:1997
A multi-gabled, stucco sided, modified L-plan with corner entry. Original tall and narrow multi-paned windows are present with some double-hung windows.

512 N. Lemon — *1923 Hip Roof Cottage*   NRHP:1997

A small, wood lapped sided residence with single gable roof, box plan. Front entry has slope, small decorative overhang.

528 N. Lemon — *1923 Hip Roof Cottage*   NRHP:1997
A small box plan Bungalow residence with front gable over front porch. Small columns on concrete piers hard up front gable. A pair of oversize single windows with mullioned top flank at the entry. Garage emulates front house roof line.

536 N. Lemon — *1920 Hip Roof Cottage*   NRHP:1997
A stucco modified box plan, with shed roof over entry and peaked roof over shed roof. Recessed entry with front porch.

544 N. Lemon — *1921 Hip Roof Cottage*   NRHP:1997
A stucco residence with 2 front facing gables, one covering front entry . Stone has been added on corner facade.

554 N. Lemon — *1923 Hip Roof Cottage*

568 N. Lemon — *1923 Hip Roof Cottage*   NRHP:1997
A wood lapped sided Bungalow, rectangular plan, two front facing gables. Front porch enhanced by small elephantine pillars on concrete piers. Front entry flanked by a large picture window.

578 N. Lemon — *1923 Hip Roof Cottage*   NRHP:1997
A small wood lapped sided Bungalow with two front facing gables in box plan. Porch leading to entry flanked by two large picture windows.

580 N. Lemon — *1922 Hip Roof Cottage*   NRHP:1997
Two front facing gables on a wood lap sided, box plan bungalow home. Two pillars concrete piers hold up front gable. Entry is flanked by a pair of double hung windows.

592 N. Lemon — *1924 Hip Roof Cottage*   NRHP:1997
A small wood lap sided Bungalow, box plan style with front gable covering entry. Two layer windows flank entry. An extension of roof line suggests possible

addition.

594 N. Lemon — *1922 Hip Roof Cottage*   NRHP:1997
A small wood lap sided, box plan residence, no gables.
Flat front with two windows flanking front door.

SAVI: weir-box, located on the corner.

MAPLE AVENUE — EAST
—Maple is named for one of the horticultural trees—

112 E. Maple — *1912 Brick Commercial*   NRHP:1997
A large brisk commercial single-story box plan building. Distinctive entablature with projecting cornice is present. A large bay single-paned window flanks the entry.

118 E. Maple — *1920 Bungalow*

137 E. Maple — *1905c Classic Box*   NRHP:1997
A large, two-story box plan house with multi-hip and gable roof built in a modified Classic Box tradition. The house is considerably altered from its original form with the addition of a chapel building adjacent and a first-story storefront. The remaining portions of the house have also since been stuccoed. Since the 1982 survey, this structure has been altered to make the storefront a little more compatible.

203 E. Maple — *1920c Bungalow*   NRHP:1997
A single-story bungalow with lap siding and single-gable roof with side-facing gables. A smaller, front-facing gable entry portico is supported by colonial-like columns. The original hardwood door with plate glass windows is still present and is flanked on either side by 3-part transomed windows.

211 E. Maple — *1915c Craftsman*   NRHP:1997
A large two-story house with clapboard siding and multi-gable roof. The second story is located over the rear half of the house. A full-width front porch, comprised of a front-facing gable overhang, is supported by wide piers with brick bases and wood posts on top. These piers are connected by a slatted balustrade whose theme is carried out in the upper gable face above.

225 E. Maple — *1915c Craftsman*   NRHP:1997
This house is identical to the one at 211 E. Maple.

227 E. Maple — *1910 Craftsman Bungalow*   NRHP:1997

A single-story bungalow with wide lap siding and double, front-facing gable roof. The foremost gable originally formed the entry porch overhang but has since been enclosed. The original tapered piers are still present. The other front-facing gable results in an angled bay window and is adorned by three large windows on either of the panes. Ornamental purlins and ornamental transoms in the upper gable faces further adorn the house.

235 E. Maple — *1906 Hip Roof Cottage*   OTPA:1997
OWNER: Charles & Mary Baker
BLDR: Charles Baker

Mary Baker with the Dr. Brooks family
This photo was taken on their lawn,
and shows the house and church across the street.

Bee Keeper Baker was a rancher who went into bee keeping in the canyons of the Santa Ana mountains. Baker Canyon is still on the maps. His wife Mary lived on in the home past his death in 1919 and married J.E. Park. He died in 1948.

A one and one-half story clapboard house with multi-gable and hip roof. The house has a full wrap-around porch on one corner which is supported by wide clapboard piers. A small hipped dormer with two sash windows is present on the front portion of the roof, as is a small pedimented gable with shingle embellishment.

319 E. Maple — *1900c Hip Roof Cottage*   NRHP:1997
Modified Style
A one-story house with a steep-pitched, hip and gable roof. A pedimented gable with fish-scale shingles and a louvered transom extend forward to form the entry porch overhang. This overhang is supported by ornate turned columns, typical of the Victorian era. Except for the porch posts, the entire house below the eaves has been altered through the replacement of the windows and door and by stuccoing the facades.

320 E. Maple — *1916 Bungalow*   NRHP:1997
Modified Style
A single-story bungalow with ornamental lap siding and tri-gable roof. The main portion of the house is covered by a single-gable roof with side-facing gables. A full-width, front-facing gable forms the entry porch overhang. This is supported by wide piers with concrete bases and wood posts on top. The original wood door with plate glass windows is still present on the center of the front facade.

327 E. Maple — *1917 Bungalow*   NRHP:1997
A single-story bungalow with ornamental lap siding and multi-gable roof. The house was built on a modified L-plan, the entry being in the apex of the ell. The brickwork on the lower foundation of the house was probably a later addition.

335 E. Maple — *1920 Mediterranean Revival*   NRHP:1997
OWNER: Clarence & Alma J. Walker
BLDR: Orange Contracting & Milling Co.
 The Walkers moved to Orange in 1921 and into this home to retire. Active in the Orange Presbyterian Church until Clarence died in 1932. Married for 54 years, the Walkers had no children, with Alma passing in the 1940s.

Clarence & Alma Walker Home - 1920s

A single-story box plan house with stucco facades and flat roof. The house is fashioned in a symmetrical manner with the center portion of the front facade devoted to a large entry portico which features large, arched openings and a raised parapet with Mission influence. On either side are large, transomed picture windows over which hang adobe tile hoods. Ornamental attic vents are present just above these hoods. The original door with multi-paned windows is still present and is flanked on either side by sidelights.

336 E. Maple — *1915 Bungalow*   NRHP:1997
A single-story clapboard bungalow with double, front-facing gable roof. The forwardmost gable forms the entry porch overhang and is supported by tapered piers. The main entry is beneath, featuring a very elaborate wood screen do or with spindlework. Large, transomed picture windows are located on either side of the door.

405 E. Maple — *1915c Bungalow*   NRHP:1997
A single-story bungalow with rectangular plan, wide lap siding and a single-gable roof with side-facing gables. The centermost portion of the front facade features an extension of the roof which culminates in an entry porch over hang supported by slim wood

posts. Main entry is beneath at center and is flanked on either side by sidelights.

413 E. Maple — *1911 Bungalow*   NRHP:1997
A single-story bungalow with wide lap siding and multi-gable roof. The house is built in a modified L-plan with the short leg of the ell resulting in the entry porch overhang. This is supported by wide piers. The original door with plate glass windows is still present. Ornamental purlins and an ornamentally framed transom vent, as well as two ornamental brick chimneys, adorn the house.

419 E. Maple — *1909 Craftsman*   OTPA:1997
owner: Walter & Cora Gregg
A one and one-half story clapboard house with single-gable roof with side-facing gables. A shed dormer rises out of the front portion of the roof and includes 3 sash windows. One-half of the front facade is devoted to a large recessed porch supported by wide clapboard piers. The remaining portion of the front facade is composed of an angled bay window with a single sash window in each of the bay panes.

427 E. Maple — *1915 Craftsman*   NRHP:1997
A one and one half story house with wide lap siding and gable roof. A large, front -facing gable dormer is present on the front portion of the roof. The main roof extends forward to form a full-width porch overhang and is supported by wood piers. The original door with multi-plate glass windows is still present.

437 E. Maple — *1905 Classic Box*   NRHP:1997
An ample two-story clapboard house with combination hip and gable roof. The house features a large, corner wrap-around porch supported by classical columns atop a clapboard porch wall. The frontmost leg of the house includes a front-facing gable with shingles and ornamental transomed vent. The original door and screen door are still present on the house. Since the 1982 survey, this structure has been altered with

appropriate rear addition.

515 E. Maple — *1923 Mediterranean Revival*   OTPA:1997
TREE: Ceder of Lebannon. Planted by Dr. Domann.
OWNER: Dr. Arthur & Bertie Domann, Medical Doctor

Dr. Arthur & Bertie Domann Home

Dr. Domann came to Orange in 1911 starting construction on this large home during the following decade. Later, the home was a Missionary House.

This is a two-story Mediterranean Revival style house with specific Italianate influence. The house features an adobe tile, hip roof with a small arched dormer. The house is constructed in brick which is unique in Orange. Built on a box plan, a symmetrical format is utilized in the arrangement of the central entry and the fenestration. The door is sheltered by a wide portico with a shallow arch; this portico is supported by decorative scroll brackets like those beneath the wide eaves at the cornice line. Each of the windows and the cornice line is ornamentally framed in contrasting brick; this same brick work is carried out in the cornice of the chimney. The house is excellently maintained and remains in its original state.

516 E. Maple —   .
TREE: White Sapota *Caasimiroa edulis* 20" 35' 40'. A rare tree, this is the only one in Orange.

526 E. Maple — *1922 Bungalow*   NRHP:1997

OWNER: John M. & Joanna Helmrich, School Principal
BLDR: Orange Contracting & Milling Co.
Principal of the Immanual Lutheran School.

John M. & Joanna Helmrich Home

A single-story bungalow with rectangular plan and single-gable roof. The original siding has since been covered by asbestos shingles. The house has an unusual entry which is comprised of a gabled portico within the large arched opening. Below is a large door with ornamentally paned side lites and a large, arched transom above. Two small eyelid dormers with lattice venting are present on the front portion of the roof.

527 E. Maple — *1914 Craftsman*   NRHP:1997

A large two-story house with ornamental lap siding and multi-gable roof . The second story portion of the house is located over the rear half of the structure. The lower front is comprised of two front-facing gables, the forward most of which forms a large entry porch overhang. This is supported by piers comprised of brick bases and wood posts on top.

535 E. Maple — *1915c Bungalow*   NRHP:1997

A single-story bungalow with wide lap siding and multi-gable roof. The main portion of the front of the house is comprised of two front-facing gables; the forwardmost one acts as an entry porch overhang. Cross-ties and triangular bracket supports adorn the upper gable faces; below the original wood door with plate glass windows is still present.

536 E. Maple — *1914 Bungalow*   NRHP:1997

A single-story bungalow with wide lap siding and multi-gable roof. The front of the house is articulated by double front-facing gables, the forwardmost of which acts as the entry porch overhang. It is supported by wide piers composed of bricks; the bricks are connected by a slatted ballustrade.

604 E. Maple — *1931 Spanish Colonial Revival* NRHP:1997

A single-story house built on an L-plan with stucco facades and gable roof with adobe tiles. Entry is at the apex of the ell and sheltered by a small, adobe tiled hood. An ornamental chimney is on the side.

605 E. Maple — *1913 Post Victorian*   OTPA:1997

OWNER: David & Hattie Claypool

The Claypool home - 'teens

Built by Claypool, this was one of many that held the large family. Young Ken went on to own the Radio Shop in the Plaza District.

A two-story house with steep-pitched, gable roof and a full-width front porch present at the first story of the lower front facade. This porch has its own separate roof overhang which is supported by wood posts.

613 E. Maple — *1914 Craftsman*   NRHP:1997

A one and one-half story house with wide lap siding and single-gable roof with side-facing gables. A large, front-facing, gabled dormer is also present. The main roof extends forward to form a full-width porch overhang, supported by tapered piers on the outermost extremities and by narrow turned posts in the center portion of the porch. These posts harken back to the Victorian-type embellishment. The original door with plate glass windows is still present and is flanked on either side by a trio of sash windows.

616 E. Maple — *1908 Hip Roof Cottage*   NRHP:1997

Arthur Barnhart built this house as a retirement home with his daughter Grace and her husband John Knolla, moving here in 1919 to care for him. They stayed on after his death that year, until 1944.

A two-story clapboard house with multi-hip and gable roof. The high hip dormer is present on the front facade. What was originally a recessed corner porch was enclosed circa 1930 and replaced by gabled porticos supported by wide ornamental posts. Since the 1982 survey, this structure has been altered with appropriate porch rail and columns.

621 E. Maple — *1915c Bungalow*   NRHP:1997

A single-story bungalow with wide lap siding and single-gable roof with side-facing gables. A low shed dormer is also present on the front portion of the roof. One-half of the front facade is devoted to a large recessed porch supported by brick piers. The house features a double entry, each with the original door.

633 E. Maple — *1909 Craftsman*   NRHP:1997

A two-story Craftsman home with wide lap siding and multi-gable roof. A wide shed dormer with two pairs of transomed windows is present on the front portion of the roof. The main roof extends forward to form a full-width porch, sup ported by stone piers connected by a long, low stone wall. This same stone work is featured in the chimney at the rear of the house. The original door is still present and is flanked on either side by a trio of sash windows.

704 E. Maple — *1905c Hip Roof Cottage*   NRHP:1997
A single-story clapboard house with hip and gable roof. The house features a large, corner, wrap-around porch supported by classical columns with Corinthian capitals. Both the front and side wings of the house have gables and feature large transomed windows with ornamental transoms in the upper gable faces.

714 E. Maple — *1920 Victorian*   NRHP:1997
Two-story, multi-gabled Victorian with covered porch entry and secondary entry on side. Front facing window is large with leaded glass mullion. Clap board siding with wrapping eaves. Porch overhang is supported by two ornate columns.

1025 E. Maple — *1920s School*   NONC
One of six grade schools built in Orange prior to 1940.

Maple Avenue Grade School - 1920s

MAPLE AVENUE — WEST

115 W. Maple — *1923 Bungalow*   NRHP:1997
A single-story clapboard bungalow with double front-facing gable roof. A small attached porch is located between the forwardmost and rear gables, and the entry is just beneath. Since the 1982 survey, this structure has undergone restoration.

123 W. Maple — *1917 Brick Commercial*   NRHP:1997
Sunshine Apartments
This is a two-story brick apartment building built on a rectangular plan. Sash windows are spaced at regular intervals across both the first and second stories. The roof is flat, but wide eaves shelter the horizontal banding at the cornice line. The two street entries are simple with just a low stoop and accompanying side walls marking their location. The building is typical of the brick commercial and multi-family buildings that were constructed during the twenties. The building is in fair condition but exhibits its original architectural integrity. Since the 1982 survey, this structure has undergone restoration.

Sunshine Apartments - 1920s

139 W. Maple — *1917*

205 W. Maple — *1905c Victorian*

224 W. Maple — *1920c Bungalow*   NRHP:1997

A single-story bungalow with wide lap siding and single front-facing gable roof. The house has been modified using stucco on the side facades and brick on the lower foundation wall.

235 W. Maple — *1920*

302 W. Maple — *1925c Bungalow*

616 W. Maple — *1920c Bungalow*

633 W. Maple — *1918 Bungalow*

MARIETTA PLACE — WEST
—*Marietta was a new development in 1924*—

402 W. Marietta — *1924 Mediterranean Revival* NRHP:1997
Small, box plan house with stucco sides, flat roof and tiles at roof edges. Front entry is at center beneath arcaded portico. Large picture windows are on either side.

408 W. Marietta — *1924 Mediterranean Revival* NRHP:1997
Small, box plan house with stucco siding and flat roof. Main entry is beneath large recessed arched opening and is flanked by large picture windows on either side.

409 W. Marietta — *1924 Mediterranean Revival* NRHP:1997
A box plan house with stucco sides and adobe tiles at roof ridges. House is distinguished by raised parapet and corner pilasters. Also included is a prominent pilastered entry and tile hoods above picture windows on either side .

414 W. Marietta — *1924 Mediterranean Revival* NRHP:1997
Small, box plan duplex with stucco siding and flat roof. Adobe tiles are at roof ridges. Each entry is beneath an arched portico.

415 W. Marietta — *1924 Mediterranean Revival* NRHP:1997
Small, box plan house with stucco siding and flat roof. Adobe tiles are at roof ridges. Main entry is at center and is flanked by three-part windows on either side.

MONTGOMERY PLACE — SOUTH
—Montgomery was renamed from Grant Street after the RR came—

428 S. Montgomery — *1920c Sidelap Cottage House*

MORELAND DRIVE — EAST

—Moreland was a new development of one block in 1928—

524 E. Moreland — *1928c Mediterranean Revival* NRHP:1997
A single-story bungalow with stucco facades and a flat roof. Entry is via a projection from the main facade defined by vertical walls with large arched openings. To either side of the porch portico is a large picture window with multi-paned transom covered by a tiled hood. The main facade of the house features a raised parapet. The porch also has a raised parapet.

536 E. Moreland — *1928c Mediterranean Revival* NRHP:1997
This house is identical to the one next door at 524 Moreland with the exception that the windows are large, three-part windows with narrow, double-hung windows flanking a large single-pane window with multi-pane transom.

604 E. Moreland — *1928c Mediterranean Revival* NRHP:1997
A single-story, box plan house with stucco facades and flat roof. Entry is at center via a portico projection which features a large arched opening. To either side are a pair of casement windows with tile hoods. The front facade has a stepped parapet and raised pilasters; the roof line all around is ornamented with adobe tiles.

608 E. Moreland — *1928c Mediterranean Revival* NRHP:1997
A single-story, box plan house with stucco facades and flat roof. Entry is via an arched portico projection flanked on either side by a large, double-hung window.

612 E. Moreland — *1915c Craftsman Bungalow* NRHP:1997
A single-story bungalow with shallow-pitched, multi-gable roof and sheathing which includes wide lap siding at the lower foundation wall and clapboard above. Entry is via a recessed gable over a porch supported by wide piers. Jigsawn ornamentation and exposed beams adorn the porch gable face. All

windows are ornamentally framed.

OLIVE STREET — SOUTH
—Olive is named for one of the agricultural grove trees—

115 S. Olive — *1908 Brick Commercial*   NRHP:1982

127 S. Olive — *1923 Brick Commercial*   NRHP:1982

139 S. Olive — *1923 Brick Commercial*   NRHP:1982

203 S. Olive — *1890c Victorian Cottage*   NRHP:1997
A one-story house with shiplap siding and a combination mansard and gable roof. The house originally was built on a slight L-plan with a large wrap-around porch. This porch was later enclosed, which significantly alters the appearance of the house. Wide eaves are embellished with simple arched brackets. A side entrance off Almond retains the original porch with ornate turned columns and slatted balustrade.

215 S. Olive — *1911 Craftsman*   NRHP:1997
A one and one-half story house with single, side-facing gable roof and smaller, front-facing gabled dormer. House is sided in clapboard, and what was probably the original front porch has since been enclosed.

224 S. Olive — *1918 Craftsman*   NRHP:1997
OWNER: Diedrich & Katherine Klanner
BLDR: Orange Contracting & Milling Co.

Diedrich & Katherine Klanner Home

This 2160 sq. ft. Craftsman style residence was built for Diedrich and Catherina Klaner in 1919.

Large, two-story home with horizontal emphasis. Second story is recessed above first story. Lower story is distinguished by two parallel front-facing gables. Frontmost gable forms entry porch overhang. Porch is supported by piers consisting of brick bases and wood post caps. Large, three-part transomed picture window is on front beneath porch.

225 S. Olive — *1922 Craftsman Bungalow*   NRHP:1997
Small, single-story house with double, front-facing gables. Frontmost gable forms entry porch overhang and is supported by wide piers. House is sheathed in clapboard with some vertical venting in gable faces.

232 S. Olive — *1922 Craftsman Bungalow*   NRHP:1997
Single-story house sheathed in clapboard on a rectangular plan. Main portion of house has side-facing gable, but two smaller, front-facing gables provide added contrast. Main roof extends to form entry porch overhang.

235 S. Olive — *1920 Craftsman*   NRHP:1997
OWNER: Louis D. & Adolphine Gunther
BLDR: Orange Contracting & Milling Co.

Louis D. & Adolphine Gunther Home

This 2 story Craftsman style residence was built, making abundant use of natural materials, for Louis Gunther in 1920.

Two-story, Craftsman home with second story located in a recessed fashion above first story. Double, front-facing gables form first story and are sheathed in arroyo stone. Frontmost gable forms entry porch overhang and is supported by arroyo stone tapered piers. Large, three-part windows adorn front, while ornamental purlins distinguish the gable eaves. Entire lower facade is faced in arroyo stone.

242 S. Olive — *1902 Victorian*   NRHP:1997
OWNER: P.W. Ehlen
Ehlen & Grote Co-owner of the "Big White Store" Ehlen & Grote Co. ran the largest operation of general merchandise in town. Wagons hauled supplies out to many areas.

This is a large, two-story house built with Classical Revival influence s. The house includes a multi-gable roof and facades sided in clapboard. Built on a modified L-plan, the main body of the house is covered by a single gable roof with side-facing gables, while the short leg of the 'L' results in a front-facing gable. The apex of this ell contains an attached overhang supported by Classical columns which form a large wrap-around porch. These columns are connected by a short balustrade with ornamental turned balusters. The front-facing gable includes an angled bay window on the lower story and considerable embellishment on the upper gable face; this embellishment consists of a return of the eaves, ornamental bargeboard and a circular, key-stoned attic vent. The house is in need of some maintenance, but exhibits its full original, architectural integrity.

245 S. Olive — *1914 Craftsman Bungalow*   NRHP:1997
Low-to-the-ground bungalow with extremely shallow pitched roof and clap board siding. Frontmost gable

forms wide entry porch overhang and is supported by wide tapered, concrete piers.

252 S. Olive — *1915 Craftsman Bungalow*   NRHP:1997
Single-story clapboard bungalow with double, front-facing gables. Forwardmost gable forms entry porch overhang and is supported by tapered piers.

253 S. Olive — *1913 Craftsman Bungalow*   NRHP:1997
Single-story, low-to-the-ground bungalow with L-plan formed by formatting of gables. Frontmost gable and main roof extension form wide porch overhang which is supported by tapered columns. Columns are slumpstone at the foundation and have wood caps.

261 S. Olive — *1914 Craftsman Bungalow*   NRHP:1997
TREE: American Hornbean *Carpinus caroliniana* 16" 40' 45' Rare Tree.
Single-story, rectangular-plan bungalow with clapboard siding and single, front-facing gable roof. Ornamental purlins accentuate front eaves. Porch is supported by elephantine piers.

262 S. Olive — *1905c Hip Roof Cottage*   NRHP:1997
Single-story clapboard house with a steep-pitched, hip roof and small, gabled dormer on front face of roof. Recessed corner porch is supported by Classical column, and a large, three-part picture window adorns the frontmost facade.

264 S. Olive — *1914 Bungalow*   NRHP:1997
Small, rectangular plan bungalow with main roof composed of a side-facing gable. Smaller, centrally located, front-facing gable extends forward to form entry porch overhang. House is sheathed in clapboard. Entry is at center front.

270 S. Olive — *1902 Rural Victorian*   NRHP:1997
Two-story clapboard house with a rectangular plan and single, front-facing gable roof. Smaller overhang at first story in front forms porch and is supported by Classical columns, the frontmost portion of which is a

pedimented gable. Large, three-part picture window is in front.

282 S. Olive — *1895*
TREE: Carob *Ceratonia siligua* 30" 45' 65' - Fair.

284 S. Olive — *1895 Hip Roof Cottage*   NRHP:1997
Small, single-story house with pyramidal roof and small attic gable in front. Corner porch is recessed beneath main roof and is supported by Classical columns. Pairs of high vertical windows indicate Victorian period.

290 S. Olive — *1910c Classic Box*   NRHP:1997
Large, full, two-story box plan house with clapboard siding and a steep-pitched, hip roof. Major alteration has been made on the front facade above the original porch overhang. The lower story porch is supported by Classical columns, and entry is at center beneath.

320 S. Olive — *1904 Victorian Cottage*   NRHP:1997
Small, single-story L-plan cottage now covered with asbestos siding. Apex of ell is location of porch overhang supported by ornamental columns characteristic of Victorian era homes.

331 S. Olive — *1923 Mediterranean Revival* NONC

339 S. Olive — *1920c Craftsman Bungalow* NONC

340 S. Olive — *1923 Craftsman Bungalow*   OTPA:1997
OWNER: J.F. & Minnie Hahn
Small, single-story bungalow, clapboard siding and double-front-facing gable roof. Foremost gable forms entry porch overhang and is supported by tapered piers. A porte cochere is located to the side and is also supported by a tapered pier.

349 S. Olive — *1915c Craftsman*   NRHP:1997
A one and one-half story Craftsman home with single, side-facing gable contrasted by smaller, front-facing gabled dormer. House is sheathed in clapboard. Main roof extends forward to form wide porch overhang and is supported by tapered piers comprised of arroyo

stone bases and wood tops. Large, transomed picture windows flank either side of main door.

350 S. Olive — *1898c Victorian, Rural*   OTPA:1997
OWNER: George & Fanny Lighthall
Teamster Lighthall built this home shortly before his death in 1905. With five children to raise alone, Fanny sold the house two years later.

Large, two-story house with rectangular plan and single, side-facing gable roof. Main entry is via recessed corner porch supported by wood posts. Ornamental fretwork comprises the balustrade and connecting links between porch posts.

356 S. Olive — *1906 Hip Roof Cottage*   NRHP:1997
Single-story, box plan house with a steep-pitched, hip roof and clapboard siding. Main roof extends forward to form entry porch overhang and is supported by wood posts. Porch posts are connected by slatted balustrade. Main entry is beneath at center.

357 S. Olive — *1895c Hip Roof Cottage*   NRHP:1997
Small, single-story box plan house with flattened hip roof and shiplap siding. Separate, smaller roof extends across full width of front facade and forms porch overhang. It is supported by wood posts connected by slatted balustrade.

364 S. Olive — *1930*

365 S. Olive — *1915 Craftsman*   NONC

373 S. Olive — *1920 Bungalow*   NRHP:1997
Single-story, low-to-the-ground bungalow with single, front-facing gable roof. Main entry is recessed beneath the porch which is supported by large tapered columns. Large transomed, picture windows flank either side of the main entry at center.

376 S. Olive — *1905c Hip Roof Cottage*   NRHP:1997
Single-story, box plan house with a steep-pitched, hip roof and smaller gable section on forwardmost portion of front facade which forms an angled bay window. A

corner porch is supported by Classical-like columns. The strongest ornamental feature of the house is the gable projection which has a recessed half moon.

392 S. Olive — *1917 Bungalow Carr*   OTPA:1997
Small clapboard cottage with U-plan and multi-gable roof. Entry is at center of U. Garage appears to be attached to house and probably a later addition.

393 S. Olive — *1915c Craftsman*   NRHP:1997
A one and one-half story Craftsman home with rectangular plan and single, side-facing, gable roof complemented by smaller, front-facing gabled dormer. Main roof extends forward to form wide porch overhang and is supported by elephantine piers. Two large picture windows with wide transoms flank either side of main entry which is at center. Ornamental purlins adorn eaves of gabled dormer.

393½ S. Olive — *1920c Bungalow*   NRHP:1997
Single-story clapboard bungalow with double, front-facing gables. Fore most gable originally formed entry porch overhang but has since been enclosed.

405 S. Olive — *1920c Craftsman Bungalow*   NRHP:1997
Single-story bungalow with double, front-facing gable roof and clapboard siding. Frontmost gable forms entry porch overhang and is supported by tapered piers. Ornamental purlins are beneath gable eaves.

406 S. Olive — *1915c Craftsman*

437 S. Olive — *1920 Bungalow*   NRHP:1997
Single-story bungalow with box plan and single, front-facing gable roof which extends forward to form main porch overhang. This overhang is supported by wood posts.

455 S. Olive — *1919 Bungalow*   NRHP:1997
Low-to-the-ground, single-story bungalow with rectangular plan, single side-facing roof and clapboard siding. The design of this house is given an unusual twist through the use of two smaller, gabled attic

dormers which project from the main roof.

465 S. Olive — *1910 Vernacular*   NRHP:1997

A full two-story home sheathed in clapboard with a rectangular plan and single side-facing gabled roof complemented by a smaller pedimented gable in front. The entry is beneath a gabled portico which projects forward and is enclosed. Three-part windows adorn the facade in various places.

475 S. Olive — *1920 Bungalow*   NRHP:1997

Single-story bungalow with clapboard siding and double front-facing gable roof. Frontmost gable is location of entry.

485 S. Olive — *1920c Craftsman Bungalow*   NRHP:1997

Low-to-the-ground, rectangular plan Craftsman Bungalow with single, side-facing gable roof and clapboard siding. Main roof extends forward to form wide porch overhang and is supported by piers. Large, three-part transomed picture windows with multi-paned transoms flank either side of main entry which is at center. A shed attic dormer peeps up from the main roof.

OLIVE STREET — NORTH

111 N. Olive — *1922* see 131 Chapman

114 N. Olive — *1910 Western False Front* NRHP:1997
A single-story rectangular plan commercial structure with a single-gable roof and a rolled tin false front. The building has been modified but is interesting for its early history.

119 N. Olive — *1914 Brick Commercial*
The current building is relatively new. Also refer to National Register Plaza Historic District list.

123 N. Olive — *1925 Brick Commercial* NRHP:1982
Ward's Cookie Factory
See National Register Plaza Historic District list.

204 N. Olive — *1905c Victorian* NRHP:1997
A two-story house with steep-pitch, multi-gable roof and probably clapboard siding which is now covered by asbestos shingles. There is a full-width and partial wraparound porch on the lower front facade covered by its own separate roof extension which includes a pedimented gable with ornamental shingles. A large 3-part window ornaments the front facade.

213 N. Olive — *1915 Craftsman Bungalow* NRHP:1997
A single-story bungalow cottage with ornamental lap siding and double, front-facing gable roof. Forwardmost gable forms the entry porch overhang and is supported by wide wood piers. Ornamental purlins and lattice work in the upper gable faces adorn the house.

218 N. Olive — *1923 Spanish Colonial Revival* NRHP:1997
Bungalow Court A very simple one-story boxy building with flat roof and stucco facades. The structure is simple, basic, and unadorned.

236 N. Olive — *1910 Craftsman Bungalow* NRHP:1997
This is a large two-story house which plays upon the bungalow styling in a most unusual way. The house features three large front-facing gables, all arranged

in symmetrical fashion. The center entry is beneath a porch with a separate roof overhang supported by wide tapered piers. Just above is a recessed balcony with slatted balustrade.

243 N. Olive — *1908 Gable Roof Cottage*   NRHP:1997
A one and one-half story house with clapboard siding and steep pitch, gable roof. A small hip dormer is present on the front portion of the roof. The main roof extends forward to form a full width porch which is supported by classical columns. The house is an interesting variation on the Classical Revival style which incorporates some Craftsman features in the way the porch is formed by the main roof extension.

251 N. Olive — *1923 California Ranch Apartments* NRHP:1997
This is an unusual structure for Orange. It appears as though it may have originally been small apartments or some sort of lodging house. It is a single-story structure with gable roof which extends forward to form a large arcade supported by wood posts. Most notable is the wide board and batten siding.

254 N. Olive — *1905c Hip Roof Cottage*   NRHP:1997
A single-story box plan house with clapboard siding and steep pitched, hip roof. A small hip dormer is present on the front portion of the roof. Entry is via a corner recessed porch supported by a Classical column.

261 N. Olive — *1911c Bungalow*   NRHP:1997
A two-story house with steep-pitched, multi-gable roof and combination board and batten and lap siding. The front-facing gable extends forward to form an entry porch overhang which is supported by wood piers on arroyo stone bases. A small gable dormer is also present.

264 N. Olive — *1919 Bungalow*   NRHP:1997
A single-story clapboard bungalow with double front-facing gable roof. The forwardmost gable forms the

entry porch overhang·and is supported by wood piers.

272 N. Olive — *1919 Bungalow*   NRHP:1997

A single-story clapboard bungalow with double front-facing gable roof. The forwardmost gable forms the entry porch overhang and is supported by wood piers.

277 N. Olive — *191 Bungalow*   NRHP:1997

A single-story bungalow with single front-facing gable roof. A smaller parallel gable also front-facing forms a full-width porch and is supported by very wide tapered piers. The building is faced in stucco and features a double entry indicating original duplex usage.

287 N. Olive — *1921 Bungalow Court*   NRHP:1997

A bungalow court of simple, single-story bungalow with clapboard siding and single front-facing gable roof. The first entry is via a recessed corner porch supported by wood posts and connecting slatted balustrade. The second entry is in the rear.

288 N. Olive — *1895 Victorian Queen Anne* NRHP:1997

OWNER: D. C. Pixley

Influence Pioneer merchant Pixley came to Orange in 1881, running a general store until he constructed the Pixley Building and opened a furniture store. He also was on the County Board of Supervisors.

This is a large two and one-half story Victorian house with a Classical Revival entry porch. As is typical of the Victorians and of the Queen Anne Victorians in particular, the house is large and has irregular proportions and an irregular roofline. The roof includes hip, gable and conical sections. The house is sided in ship-lap siding except for the pedimented entry gable which features wavy shingles. The front-facing gable includes a conical hood, paired sash windows and an ornamental moulding between the windows on the first and second level. The entry porch features a pedimented gable supported by Classsical columns. It appears that this porch has been partially enclosed, but was probably done so in the early part of the century. The house is in excellent condition and exhibits its original architectural appearance.

291 N. Olive — *1921 Frame Bungalow*   NRHP:1997
A single-story clapboard bungalow with multi-gable roof. The house is predominantly covered by a single-gable roof with side-facing gables, while three front-facing gables are also present. The main roof extends forward to form a full-width porch and is supported by Colonial columns. Main entry is at center and is flanked on either side by a series of multi-paned windows.

304 N. Olive — *1920c Bungalow*   NRHP:1997
A single-story clapboard bungalow with double front-facing gable roof. The main entry door is shielded by a slight canopy overhang flanked on either side by casement windows.

312 N. Olive — *1920c Bungalow*   NRHP:1997
A single-story clapboard bungalow with single front-facing gable roof. What was originally a full porch has since been enclosed. The house is otherwise simple and unembellished.

320 N. Olive — *1920 Bungalow*   NRHP:1997
A single-story bungalow with lap siding and double front-facing gable roof. The forwardmost gable forms the entry porch overhang and is supported by ornamental iron piers, a replacement for the original.

321 N. Olive — *1915 Bungalow*   NRHP:1997
A single-story bungalow with shallow pitch, gable roof. Centrally located front-facing gable extends forward to form an entry porch and is supported by tapered piers.

331 N. Olive — *1921 Bungalow*   NRHP:1997
A single-story bungalow with wide lap siding and shallow-pitch, multi-gable roof. The front facade of the

structure results in a front-facing gable which extends forward to form the entry porch overhang. This overhang is supported by tapered piers and a connecting balustrade.

332 N. Olive — *1911 Bungalow*   NRHP:1997
A single-story bungalow with multi-gable roof. The original sizing has been covered with asbestos shingles. Centrally located front-facing gable extends forward to form the entry porch and is supported by piers.

336 N. Olive — *1915 Bungalow*   NRHP:1997
A single-story bungalow with lap siding and single front-facing gable roof. One-half of the front facade is devoted to a recessed porch supported by a tapered pier.

341 N. Olive — *1915 Bungalow*   NRHP:1997
A single-story bungalow with single shallow-pitch, front facing gable roof. The main roof extends forward to form a full-width porch and is supported by wide piers. The house has been stuccoed, which is a modification of the original siding.

348 N. Olive — *1909 Bungalow*   NRHP:1997
A single-story bungalow with single front-facing, gable roof. The original siding has been covered with asbestos shingles. Small entry portico is supported by wood posts.

404 N. Olive — *1920c Bungalow*

412 N. Olive — *1920 Bungalow*   NONC
A single-story bungalow with wide lap siding and double front-facing gable roof. The forwardmost gable forms the entry porch overhang and is supported by wood posts. The main entry is flanked on either side by a pair of casement windows.

428 N. Olive — *1914 Bungalow*   NRHP:1997
A single-story house with wide lap siding and single side-facing, gable roof. The main roof extends forward

to form a nearly full-width porch and is supported by classical columns on concrete bases.

429 N. Olive — *1914 Bungalow* NRHP:1997
A single-story bungalow with double front-facing, gable roof. The lower gable forms the entry porch overhang and is supported by slender wood posts. The house has been stuccoed, which is a modification of its original character. Since the 1982 survey, this structure has added a somewhat compatible second unit.

436 N. Olive — *1917 Bungalow* NONC
A one and one-half story house with wide lap siding and principally a single side-facing, gable roof. A small, front-facing gable dormer is also present. The main roof extends forward to form a full width porch and is supported by 2' x 4's.

437 N. Olive — *1920c Bungalow* NRHP:1997
A single-story bungalow with wide lap siding and shallow-pitch, multi-gable roof. The centrally located front-facing gable extends forward to form the entry porch overhang and is supported by tapered piers.

445 N. Olive — *1924c Bungalow* NRHP:1997
A single-story bungalow with wide lap siding and shallow-pitch, gable roof. The house is covered by a single side-facing, clipped gable roof for the most part, while a centrally located, front-facing gable shelters a recessed entry porch. The main door consists of a large mullioned plate glass window and is flanked on either side by mullioned sidelights.

446 N. Olive — *1914 Bungalow* NRHP:1997
A single-story clapboard bungalow with single , front-facing gable roof. A lower, smaller front-facing gable forms the entry porch overhang which is supported by wood posts. A low connecting clapboard porch wall is also present.

454 N. Olive — *1920*

460 N. Olive — *1921*   NRHP:1997
Multi-gabled stucco L-shaped home with matching double hung windows and a covered flat roof porch with small wood supports.

468 N. Olive — *1916*   NRHP:1997
Small and simple brick box-shaped residential home.

474 N. Olive — *1918 Bungalow*   NRHP:1997
A single-story clapboard bungalow with single side-facing gable roof. A small front-facing gabled portico shelters the entry. The brick siding along the foundation wall is probably a later addition.

480 N. Olive — *1923 Bungalow*   NRHP:1997
A single-story clapboard bungalow with double front-facing, gable roof. The forwardmost gable forms the entry porch overhang and is supported by tapered piers. The original door is still present which features mullioned glass plates.

486 N. Olive — *1920*   NONC

492 N. Olive — *1918 Bungalow*   NRHP:1997
A single-story clapboard bungalow with double front-facing gable roof. The forwardmost gable houses the entry and may have originally supported an open porch. Sunray wood embellishment articulates each of the front gable faces.

495 N. Olive — *1916 Bungalow*   NRHP:1997
A single-story bungalow with wide lap siding and double front-facing gable roof. The forwardmost gable forms the entry porch overhang and is supported by slender tapered piers. Entry is beneath at center and is flanked on either side by a pair of casement windows with mullioned transoms.

ORANGE STREET — SOUTH
—Orange is named for one of the agricultural grove trees—

111 S. Orange — *1910 Brick Commercial*   NRHP:1982
Barger's Hall

120 S. Orange — *1915c Brick Commercial*   NRHP:1997
Single-Story This is a very small, single-story, rectangular plan brick structure with ornamental brick used at the cornice line.

124 S. Orange — *1914 Brick Commercial*   NRHP:1982
Alfred Kuhn Building

182 S. Orange — *1891 Carpenter Gothic, Victorian*   NRHP:1996
First Baptist Church

TREE: Swamp Mahogany Brown Gum *Eucalyptus robusta* 20" 50' 40' -
The North half of this church was first constructed in 1891 with the stained glass coming from Belgium in 1893. Enlarged in 1920 to the present form, the steeple toppled in the 1932 Long Beach earthquake. Recently refurbished with steeple now intact.

Courtesy PJs Abbey

First Baptist Church - 1920s

This vernacular church incorporates Victorian and Gothic influences. This is a one-story church building with multi-gable roofline and combination shiplap and shingle siding. The building includes three, street-facing gables contrasted by the corner entry tower. This tower, like many in the Gothic tradition, is comprised of a raised box crowned by a mansard roof. Pointed arch transoms on the lower level and arched louvers on the upper level embellish the tower a long with the moulding on the cornice.

The remaining portions of the facade are characterized by large, arched, stained glass windows with tracery and ornamental fish-scale shingles in the upper gable faces. The building has been restored and converted to restaurant use. The building is excellently maintained and exhibits its original architectural integrity. In the rear is a compatible addition. This building was recently added to the National Register of Historic Places.

191 S. Orange — *1924 Brick Commercial* NRHP:1997
This is a single-story brick building with flat roof. There are two portions of the front facade on either end which project forward, and the center portion in between is articulated by a tile hood roof.

204 S. Orange — *1915c Craftsman* NRHP:1997
A large, two-story house with lap siding and a single, front-facing gable roof. Entry is via a corner cut-out porch. A side porch with brick piers is present off Almond Street. The house is simple and unadorned.

205 S. Orange — *1896 Victorian* NRHP:1997
Though this Victorian-era home has undergone some modifications, it retains much of its original formatting and style. This is a two-story house built on an L-plan with the frontmost portion of the ell resulting in an angled bay window with a gable face above. Originally there was a large corner, wrap-around porch supported by thin wood posts and a connecting balustrade with ornament alabasters. The porch has since been enclosed.

212 S. Orange — *1911 Craftsman* NRHP:1997
A large, two-story Craftsman with side-facing gable

topped by a narrow, front-facing gable with heavy sticks work. Chicago style windows and front door are framed with tapered, flat board trim. Across the front is an under roof porch with wood posts on brick piers.

215 S. Orange — *1918 Craftsman Bungalow*   NRHP:1997
A low, single-story bungalow with shallow-pitched, multi-gable roof and wide lap siding. Entry is via a large gable extension of the main roof and is supported by tapered piers. The roof extends on the side, covering a bay projection and also a pergolaon either side of the bay.

220 S. Orange — *1911 Craftsman*   NRHP:1997
A one and one-half story Craftsman house with a single-gable roof, side-facing gables and wide lap siding. A gable roof dormer on the front is ornamented with cross-ties on the bargeboard and ornamental purlins. The main roof extends forward to form the porch overhang supported by wide tapered piers. It appears that half of the porch has since been enclosed.

221 S. Orange — *1895c Victorian*   NRHP:1997
This is a single-story cottage-scale house with narrow shiplap siding and a flattened hip roof. The main entry is via a corner recessed porch supported by ornamental turned posts and ornamental brackets above. A front-facing gable is located on the opposite portion of the front facade and features fish scales shingles, spindle work and ornamental jigsawn bargeboard.

230 S. Orange — *1913 Craftsman*   NRHP:1997
A two-story clapboard house with multi-gable roof. The second story portion is recessed over the rear half of the house while the front half is defined by two front-facing gables. The forwardmost gable is flanked by double-hung windows across the front which is contrasted by brick piers and a connecting wall.

233 S. Orange — *1923 Mediterranean Revival*   NRHP:1997
OWNER: Roland G. Bookless

1923 Apartments; cost: $25,000
Built by Bookless after his coming to Orange, Roland Court offered nine three-room apartments. He, his wife and child lived in Orange while operating the Music store in town.

This is a one-story bungalow court built on a U-plan. The roof is flat with adobe tiles along the cornice line; the facades are sided in stucco. The most distinguishing feature of the building is the three-part, arched entry gate; a large central arch with an ornamental parapet is flanked on either side by a smaller arch. The interior entries are all articulated by entry porticos with adobe tiles. The building is simple and relatively unembellished but representative of the Twenties era bungalow courts. The building is in excellent condition and exhibits its original architectural integrity.

238 S. Orange — *1913 Craftsman*   NRHP:1997
TREE: King Palm *Seforthia* 12" 40' - Good. May be duplicate at 238 S Center.
Builder Clyde Newton had bought the bicycle business from D.C. Pixley in 1907 and constructed this home a few years later. Active in the community and City Council, Newton even coached a local basketball team.

A one and one-half story Craftsman house with wide lap siding and single-gable roof with side-facing gables. Front portion of the roof also features a shed dormer. The main roof extends to form a full-width porch which is supported by tapered piers with arroyo stone bases and an arroyo stone connecting wall.

239 S. Orange — *1920c Bungalow*   NRHP:1997
A single-story bungalow with lap siding and double, front-facing gable roof. The smaller, forwardmost gable forms the entry porch overhang supported by wood posts atop wide piers. Vertical venting and dentils as well as exposed beams ornament the upper gable faces.

256 S. Orange — *1917 Craftsman*   NRHP:1997
OWNER: ALFRED A. EVANS
A one and one-half story Craftsman house with side-facing, gable roof with a front-facing, gable roofed dormer with an ornamentally framed window and louvered vent and ornamental purlins beneath the eaves. The main roof extends forward to form a full-width porch overhang supported by wide brick piers. The house is now sheathed in asbestos siding.

Alfred A. Evans Home

257 S. Orange — *1915 Craftsman*   NRHP:1997
A one and one-half story Craftsman house with side-facing, gable roof contrasted by a front-facing, gable roof dormer. The house is now sheathed in asbestos siding. The main roof extends forward to form a full-width porch supported by tapered piers and a low connecting porch wall. Entry is at center, flanked on either side by a large, three-part window with horizontal transom.

265 S. Orange — *1900c Victorian*   NRHP:1997
A two-story house built in a simple, rural farmhouse style. The main roofline is comprised of a hip roof. Beneath, at the first story, there is a roof projection which forms a full-width porch supported by wood posts. Pairs of narrow vertical windows adorn the front facade.

270 S. Orange
TREE: Evergreen Maple *Acer oblongum* 10" 20' 30' - Good.

272 S. Orange — *1905c Victorian*   OTPA:1997
OWNER: C.B. Campbell

A large, two-story house with clapboard siding and multi-gable roof. The house is built somewhat on a T-plan with the stem of the T forming the front most facade, resulting in a circular bay window on the first story and a gable face on the upper story. Entry is via a corner porch supported by clapboard piers. Ornamental bargeboard on the front gable face along with exposed beams at the first story provide ornamentation.

282 S. Orange — *1911 Hip Roof Cottage*   NRHP:1997

A single-story house with hip and gable roof and wide lap siding. The front-facing gable forms the entry porch overhang and is supported by slim tapered piers. On either side of the main entry is a large, three-part window with multi-pane transom. The front gable features ornamental shingles and a louvered vent.

292 S. Orange — *1905c Hip Roof Cottage* NRHP:1997

A single-story, box plan house with clapboard siding and a steep-pitched, hip roof with a smaller hip roof over a dormer on the front portion. What was originally a corner recessed porch has since been screened in, but the original Classical column with Corinthian capital is still present. The house features very wide eaves adorned with ornamental brackets.

315 S. Orange — *1919 Prairie Style Influence*   OTPA:1997
OWNER: Leroy Palmer

This is a two-story house with a distinct Prairie style (Frank Lloyd Wright inspired) quality about it. The house features a flat roof with multi-planed, stucco siding on the facades. A porch projects forward and is supported by very wide round columns. Pairs of French doors are present in four places on the front facade. Horizontal banding, typical of the Prairie style, is present on the house. This style is rare for Orange.

325 S. Orange — *1915c Craftsman*   NONC
TREE: California Pepper *Schinus molle. Note old gnarled trunk.*

331 S. Orange — *1904 Hip Roof Cottage*   NRHP:1997
This house has undergone modifications over the years. Most visible is the stucco siding. It is a box plan house with steep-pitched hip roof and a recessed corner porch supported by wood posts with ornamental brackets.

339 S. Orange — *1913 Craftsman Bungalow*   NRHP:1997
A single-story clapboard bungalow with multi-gable roof. The front facade is defined by a full-width porch with a gable overhang supported by tapered piers on brick bases. The piers are connected by a slatted balustrade. Entry is at center and flanked on either side by a large, three-part window with multi-paned transom.

344 S. Orange — *1917 Hip Roof Cottage*   NRHP:1997
A single-story house with shiplap siding and pyramidal roof. What was formerly a nearly full-width porch has since been enclosed. A separate roof extension covers the porch on the front facade, supported by thin wood posts atop a connecting porch wall.

347 S. Orange — *1914 Craftsman Bungalow*   NRHP:1997
A single-story bungalow with lap siding and double, front-facing gable roof. The forwardmost gable forms the entry porch overhang and is supported by thin tapered piers. The upper gable faces are adorned with dentils, ornamentally framed windows and vents, and ornamental purlins.

355 S. Orange — *1921 California Bungalow*   NRHP:1997
A low, single-story clapboard bungalow with single-gable roof with side -facing gables. A small overhead

extension on the center of the front facade forms the entry portico and is supported by wood posts. Entry is beneath at center.

356 S. Orange — *1905c Victorian*   NRHP:1997
This is a two-story house with multi-planed roof and shiplap siding. The roof is comprised of both gable and hip elements. Full-width porch at the first story is defined by an attached roof overhang with a small pedimented gable. The entire porch overhang is supported by wide piers with wood posts on top. These piers are connected by a slatted balustrade.

360 S. Orange — *1938 Prairie*

363 S. Orange — *1914 Craftsman Bungalow*   NRHP:1997
OWNER: Samuel & Alice L. Armor (Armor Building)
BLDR: Orange Contracting & Milling Co.
Both teachers, Armor and wife both pioneers came in 1875 to Orange. He went onto the City Council and County Board of supervisors. He later constructed the Armor Building; she published the Orange Post newspaper from 1892-1915.

Samuel & Alice L. Armor Home

This is a one-story bungalow with a double, front-facing gable roof and wide lap siding on the facades. The forwardmost gable forms the entry porch overhang supported by elephantine piers on brick bases. A low, slatted balustrade connects the full-height and half-sized piers. Ornamental, triangular bracket supports grace the eaves. A small mullioned transom is present in the front most gable face. The original door with vertical glass panes is still present. The house is in good condition and retains the full body of its original architectural integrity.

371 S. Orange — *1920 California Bungalow*   NRHP:1997
A single-story clapboard bungalow with the main portion of the house covered by a single-gable roof with side-facing gables. The center front of the house features a gable porch overhang supported by Colonial columns and some horizontal wood ornamentation on the gable face. The front door consists of a single glass plate with 15 small glass panes. The door is flanked by glass sidelights.

378 S. Orange — *1890 Hip Roof Cottage*   NRHP:1997
This is a small Hip roof cottage with an L-plan, shiplap siding and a combined flattened hip and gable roof. The porch is formed in the apex of the ell. It has its own separate roof overhang supported by wood posts. The frontmost leg of the ell features a gable-face embellished with ornamental shingles and jigsawn embellishments in the bargeboard. Also present is a large picture window with ornamental framing.

384 S. Orange — *1914 Craftsman*   NRHP:1997
A two-story Craftsman home with wide lap siding and multi-gable roof. The second story portion of the house is over the rear half, while the lower story is defined by a wide, shallow-pitched gable overhang which forms the porch. This is supported by wide piers with ornamental capitals; the upper gable face includes vertical slatting which is repeated on the porch balustrade below.

394 S. Orange — *1909 Gable Roof Cottage*   OTPA:1997
Housekeeper Miss Northrop bought the C.Z. Culver Hotel tract Lot #8 in March of 1903. The home was

erected the following year but Louisa died in 1913. William H. Bruns bought the home and with his wife and 9 children, stayed some 40 years.

Miss Northrop Home

A single-story clapboard house with multi-gable roof. A large corner porch is formed by the main roof extension and is supported by Classical columns with Corinthian capitals. The other half of the front facade results in an angled bay window with a shingled gable above. A curved bay window is present on the side of the house. Ornamental rafter tails and brackets adorn the wide eaves.

395 S. Orange —
TREE: Indian Laurel *Ficus nitida* 24" 50' 60' - Good.

404 S. Orange — *1909 Craftsman Bungalow*   NRHP:1997
A single-story clapboard bungalow with single, front-facing gable roof. The upper gable face is sheathed in shingles with a row of fish scale shingles just beneath. Entry is via a corner recessed porch supported by a wide clapboard pier. Dentils and ornamental purlins and a spire in the peak of the gable further embellish this house.

412 S. Orange — *1920c Craftsman Bungalow*   NRHP:1997
A single-story bungalow with double, front-facing gable roof and ornamental lap siding. The entry porch

is formed by a small, front-facing gable which runs parallel to the main roof gable and is supported by elephantine piers which have since been remodeled using wood.

413 S. Orange — *1905c Victorian*   OTPA:1997
This two-story, L-shaped plan, simple Victorian house has boxed cornices with short returns at the gable ends, and has shiplap siding. A shed roof covers the narrow porch in the 'L.' Two doors open onto the porch. In the front wing is a double-hung, single-pane window on each floor. There is decorative wood trim in the peak of the gable and under each window sill.

420 S. Orange — *1913 Craftsman Bungalow*   NRHP:1997
This one-story Craftsman bungalow has a side-facing gable roof with shed dormer. Across the front is an under roof porch. The porch has field stone piers at the end corners. Flanking the concrete steps to the porch are field s tone wing walls and short fieldstone piers. Wood posts on the piers support the arched header beam.

421 S. Orange — *1914 Craftsman Bungalow*   NRHP:1997
TREE: Bottle Tree *Brachychiton populneum* 24" 50' 60'.
A single-story bungalow with lap siding and double, front-facing gables. A small entry porch is formed in one corner portion of the forwardmost gable.

428 S. Orange — *1886 Victorian*   OTPA:1997
Levanworth House.
This is the second oldest home in Old Towne Orange. This is a two-story Victorian house with a multi-gable roof and combination shiplap/shingle siding. What was the original porch has since been enclosed. The front gable face is adorned with ornamental, square butt shingles and ornamental framing around both the attic vent and windows.

429 S. Orange — *1938*
TREE: Bottle Tree *Brachychiton populneum* 24" 50' 60'.

435 S. Orange — *1908 Hip Roof Cottage*   NRHP:1997
TREE: Bottle Tree *Brachychiton populneum* 24" 50' 60'.
A single-story clapboard bungalow with multi-hip roof and a small recessed entry porch beneath the front facade. The house is otherwise simple and unadorned.

436 S. Orange — *1910 Craftsman*   NRHP:1997
A one and one-half story craftsman house with a single, side-facing gable roof contrasted by front-facing gable dormer. A full-width porch is formed by the extension of the main; this is supported by tapered piers on the outside edges and Classical columns on the inside portions. All of the piers and columns have arroyo stone bases. Also, the foundation of the house is of arroyo stone. Ornamental purlins grace the eaves.

442 S. Orange — *1905 Classical Revival*   NRHP:1997
A two-story house with multi-gable roof and clapboard siding. Entry is via a corner recessed porch supported by Classical columns. An unusual appearance to the house is derived from a large, flush front-facing gable face. This gable features a return at the eaves and a pair of double-hung windows in the upper portion of the gable. It appears as though the original door is still present.

443 S. Orange — *1922 Bungalow*   NRHP:1997
A single-story, tri-gable bungalow with clapboard siding. The main portion of the house is comprised of a single-gable roof with side-facing gables. A centrally placed, front-facing gable with return at the eaves forms the entry porch overhang and is supported by wide wood posts. A three-part louvered vent is present in this gable face.

450 S. Orange — *1914 Bungalow*   NRHP:1997
A two-story clapboard house with single, front-facing gable roof. A smaller roof extends forward from the front facade and aids in forming the recessed porch supported by wood posts atop wide concrete piers.

453 S. Orange — *1915 Craftsman Bungalow*   NRHP:1997

TREE: Bottle Tree *Brachychiton populneum* 24" 50' 60'.
A small, single-story bungalow with a single, shallow-pitched, front-facing gable roof and ornamental lap siding. A recessed porch occupies one-half of the front facade; its overhang is supported by a pier with concrete base and wood posts on top. Exposed beams act as ornamentation on the porch overhang.

459 S. Orange — *1903 Victorian*   NRHP:1997
TREE: Bottle Tree *Brachychiton populneum* 24" 50' 60'.
A Victorian cottage with multi-planed roof and shiplap siding. The house is treated in the usual Victorian manner by having a complex and dynamic roof comprised of hip and gable sections and combined shiplap siding with ornamental shingles in each of the front-facing gables. A small pedimented, front-facing gable forms an entry porch overhang and is supported by ornamental turned posts. Decorative bargeboard is also in this porch gable.

460 S. Orange — *1912 Craftsman*   NRHP:1997
TREE: Bottle Tree *Brachychiton populneum* 24" 50' 60'.
A one and one-half story Craftsman house with lap siding and single-gable roof with side-facing gables. The front portion of the roof features a front-facing gable dormer with ornamental purlins and an ornamentally framed, multi-paned transom window. The main roof extends forward to form a full-width porch supported by arroyo stone piers. Half piers flank either side of the entry stoop. The main door is at center; on either side are located large, three-part windows with transoms.

468 S. Orange — *1909 Craftsman*   NRHP:1997
A one and one-half story Craftsman house with a single-gable roof with side-facing gables contrasted by a smaller, front-facing gable dormer. The lower portion of the house is sheathed in slump stone; the dormer is sheathed in shingles. The main roof extends forward to form a wide porch overhang and is

supported by piers. The dormer features half timbering and exposed beams. Entry is off-center and a large, three-part picture window with transom is on the front facade.

469 S. Orange — *1900c Gable Roof Cottage* NRHP:1997
TREE: Bottle Tree *Brachychiton populneum* 24" 50' 60'.
A small, single-story cottage with shiplap siding and single, front-facing gable roof. A full-width porch is formed by a separate hip extension and is supported by wood posts. Entry is center and flanked on either side by a double-hung window.

476 S. Orange — *1912 Craftsman* NRHP:1997
A one and one-half story Craftsman house with wide lap siding and single-gable roof with side-facing gables. A front-facing, gable dormer is present and is ornamented with cross-ties in the upper gable face and ornamental purlins below. The house features only a half porch which is supported by a pier. The original wood door with three, small rectangular panes is present; on each portion of the front facade there is a large, three-part window with diamond-paned transom.

477 S. Orange — *1908 Craftsman Bungalow* NRHP:1997
TREE: Bottle Tree *Brachychiton populneum* 24" 50' 60'.
A single-story, rectangular plan house with wide lap siding and single-gable roof with front-facing gable. What was probably a corner recessed porch has since been enclosed. The foundation of the house is sheathed in arroyo stone and half-size piers line either side of the entry stoop.

485 S. Orange — *1916 Craftsman Bungalow* NRHP:1997
A one and one-half story house with wide lap siding and roof comprised of a single-gable section with side-facing gables. This is contrasted by a front-facing, gable dormer ornamented with cross-ties, purlins and a multi-pane, transom window. The main window extends forward to form a full-width porch supported

by tapered piers connected by slatted balustrade. Entry is at center, flanked on either side by a pair of double-hung windows with transom.

493 S. Orange — *1911 Craftsman*   NRHP:1997
TREE: Bottle Tree *Brachychiton populneum* 24" 50' 60'.
A single-story house with single-gable roof with side-facing gables. There is a smaller shed dormer with three-part louvered opening at the front portion of the roof. The main entry is via a corner recessed porch supported by a tapered pier. The house is currently sheathed in asbestos siding.

515 S. Orange — *1919 Bungalow*   NRHP:1997
A small, single-story clapboard bungalow with single, side-facing gable roof. The main entry is distinguished by a pergola overhang in the central portion of the front facade. Located on either side are large, three-part windows with central transoms.
Nutwood Place 1906 Arroyo Stone Marker

525 S. Orange — *1919*   NRHP:1997
A small box shaped stucco sided home with a wood-trimmed flat roof and three vertical windows offset from covered entry and includes a large picture window.
Nutwood Place 1906 Arroyo Stone Marker

535 S. Orange — *1918 Craftsman Bungalow*   NRHP:1997
A single-story bungalow with wide lap siding and shallow-pitched, multi-gabled roof. One-half of the front facade is devoted to a projecting gable which forms the entry porch overhang. This gable is supported by piers composed of wide bases and smaller posts on top. Cross-ties in the upper gable face add embellishment. The original door with plate glass windows is still present. .

545 S. Orange — *1923 Bungalow*   NRHP:1997
A single-story clapboard bungalow with shallow-pitched, multi-gabled roof. The central portion of the front facade features a projecting gable which acts as

an entry overhang. This is now supported by ornamental iron posts, a replacement of the original. The original door with plate glass windows is still present and is flanked on either side by large, three-part picture windows.

604 S. Orange — *1925 California Bungalow*   NRHP:1997
A single-story clapboard bungalow with single-gabled roof with side-facing gables. The entry is located at the center and is articulated by a small gabled portico with an inner arched bracket support. The house is otherwise simple and unembellished.

609 S. Orange — *1915 Craftsman*   NRHP:1997
A one and one-half story house with wide lap siding and single, side-facing gabled roof. A small shed dormer is located on the front portion of the roof. The main roof extends forward to form what was once a full-width porch but has since been enclosed on one-half.

612 S. Orange — *1914 Craftsman*   NRHP:1997
A one and one-half story house with wide lap siding and single, side-facing gabled roof. The front-facing gable dormer with purlins and louvered transom is present. The entry is recessed beneath the main roof; no porch is present. It appears that there has been some modification on the front facade, specifically this includes the brick facing along the lower half of the front facade .

615 S. Orange — *1927 Provincial Revival* NRHP:1997
A L-plan single-story residence with stucco facade and gable roof. The entry is at the apex of the wall beneath an extension of the front facing gable. A picture window framed by a set of 3 double-hung mullioned windows is present on the front facade.

620 S. Orange — *1915 Craftsman Bungalow*   NRHP:1997
A single-story bungalow with wide lap siding and single-gabled roof with side-facing gables. The house takes on an unusual appearance based on the entry

which is defined by a shallow-pitched, gabled projection. This projection is supported by large, battened stone columns at the corners. The porch is enclosed by a double door entry with wide sidelights on either side. On either side of these are large, transomed picture windows.

621 S. Orange — *1915c Craftsman*   NRHP:1997

A large, two-story Craftsman house with wide lap siding and single, side-facing gabled roof. Two gable dormers are present, of which the forwardmost is the larger and most elaborate. It features exposed beams, triangular bracket supports, and a large mullioned window. The main roof extends forward to form a full-width porch supported by piers constructed of wide concrete bases and wood posts on top.

626 S. Orange — *1913 Bungalow*   NRHP:1997

A rectangular plan, single-story bungalow with gable roof and wide-lap siding. The large front facing gable may have formed a front porch which has since been enclosed. The upper gable face is ornamented with small brackets and vertical wood slats framing a small window.

629 S. Orange — *1915 Bungalow*   NRHP:1997

TREE: Coastal Live Oak *Quercus agrifolia* 25" 40' 65'. Only large oak in Orange.

A single-story rectangular plan bungalow residence with multi gables and wide-lap siding. The large front facing gable forms the entry porch which almost extends the full length of the structure. Wooden columns atop massive brick piers which support the porch roof at the corners. The brick piers repeat at a smaller scale at the lower steps of the porch and at the entry opening. A single board between the piers forms the porch wall.

636 S. Orange — *1920 Craftsman*   NRHP:1997

A two-story house with ornamental lap siding and shallow-pitched, multi-gabled roof. The second story is on the rear half of the house; the front story is characterized by two, front-facing gables. The forwardmost gable forms the entry porch overhang and is supported by a combination of wood posts with angular brace supports. Large, mullioned picture windows are present on either side of the main door.

700 S. Orange — *1938 Spanish Colonial*
Band Shell
BLDR: WPA
Along with the Plunge, the Band Shell came shortly after the park dedication in 1937, during the depression in the US (1929-1940.) Styled WPA Spanish Colonial architecture, the shell is but one of many structures in Orange built through the Works Progress Administration that constructed projects as an innovative way to give work to artists an designers.

The Burnett Family in front of the 1938 Band Shell

Orange Street — North

145 N. Orange — *1873c*

TREE: California Pepper *Schinus molle* 72" 67' 70'.
Behind the YWCA (1945) is this magnificent Pepper tree from the founding days of Orange. Robert Crowder opened one of the first stores of the community of Orange, sometime during or after 1873, on the northeast corner of Glassell Street at the Plaza. Crowder bought out the store on the northwest corner and moved his there in 1880. By 1882, Crowder's failing health forced him to sell out to D.C. Pixley. Early on, Crowder planted Pepper trees on Orange Street. The remaining pepper tree on Orange had to have been planted prior to 1882, and possibly as early as 1873. Crowder had the only safe in town which was robbed in 1880.

213 N. Orange — *1920c Bungalow*   NRHP:1997

A single-story bungalow with multi-gable roof and wide lap siding on the facades. The house is built in an L-plan with the short leg resulting in a front-facing gable. To the side is a gabled entry portico supported by colonial columns and fashioned in the Colonial Revival style.

217 N. Orange — *1920 Bungalow*   NRHP:1997

A single-story house with wide lap siding and single-gable roof. The center portion of the house is articulated by a front-facing, gabled porch overhang supported by slender wood posts. Double doors indicate duplex usage. The house is simple, small and unadorned.

221 N. Orange — *1874 Victorian Pioneer*   NRHP:1997

Shaffer House
The Shaffer House is the oldest house in Old Towne Orange. Peter J. Shaffer (Shaffer St.) came in 1871, hired Leon Shadel to build this home at a cost of $2000. Shaffer married Eva Harwood, daughter of first postmaster, Nathan Harwood (Harwood St.) Farming

some 200 acres around Orange, Shaffer became a noted horticulturist on several crops.

Shaffer House - 1886

This is a large, two-story house with shiplap siding and multi-gable roof. The house has undergone some alterations done in an uncomplimentary manner circa 1925. The house is currently built in a U-plan with the center of the U forming the entry, embellished on the entry exterior by a gabled portico supported by classical columns. A double-story bay window is present to the side of the entry and features typical Victorian embellishment above and below the windows. Since the 1982 survey, it appears that a pyramid roof has been removed. Originally located around the corner at 137 E. Maple, the house was moved here in the 1920s.

230 N. Orange — *1908 Bungalow*   NRHP:1997
A single-story bungalow with combination lap and shingled siding and a roofline comprised of double front-facing gables. The entry is to the side of the frontmost gable. Ornamental bargeboard and rafter tails distinguish the eaves.

233 N. Orange — *1920c Bungalow*   NRHP:1997
TREE: CAROB *Ceratonia siligua*.
A single-story clapboard bungalow with multi-gable roof. The front facade is comprised of three front-

facing gables, of which the two outermost gables form entry porch overhangs supported by tapered piers. There is an entry beneath each porch, indicating duplex usage of the house.

237 N. Orange — *1917 Bungalow*   NONC

238 N. Orange — *1908c Bungalow*   NRHP:1997
This is a single-story bungalow with double front-facing, gable roof. The forwardmost gable forms the entry porch overhang. The original siding of the house has since been covered with asbestos shingles. The original door with plate glass windows and large, beveled transomed window to the side are still present. An earlier house may have been constructed on this site, which may form the skeleton for this present facade.

243 N. Orange — *1914 Bungalow*   NRHP:1997
Jane Mather purchased the lot in 1913 with the requirement that she build a house of at least $1,200 in value. A widow she stayed until she died in 1923 at 75.

A single-story bungalow with wide lap siding and double, front-facing, gable roof. The forwardmost gable forms the entry porch overhang and is supported by tapered piers with cast concrete bases. A low porch wall and half-sized piers are also composed of cast concrete. The original door with plate glass windows is still present. Adjoining it is a large picture window with a transom window.

246 N. Orange — *1906c Bungalow*   NRHP:1997
A single-story bungalow with wide lap siding and double, front-facing gable roof. The forwardmost gable forms the entry porch overhang which is supported by tapered piers above a stone base. Ornamental purlins grace the eaves. An earlier structure was probably built on this site in 1906 and later remodeled into the present facade around 1915.

254 N. Orange — *1910c Hip Roof Cottage*   NRHP:1997
A single-story clapboard house with box plan and steep-pitched, hip roof. There is also a hipped dormer present on the front portion of the roof. Entry is via a large corner recessed porch supported by brick piers which are probably a later addition.

259 N. Orange — *1914 Craftsman*   NRHP:1997
Retirement home of long-time resident Kenneth Claypool

A one and one-half story house with wide lap siding and single, side-facing gable roof. A front-facing gabled dormer is also present and features ornamental purlins. One-half of the front facade is comprised of a recessed entry porch supported by wide piers. A grouping of four transomed windows is also present on the front facade.

261 N. Orange — *1916 Altered Bungalow*   NRHP:1997
A single-story bungalow with wide lap siding and multi-gable roof. The front facade is comprised of a single, front-facing gable supporting a three-quarter size recessed porch. The porch is supported by piers with a small connecting, slatted balustrade. The remaining half of the front facade is almost fully enclosed by windows. Brickwork is probably a later addition.

262 N. Orange — *1908 Hip Roof Cottage*   NRHP:1997
A single-story box plan house with clapboard siding and steep-pitched, hip roof. A small hipped dormer is present on the front portion of the house. Entry is via a corner recessed porch supported by a single classical column.

267 N. Orange — *1915c Bungalow*   NRHP:1997
A single-story bungalow with lap siding and double, front-facing gable roof. The forwardmost gable forms the entry porch overhang and is supported by piers with wood posts on top.

270 N. Orange — *1910 Bungalow*   NRHP:1997
A single-story bungalow with wide lap siding and double, front-facing gable roof. The forwardmost gable forms the entry porch overhang and is supported by wood posts. Exposed beams in the upper gable faces act as embellishment as well as serve a functional purpose.

275 N. Orange — *1915 Colonial Revival*   NRHP:1997
A colonial revival residence with distinctive gambrel roof on a rectangular plan. Kneebraced canopied over door, double-hung windows with 6/1 windows, and detailed crown molding are present.

278 N. Orange — *1912 Hip Roof Cottage*   NRHP:1997
A single-story clapboard house with combination hip and gable roof. The house is built on a modified L-plan with the front leg of the ell resulting in a small pedimented gable with a recessed entry porch beneath. This porch is supported by a slim wood post. The front portion of the house is covered by a grouping of sash windows.

283 N. Orange — *1918 Bungalow*   NRHP:1997
A single-story bungalow with ornamental lap siding and double, front-facing gable roof. The forwardmost gable forms the entry porch overhang and is supported by tapered piers.

286 N. Orange — *1910 Hip Roof Cottage*   NRHP:1997
A single-story clapboard house with combination hip and gable roof. A large corner wrap-around porch is the primary feature of this house. The porch is articulated by a pedimented gable overhead, supported by piers with clapboard bases and wood posts on top. Wide eaves are embellished with ornamental brackets.

294 N. Orange — *1908 Hip Roof Cottage*   NRHP:1997
A single-story clapboard house with combination hip and gable roof. The house features a large corner wrap-around porch supported by classical columns. A

portion of this porch has since been enclosed. The house is built on a modified L-plan with the frontmost leg of the ell resulting in a pedimented gable ornamented with fishscale shingles.

295 N. Orange — *1920 Bungalow*   NRHP:1997

A single-story bungalow with wide lap siding and gable roof. A low shed dormer with shingle facing is present on the front portion of the roof. Entry is beneath an arched portico supported by classical columns. To either side are large 3-part picture windows.

PALM AVENUE — EAST
—Palm is named for one of the horticultural trees—

114 E. Palm — *1915c Bungalow*   NRHP:1997
A single-story bungalow with wide lap siding and tri-gable roof. The main portion of the house is covered by a single gable roof with side-facing gables. A narrow front-facing gable forms what was once an entry porch overhang. It has since been enclosed with glass windows.

230 E. Palm — *1920c Bungalow*   NRHP:1997
A single-story bungalow with wide lap siding and double, front-facing gable roof. The forwardmost gable forms the entry porch overhang and is supported by tapered piers. Ornamental purlins grace the eaves.

236 E. Palm — *1915c Bungalow*   NRHP:1997
A single-story bungalow with wide lap siding and multi-gable roof. The main portion of the house is covered by a single gable roof with side-facing gables accented by a smaller gabled porch on the side of the house. A wide, front-facing gable forms a full entry porch overhang supported by tapered piers.

421 E. Palm — *1917 Bungalow*   NRHP:1997
A single-story clapboard bungalow with single, front-facing gable roof. A smaller, front-facing gable forms the entry porch overhang and is supported by wide piers with concrete bases. The original hardwood door with plate glass windows is still present in the center of the front facade.

522 E. Palm — *1913 Bungalow*   NRHP:1997
A single-story bungalow with ornamental lap siding and single-gable roof with front-facing gable. A small gabled entry portico is present which is adjoined by a pergola on either side to form a full-width porch in front. The original door·with plate glass windows is still present.

537 E. Palm — *1914 Church Building*   NRHP:1997

A single-story box plan structure with wide lap siding and steep-pitched, hip roof. The front entry to the church is distinguished by a large, hipped projecting wing which acts as a modified cupola.

537 E. Palm — *1918 Church Building*

603 E. Palm — *1915c Bungalow*   NRHP:1997
A single-story bungalow with wide lap siding and single-gable roof with side-facing gable. The main roof slopes forward to form a full-width porch supported by slender wood posts. A small shed dormer is on the front portion of the roof. Since the 1982 survey, this structure has been altered with inappropriate bay window and porch screen.

608 E. Palm — *1922*

613 E. Palm — *1914*

623 E. Palm — *1895c Victorian cottage*   NRHP:1997
A two-story house with shiplap siding and steep-pitched, multi-gable roof. The house is built on a modified L-plan with entry on the apex of the ell. There is a small shed overhang which forms a porch over the entry. High narrow windows are characteristic of the Victorian period.

631 E. Palm — *1917 Bungalow*   NRHP:1997
A small, single-story bungalow distinguished by double, front-facing gable roof. The original siding has since been covered with asbestos shingles. The smaller, forwardmost gable forms the entry porch overhang and is supported by tapered piers on concrete bases. Vertical slatting above ornaments the gable .

640 E. Palm — *1900c Board & Batten Cottage*   NRHP:1997
Hip Roof This is a small pioneer type, probably hand built, structure with a simple box plan and steep-pitched, hip roof echoing the classical revival tendency of the period. Board and batten siding, however, is an indication that it is probably not contractor built.

There is a nearly full-width porch in the front which has its own separate shed roof overhang supported by wood posts with ornamental brackets in between.

641 E. Palm — *1905 Hip Roof Cottage*   NRHP:1997
This is the typical turn-of-the-century house with box plan, clapboard siding and steep-pitched, hip roof. Entry is via a corner recessed porch supported by a single classical column. A hipped dormer is on the upper front portion of the roof.

648 E. Palm — *1923 Bungalow*   NRHP:1997
This is a single-story clapboard bungalow with single, shallow-pitched gable roof with side-facing gables. The center portion of the front facade is adorned by an entry porch portico with a gable roof supported by slender wood posts.

654 E. Palm — *1923 Bungalow*   NRHP:1997
A single-story bungalow with rectangular plan and single-gable roof wit h side-facing gables. Original siding has since been covered with asbestos shingles. The center portion of the front facade is distinguished by a gabled entry portico with tapered piers. Original door with plate glass panes is still present. Since the 1982 survey, the clapboard siding has been restored.

705 E. Palm — *1923 Bungalow*   NRHP:1997
This is a single-story clapboard bungalow with double, front-facing gable roof. The smaller, front-facing gable forms an entry porch overhang over recessed corner porch. The porch overhang is supported by tapered wood piers on brick bases. There is a dramatic entry presented by a plate glass window door flanked on either side by mullioned side lites.

709 E. Palm — *1923 Bungalow*   NRHP:1997
A single-story clapboard bungalow with multi-gable roof. The front-facing gable forms an entry porch overhang supported by wood posts. Vertical slatting in the upper gable face acts as embellishment. Since

the 1982 survey, this structure has been altered with inappropriate solid porch rail.

715 E. Palm — *1912 Bungalow*   NRHP:1997
A single-story bungalow with lap siding and a single, front-facing gable roof. The house is basic and unembellished.

725 E. Palm — *1915 Bungalow*   NRHP:1997
A single-story bungalow with wide lap siding and double, front-facing gable roof. The forwardmost gable forms the entry porch overhang supported by slender wood posts atop a low porch wall.

732 E. Palm — *1923 Mediterranean Revival*   NRHP:1997
This house is one of several in Orange which is a simplified take-off on the Mediterranean Revival bungalows. A simple, rectangular plan house with stucco siding on the facades and with a flat roof. A projection on the front part of the house forms an entry porch portico. *Please note: there is a large remodeled side addition on the house.*

740 E. Palm — *1923 Mediterranean Revival*   NRHP:1997
This house is identical to that at 732 E. Palm Ave. A simple, rectangular plan house with stucco siding on the facades and with a flat roof. A projection on the front part of the house forms an entry porch portico. *Note: there is a large remodeled side addition on the house.*

817 E. Palm — *1927c Mediterranean Revival*   NRHP:1997
A single-story, Mediterranean Revival bungalow with stucco siding on the facades and with a flat roof with raised parapets on the corners. The house is built on a modified L-plan, the entry being in the apex of the ell enclosed by an arched entry portico. A tile hood is present over both the entry portico and the picture windows in the front facade.

827 E. Palm — *1921 Bungalow*   NRHP:1997
A single-story clapboard bungalow with shallow-

pitched, multi-gable roof. Main portion of the house is covered by a single-gable roof with side-facing gables. A wide front-facing gable forms the entry porch overhang supported by wood piers atop brick bases. Main entry consists of a mullioned plate glass door with mullioned side lites.

837 E. Palm — *1921 Bungalow*   NRHP:1997
A single-story bungalow with shallow-pitched, multi-gable roof. The original siding has since been covered with asbestos shingles. The roof line is composed of two juxtaposing gables, one side-facing and the other a small front-facing gable which also acts as an attic dormer vent.

917 E. Palm — *1931 Bungalow*   NRHP:1997
A single-story clapboard bungalow with double, front-facing gable roof. The forwardmost gable forms the entry porch overhang and is now supported by wrought iron posts, a replacement for the original.

926 E. Palm — *1924 Bungalow*   NRHP:1997
A single-story clapboard bungalow with shallow-pitched, multi-gable roof. Main portion of the house is covered by a single-gable roof with side-facing gables. A front-facing gable acts as an entry porch overhang supported by wrought iron piers, a replacement for the original.

931 E. Palm — *1923 Bungalow*   NRHP:1997
A rectangular plan house with multi-gables and clapboard siding. The main portion of the house is covered by a side to side gable. A front facing gable extends forward to form the entry porch overhang. This is supported by classical columns and dentils running across the lower gable face. The front facade is embellished by 3 sets of paired windows.

—Outside Old Towne—

1319 E. Palm — *1938 Streamline Moderne*

BLDR: W.H. Wolting Construction
Wolting both designed and built this house in 1938. As a construction supervisor, he had a hand in building many homes in Orange. A style of architecture which came from a wave of art and design known as: *L'Exposition Internationale des Arts Decoratifs et Industriels Modernes' a Paris* (1925). Both Art Deco and Streamline Moderne became architecture styles although for residential, most often the latter form only. Large blocks with curved surfaces, a flat roof with parallel line forms and small square window sets.

Palm Avenue — West

118 W. Palm — *1920c Bungalow*   NRHP:1997

A single-story clapboard bungalow with multi-gable roof. The roof is fashioned in an L-plan with the short leg resulting in a front-facing gable which forms the entry porch overhang. This gable is supported by slender wood posts atop ornamental concrete bases. There is a connecting slatted balustrade contrasted by slatting in the upper gable face. This bungalow house has a built-in garage which was probably a later addition.

133 W. Palm — *1915c Bungalow*   NRHP:1997

A single-story clapboard bungalow with single front-facing gable roof. The main roof extends forward to form a full-width porch which is supported by tapered piers atop wood bases. The lower foundation wall and half-piers near the porch stoop are also of brick. The double entry indicates the house was originally intended for duplex usage.

141 W. Palm — *1915 Bungalow*   NRHP:1997

A single-story clapboard bungalow with double front-facing gable roof. The forwardmost gable forms the entry porch overhang and is supported by tapered piers on brick bases. The main entry is flanked on either side by a trio of sash windows with ornamental upper sashes. This is complemented by the leaded glass transom in the porch gable face.

230 W. Palm — *1915c Bungalow*   NRHP:1997

A single-story bungalow with wide lap siding and multi-gable roof. The centrally located front-facing gable extends forward to form the entry porch overhang and is supported by tapered piers on concrete bases. The original door with plate glass windows is beneath and flanked on either side by windows with mullioned transoms.

233 W. Palm — *1912 Bungalow*   NRHP:1997

A single-story bungalow with ornamental lap siding

and double front-facing gable roof. The lower, smaller front-facing gable runs parallel to the main roof gable and acts as an entry porch overhang supported by tapered piers. Vertical slatting provides ornamentation in the upper gables.

238 W. Palm — *1915c Bungalow*   NRHP:1997
A single-story bungalow with wide lap siding and shallow-pitch, multi-gable roof. The front facade features three front-facing gables of which the widest acts as an entry porch overhang defining a wrap-around porch. Porch gables are supported by wood posts on concrete bases.

545 W. Palm — *1920c Brick Industrial*
Western Cordage Company
A large, single-story brick cordage plant, adjacent to the railroad. This was one of three companies to produce rope and cable in the town of Orange.

730 W. Palm — *1914 Bungalow*

803 W. Palm — *1907 Bungalow*

806 W. Palm — *1920c Provincial Revival*

—Outside Old Towne—

1174 W. Palm — *1927 Mediterranean*
BLDR: Herman Lembcke, Carpenter
Frickel, a very tall individual, built this house to his proportion. Every element of the interior is built to a larger size. Frickel never finished and Herman Lembcke completed the home. Hugo Lembke's widow still lives there.

An idyllic flat roofed structure with parapets and corner tower door entry. Arched, thick-walled doorway and tower window with a tiled roof.

PALMYRA AVENUE — EAST
—Palmyra is named for pioneer Charles Z. Culver's hometown in NY—

205 E. Palmyra — *1887 Victorian*   OTPA:1986
   BLDR: C.Z. Culver $1,700
   Built by promoter Culver (Culver Ave.) as an overflow
   to his Palmyra Hotel, now gone. Hailing from Palmyra
   NY (Palmyra Ave.) Culver lasted only two years in
   Orange, a victim of the 1880s bust after the boom.

This is a large, three-story Victorian house with a
multi-gable roofline. The original siding has since been
covered with asbestos shingles. The house is
comprised of robust and dynamic massing, typical of
the Queen Anne style Victorians. Built on a modified
box plan, the house features several bay projections.
A larger, wrap-around porch extends the full width of
the front facade and around the east side. This porch
is characterized by an attached roof with a gable
portico at the point of entry. The porch is supported
by ornate turned columns with ornamental brackets.
The third story dormer in front includes a balcony
with ornamental balustrade. The house is in excellent
condition and retains its original architectural
integrity except for the newer siding. Added to the
National Register of Historic Places in 1986.

214 E. Palmyra — *1909 Hip Roof Cottage*   NRHP:1997
   OWNER: George J. Schnackenberg

George J. Schnackenberg Home

BLDR: Orange Contracting & Milling Co.
A single-story Classical-Revival house with wide lap siding and pyramidal roof. The roof extends forward to form a large corner, wrap-around porch supported by Classical columns. A modified gambrel dormer is present on the front portion of the roof.

220 E. Palmyra — *1900c Hip Roof Cottage*   NRHP:1997
A single-story house with flattened hip roof and gable roof portions on the rear of the house. What was once a full-width porch has since been enclosed, although it appears to have been done in earlier days of the house. What was the porch overhang is a separate roof extension and is supported by wood posts.

221 E. Palmyra — *1915 Craftsman Bungalow*   NRHP:1997
A single-story bungalow with double, front-facing gable roof and ornamental lap siding. The forwardmost gable forms the entry porch overhang supported by round columns connected by slatted balustrade.

225 E. Palmyra — *1920c Bungalow*   NRHP:1997
TREE: Southern Magnolia *Magnolia Grandiflora* 24" 50' 50'.
A single-story house with multi-gable roof and entry beneath a corner recessed porch supported by wide tapered piers. The shiplap siding indicates pre-1900 origins.

230 E. Palmyra — *1908 Hip Roof Cottage*   NRHP:1997
A single-story clapboard house with pyramidal roof and corner recessed porch supported by a single round Classical column.

235 E. Palmyra — *1919 Craftsman Bungalow*   NRHP:1997
A single-story clapboard bungalow with a multi-gable roof. This house has an unusually complex roofline, one portion of which extends forward to form a porch overhang supported by a wide pier. The main door is the original hardwood door with small rectangular pane and is flanked on either side by side vents .

238 E. Palmyra — *1909 Hip Roof Cottage*   NRHP:1997
TREE: Arizona Cypress *Cupressus globra* 35" 65' 30'.
Single-story, box plan, clapboard house with steep-pitched hip roof and small, hip dormer in front. Entry is via a corner recessed porch supported by a classically treated wood post. A low slatted balustrade connects the posts and house. A large picture window with mullioned transom distinguishes the front facade.

238 E. Palmyra — *1909 Cottage, Hip Roof*

305 E. Palmyra — *1905c Hip Roof Cottage*   NRHP:1997
A single-story clapboard house with a steep-pitched, hip and gable roof. The most notable feature is the corner, wrap-around porch supported by wide Classical columns. The window on the facade curves with the curvature of the porch. Either side of the house contains a gable face with an angled bay window and ornamentation in the upper gable face.

313 E. Palmyra — *1908 Hip Roof Cottage* NRHP:1997
A single-story house with pyramidal roof and smaller, front-facing gable which articulates the corner recessed porch. The porch is supported by Classical columns and the front facade contains a large, three-part window with multi-pane transom.

314 E. Palmyra — *1923 Mediterranean Revival*   NRHP:1997
A single-story, stucco bungalow with flat roof. Main entry is at center via a recessed porch defined by a large arched opening. Main door is flanked by sidelights. On either side of the porch entry is a large, fixed-pane, picture window with adobe tiled hood.

321 E. Palmyra — *1904 Hip Roof Cottage* NRHP:1997
A single-story clapboard house with combination hip and gable roof. Entry is via a corner recessed porch supported by Classical columns. Two gables, one on the side and one on the front, are embellished with ornamental shingles and an attic vent transom. A smaller, hip dormer is on the front facades. Exception

ally wide eaves are ornamented with brackets.

322 E. Palmyra — *1903 Hip Roof Cottage* NRHP:1997
A single-story clapboard house with hip roof and small hip dormer on the front portion of the roof. Main entry is via a corner recessed porch supported by Classical columns with Corinthian capitals.

329 E. Palmyra — *1910c Transitional* NRHP:1997
A one and one-half story house with shiplap siding and multi-gable roof. The large gable face on the front facade is defined by a return at the eaves and a small corner, recessed porch with separate roof overhang supported by thin wood posts.

330 E. Palmyra — *1912 Craftsman* NRHP:1997
A single-story clapboard bungalow with double, front-facing gables of which the forwardmost gable forms the entry porch overhang. This overhang is supported by tapered piers connected by a low porch wall. Ornamental purlins grace the eaves.

330 E. Palmyra — *1912 Craftsman Bungalow*

338 E. Palmyra — *1905 Hip Roof Cottage* NRHP:1997
A single-story house originally with clapboard siding, much of which has now been covered with asbestos siding. The roof is defined by several hip portions. The main portion of the roof results in a large, wrap-around corner porch. There is a small hip dormer present on the front portion of the roof. Porch supports are Classical columns with Corinthian capitals.

339 E. Palmyra — *1907 Transitional* NRHP:1997
A two-story clapboard house with multi-gable roof of which the front facade is defined by a large, front-facing gable with a return at the eaves. Entry is via a corner recessed porch supported by a Classical column. The side of the house is defined by a large, projecting gable dormer on the second story which results in an angled bay window on the first story.

Ornamental brackets are on the front gable base.

403 E. Palmyra — *1904 Hip Roof Cottage*   NRHP:1997
TREE: BLACK Acacia *Acacia melanoxylon* 24" 55' 40'. There
are today eight remaining Black Acacias on this block
from an original planting of 12.
A single-story clapboard house with hip roof and two
hip dormers and a corner, wrap-around porch
supported by Classical columns. A concrete hitching
post is present in the front yard of this contributing
residence. This is one of only two original hitching
posts remaining in their original location within the
district.

414 E. Palmyra — *1904 Transitional*
TREE: Black Acacia *Acacia melanoxylon* 24" 55' 40'.
Concrete Hitching Post.

417 E. Palmyra — *1922 Bungalow*   NRHP:1997
A single-story clapboard bungalow with shallow-
pitched, multi-gable roof. Entry is via a corner
recessed porch supported by a wood post.

421 E. Palmyra — *1913 Craftsman Bungalow*   NRHP:1997
TREE: Black Acacia *Acacia melanoxylon* 24" 55' 40'.
A one and one-half story bungalow with wide lap
siding and multi-gable roof. The front-facing gable
defines the porch overhang and is supported by tape
red piers. The upper, front-facing gable face is
embellished with a three-part window with transom,
with purlins beneath the eaves and lattice work for
attic venting.

422 E. Palmyra — *1915 Craftsman Bungalow*   NRHP:1997
A single-story bungalow with double, front-facing
gable roof. The house was originally sided in
clapboard, no doubt, but is now covered by asbestos
siding. The forwardmost gable forms the entry porch
overhang and is supported by piers of concrete bases
with wood posts on top.

429 E. Palmyra *1928 Mediterranean Revival*   NRHP:1997

TREE: Black Acacia *Acacia melanoxylon* 24" 55' 40'.
A single-story stucco house with a flat roof. The entry is via a porch with a large, ornamental opening and a tile hood above. The arch of the porch opening is carried out on the adjacent three-part picture window.

430 E. Palmyra — *1916 Prairie Influenced*   NRHP:1997
OWNER: Rudolph W. & Fay Miller
BLDR: Orange Contracting & Milling Co.
A single-story house with stucco siding and flat roof. Entry is via a large recessed porch built beneath the main portion of the house and supported by wide concrete piers. A large picture window with transom is on either side of the porch. Entry is at center. The original door is still present and is flanked by original sidelights.

Rudolph W. & Fay Miller Home

435 E. Palmyra — *1890c Victorian*   NRHP:1997
TREE: Black Acacia *Acacia melanoxylon* 24" 55' 40'.
Entire block (8)
OWNER: L.T. & Martha Barwise
Barwise bought the corner lot and moved the home here in 1900. After his death, Martha stayed on until 1917. John Black bought the home in 1921 and ran the Pacific Electric Railway as Agent for some 30 years.

A large, two-story home set on a corner which played an anchor role in the neighborhood. The house has shiplap siding and a multi-gable roof treated in the Victorian manner. A porch at the first story is defined by a separate roof overhang now supported by wrought iron posts which have been modified from the original. Windows around the house are the large, narrow Victorian windows and are ornamentally framed in the Victorian manner. A modified Palladian window is present in the upper, front-facing gable face. Ornamental jigsawn brackets grace the eaves around the house.

440 E. Palmyra — *1903 Transitional*   NRHP:1997
A two-story house with combination slump stone, clapboard and shingle siding and a large gable roof. Entry is via a corner recessed porch supported by Classical columns. The remaining half of the front facade on the first story is defined by an angled bay window with a large window on each bay side. The low porch wall is of slump stone, the first story is in clapboard, and the upper gable face is embellished with shingles. Brackets grace the eaves at the first story; a large, arched three-part window is featured in the upper gable face.

504 E. Palmyra — *1913 Bungalow*   NRHP:1997
A single-story bungalow house with wide lap siding and single, side-facing gable roof. Small dormer gable is present in front. The main roof extends forward to form a full-width porch overhang and is supported by wood posts. The front door is the original door with window panes and is flanked in an unusual way by multi-paned sidelights. A large, three-part window with transom is present on the other half of the front facade.

505 E. Palmyra — *1909 Bungalow*   NRHP:1997
This is a very large, two-story house with clapboard siding and combination hip and gable roof. The most

notable feature of the house is the double decked corner, wrap-around porch on both the first and second floors. Each is supported by a Classical column with Corinthian capital. Wide eaves of the house are graced with ornamental brackets. Large framed windows are located through out the facade, and of a notable presence is the small, stained glass transom on the front portion of the house.

511 E. Palmyra — *1920 California Bungalow*   NRHP:1997
A single-story bungalow with clapboard siding and tri-gable roof, each gable resulting in a small clipped gable. The front-facing gable occupies the center of the front facade and may have originally supported an open porch which has since been enclosed. Large, three-part window with transom is on either side of the porch projection.

512 E. Palmyra — *1913 Craftsman Bungalow*   NRHP:1997
A single-story house with wide lap siding and single, side-facing gable roof. A wide shed dormer with windows of ornamental glass is on the front portion of the roof. One-half of the front facade is comprised of a recessed porch supported by a tapered pier.

517 E. Palmyra — *1921 Craftsman Bungalow*   NRHP:1997
A single-story house with wide lap siding and multi-gable roof with shallow-pitched gables. The front facade of the house is defined by a wide, front-facing gable extending forward to form a full-width porch supported by piers with brick bases and wood posts on top. Entry is at center, flanked on either side by a large, three-part window.

520 E. Palmyra — *1912 Craftsman*   NRHP:1997
A one and one-half story Craftsman house with wide lap siding and single, side-facing gable roof. The main roof is contrasted by a front-facing gable dormer ornamented with louvered venting, ornamental purlins and cross-ties in the upper gable face. An ornamental brick chimney is also present. The main

roof extends forward to form a full-width porch supported by arroyo stone piers with fluted posts on top.

521 E. Palmyra — *1921 Provincial Revival* NRHP:1997
OWNER: J.S. Lampert
Although Lampert is the first registered resident, A.F. Beheman lived twice in this home, finally up until the 1950s. Beheman was a teller at the First National Bank of Orange.

A single-story house with steep-pitched, multi-gable roof and stucco siding. Entry is via a centrally located, recessed porch beneath a small gable f ace. Two front-facing gables articulate the front portion of the house; each is embellished with half timbering. The arched opening to the entry and the windows on either side are framed in ornamental brick.

528 E. Palmyra — *1914 Craftsman Bungalow* NRHP:1997
A single-story house with wide lap siding and multi-gable roof, all gables side-facing. The main portion of the roof extends forward in the center to form a porch overhang and is supported by wide piers with wood posts on top. The original door with single large pane is present on the front.

535 E. Palmyra — *1918 Craftsman* NRHP:1997
A one and one-half story clapboard house with single, side-facing gable roof contrasted by a front-facing dormer gable. Entry is via a centrally located recessed porch and is flanked on either side by a large, three-part window with ornamental beveled glass transom. The front-facing dormer gable is embellished with dentils, louvered venting and ornamental purlins.

536 E. Palmyra *1913 Craftsman Bungalow* NRHP:1997
A single-story bungalow with wide lap siding and shallow-pitched, multi-gable roof. The main entry is at front center and is defined by a gable projection which forms an entry porch and is supported by brick

elephantine piers. The porch gable features exposed beams in the Oriental manner.

544 E. Palmyra — *1919 Craftsman Bungalow* NRHP:1997
A single-story, tri-gable bungalow with wide lap siding. The main portion of the house is covered by a single-gable roof with side-facing gables; a centrally located, front-facing gable forms what was originally a porch overhang. This porch has since been screened in. Tapered piers support the gable over hang which is also ornamented by a framed transom and ornamental purlins.

545 E. Palmyra — *1923 Bungalow* NRHP:1997
A single-story bungalow with clapboard siding and multi-gable, shallow-pitched roof fashioned in an L-plan with the short leg resulting in a front-facing gable face. The remaining portion of the front facade is defined by a recessed porch supported by an elephantine pier.

552 E. Palmyra — *1925 Eclectic* NRHP:1997
TREE: European White Birch *Betula nendula* 18" 45' 25' Good.
This is a large, two-story house with Provincial Revival influences. The house is comprised of stucco siding with steep-pitched, multi-gable roof fashioned in an L-plan. The short leg of the ell results in a large, front-facing gable face with the uppermost peak having been clipped. Windows are grouped largely in pairs. The front door is Cotswold style.

605 E. Palmyra — *1921 Bungalow* NRHP:1997
A single-story bungalow with wide lap siding and shallow-pitched, multi-gable roof. One-half of the front facade is comprised of a recessed porch now supported by wrought iron posts, a replacement for the original.

615 E. Palmyra — *1916 Craftsman* NRHP:1997
A large, one-story Craftsman house with wide lap siding and single, side-facing gable roof. A wide shed

dormer is present on the front portion of the roof. One-half of the front facade is comprised of a recessed porch supported by a tapered pier.

625 E. Palmyra — *1922 Craftsman Bungalow*   NRHP:1997
A single-story house with shallow-pitched, multi-gable roof arranged in an L-plan and siding now covered by asbestos. The short leg of the ell on the gable roof extends forward to form the entry porch overhang which is supported by thin wood posts. This upper gable face is ornamented with slats.

628 E. Palmyra — *1909 Hip Roof Cottage*   NRHP:1997
A one and one-half story house with shiplap siding and hip roof with a small hip dormer on the front portion. The full front of the house is comprised of a recessed porch beneath the main roof overhang supported by wood posts with a connecting porch wall. Entry is at center.

631 E. Palmyra — *1909 Vernacular*   NRHP:1997
A small, single-story clapboard house with multi-gable roof primarily comprised of side-facing gables. The center front of the house consists of a small, gable entry portico supported by tapered piers.

639 E. Palmyra — *1921 Bungalow*   NRHP:1997
A single-story clapboard bungalow with single, front-facing gable roof. A parallel gable, slightly smaller and shorter, is present on the front facade which defines what may have once been an open porch but has since been enclosed .

640 E. Palmyra — *1910c Transitional*   NRHP:1997
TREE: Avocado *Avocado* 24" 45' 40' Good.
Dr. Ida Parker Home
Dr. Parker was Orange's first woman doctor and the first female member of the Orange County Medical Association, serving as Association President in 1912. She came with her family to this area in 1870, graduated from USC. He practiced medicine here from

1895 until her death in 1917.

This is a two-story, Classical Revival style house with multi-gable roofline and clapboard siding. A large, full-width, front-facing gable is contrasted with a smaller, angled bay window on the northeast corner of the house and the large, wrap-around porch on the opposite corner. An attached roof that rounds the corner forms the porch overhang supported by simple Classical columns; a small pediment marks the entry on the porch overhang. The upper gable face in front features a semi-Palladian arrangement formed by the three-part window and louvered transom above. The house is in good condition and retains its full original architectural integrity.

701 E. Palmyra — *1905c Hip Roof Cottage*   NRHP:1997
A single-story clapboard house with hip roof and smaller, front-facing gable on the front plane of the roof. Entry is via a corner recessed porch supported by wood posts. Original screen door is still present on the house. Since the 1982 survey, this structure has been altered with inappropriate aluminum window.

713 E. Palmyra — *1911 Transitional*   NRHP:1997
A two-story house with rectangular plan and single, front-facing gable roof. Entry is via a corner recessed porch supported by wood posts. Ornamental purlins grace the eaves.

720 E. Palmyra —
TREE: CAMPHOR *Cinnamomum camphora* 60" 50' 65'.

733 E. Palmyra — *1907 Hip Roof Cottage*   NRHP:1997
TREE: California Pepper *Schinus molle* 108" 50' 60'
A one and one-half story house with combination clapboard and wide lap siding and combination hip and gable roof. The main portion of the roof extends forward to form a large corner, circular wrap-around porch supported by Classical columns. The remaining front facade is defined by a wing that extends forward

and is articulated by a pedimented gable. In this gable face there is a large window with ornamental transom.

737 E. Palmyra — *1906 Hip Roof Cottage* NRHP:1997
A one and one-half story house with clapboard siding and combination hip and gable roof. The front facade is defined by a half corner porch supported by Classical columns. Just above there is a pedimented gable with ornamental bargeboard on the front portion of the roof.

803 E. Palmyra — *1919*

815 E. Palmyra — *1922 California Bungalow* NRHP:1997
A single-story clapboard bungalow with single, side-facing gable roof. The front facade is defined by a small, arched entry portico supported by large curvalinear brackets. The main door is framed by an arched frame. Large, multi-paned windows flank either side of the main entry.

817 E. Palmyra — *1920c Bungalow* NRHP:1997
A single-story clapboard house with shallow-pitched, multi-gable roof. The house is built in a U-plan with the legs of the U resulting in front-facing , gable porch overhangs. Each has its own separate entrance, indicating duplex usage of the house. Each gable is supported by piers with brick bases and wood posts on top, arranged in an ornamental fashion to adorn these gable faces.

PALMYRA AVENUE — WEST

119 W. Palmyra — *1920c Bungalow*   NRHP:1997
Low-to-the-ground bungalow cottage with multi-gable roof and wide clapboard siding. Bungalow is built on an L-plan with entry in apex of ell.

127 W. Palmyra — *1906 Hip Roof Cottage* NRHP:1997
Single-story, box plan house with a steep-pitched, hip roof and clapboard siding. Wide entry porch has its own separate roof which extends forward and is supported by Classical columns. The house has a raised foundation, and the main entry is reached via a stoop. A small gabled pediment adorns the center front of the house.

206 W. Palmyra — *1915c Craftsman*   NRHP:1997
One and one-half story Craftsman home with single, side-facing gable roof contrasted with smaller, front-facing gabled dormer. Main roof extends forward to form entry porch overhang and is supported by elephantine piers with brick bases. A smaller gabled adjunct is on the side of the house and is also supported by an elephantine pier. Ornamental purlins grace the gable eaves.

219 W. Palmyra — *1904 Hip Roof Cottage* NRHP:1997
Small, single-story house with a steep-pitched hip roof and wood shingle siding which is a later addition to the house. A small hipped dormer graces the front portion of the roof, while an additional extension forms an entry porch overhang. The house has been modified in the front porch portions and through the use of a more contemporary siding.

222 W. Palmyra — *1897c Victorian*   OTPA:1997
OWNER: William & Ora Clayton
This Victorian era house has been remodeled in such a way as to make it even more Victorian than it originally was. What was at first a simple homestead house has been remodeled by the present owner in order to make of the house a more ornate Victorian

style. The house features a basic box plan with side-facing gable to which a front-facing gable has been added with an angled bay window and a unique Palladian transom in the uppermost portion of this front gable. Ornamental porch posts, decorative brackets and other work on the house is very characteristic of the Victorian period.

225 W. Palmyra — *1919 Bungalow*   NRHP:1997
Low-to-the-ground, single-story bungalow with shallow pitched, single, front-facing gable roof and a box plan. Smaller secondary gable to the side of the house on the front side extends forward to form an entry porch overhang and is supported by two wood posts.

226 W. Palmyra — *1913 Craftsman Bungalow* NRHP:1997
TREE: Deodor Cedar *Cedrus deodora* 24" 65' 45' Fair Only 3 or 4 in Orange.
Single-story clapboard bungalow with double, front-facing gable roof. Frontmost gable forms entry porch overhang and is supported by elephantine piers with arroyo stone bases. Ornamental purlins distinguish the eaves. Wide transomed, picture windows and handcrafted door distinguish the front facade.

236 W. Palmyra —
tree: European Linden *Tillia europea* 10" 40' 25'. The only one in Orange.

305 W. Palmyra — *1910c Hip Roof Cottage*   NRHP:1997
TREE: Arizona Cypress *Cupressus globra*
Single-story house with modified L-plan, hip roof and clapboard siding. Frontmost portion extends forward to form a gable face. Entry is beneath main roof overhang in apex of ell.

325 W. Palmyra — *1910 Rural Vernacular*

327 W. Palmyra — *1939*

335 W. Palmyra — *1916 Craftsman Bungalow* NRHP:1997
Single-story clapboard bungalow with shallow

pitched, single-gable roof. Roof extends forward to form entry porch overhang and is supported by unique combination of posts to form piers. Slatting in front gable face adds ornamentation.

604 W. Palmyra — *1925 Provincial Revival*   NRHP:1997
Two-story, stucco house with multi-gable roof. Gables are clipped. Smaller, single-story gable projections form separate wings of the house and are highlighted by curved extensions of the lower facade on the sides.

614 W. Palmyra — *1926 Provincial Revival*   NRHP:1997
Single-story house with steep pitched, multi-gable roof. House is built on a U-plan with each of the extensions of the U having a separate gable. Entry is recessed beneath center of U. Large arched picture window, which is multi-paned, adorns one of the front-facing gables.

656 W. Palmyra — *1920 Craftsman Bungalow*   NRHP:1997
Low-to-the-ground, single-story bungalow with shallow pitched, multi-gable roof and clapboard siding. Frontmost gable extends forward to form entry porch overhang and is supported by tapered piers. A porte cochere is located to the side and is also supported by tapered piers.

664 W. Palmyra — *1946 Provincial Revival*   NRHP:1997
Single-story clapboard house built on an L-plan with multi-gable roof. Frontmost portion of ell extends forward and incorporates half-timbering and a large picture window. *Please note: While the house was built post-1940, it incorporates the stylistic features of the earlier architectural periods.*

690 W. Palmyra —*1906 Vernacular*   NRHP:1997
TREE: Red Flowering Gum *Eucalyptus ficifolia* 24" 30' 25'. A large, two and one-half story vernacular farmhouse with a multi-gable roofline. The original siding has been covered with asbestos shingles. Each upper gable features ornamental exposed beams and a

transom of louvered vents and mullioned windows. A large boxy, wrap-around porch in the Mediterranean/Prairie Style was added circa 1925 which significantly disguises the original style of the house. A porte-cochere is located to the side.

704 W. Palmyra — *1900c Rural Vernacular*   NRHP:1997
Two-story, tri-gable, L-plan house with steep pitched, gable roof and shiplap siding. The main entry is beneath the porch extension at the corner of the lower story and is supported by slender ornamental posts. Windows are framed in the Victorian manner, and a small ornamental transom is in uppermost portion of front gable face.

720 W. Palmyra — *1929*

798 W. Palmyra — *1905c Craftsman*   NRHP:1997
Two-story house with a box plan and single, front-facing gable roof contrasted by smaller, side-facing gable dormers and a porch covering on lower story of front supported by Classical columns. Windows are framed in the period manner. Ornamental purlins grace the eaves.

798 W. Palmyra — *1905c Post Victorian*

PARKER STREET — SOUTH
—Parker is named for pioneer Parker—

126 S. Parker — *1923 Bungalow*

129 S. Parker — *1915 Bungalow*

142 S. Parker — *1911 Cottage, Gable Roof*

150 S. Parker — *1924 Bungalow*

167 S. Parker — *1915c Bungalow*

168 S. Parker — *1904c Board & Baton*
Ida Richardson moved in 1923. Built around 1904 as a simple residence, the original owner and location of this home are unknown. Moved in 1923 to Parker St., Mrs. Richardson lived here for the remainder of her life.

Typically a low cost, settlement type of style - this Board & Batten is one of few left of this simple construction. Vertical boards placed edge to edge with parallel bats covering the seams and no foundation were common.

195 S. Parker — *1918 California Bungalow*

328 S. Parker — *1908 Bungalow*   NRHP:1997
Single-story clapboard bungalow with double, front-facing gables. Decorative shingles are located in upper gable faces. Ornamental purlins grace the eaves. Entry is at front of rearmost gable. There is a porch overhang supported by columns. Entry is beneath.

331 S. Parker — *1927 Mediterranean Eclectic*   NRHP:1997
OWNER: Clarence Newkirk
An unusual house for Orange, for brick residences are rare. Used as a rental through the 1930s, the first permanent resident Clarence Newkirk came in 1941.

This is an unusual, single-story home constructed of brick with definite Spanish influences. House has a low-to-the-ground horizontal quality, flat roof with a large arcade entry along the front facade embellished with three large arched openings. This arcade has adobe tile hood.

338 S. Parker — *1924 Bungalow*   NRHP:1997
Single-story clapboard bungalow with single, front-facing gable roof. Smaller roof projection forms entry porch overhang. This is symmetrically placed along the front facade and is supported by tapered piers with brick bases. Ornamental purlins grace the eaves.

339 S. Parker — *1926 Bungalow*

340 S. Parker — *1926 Bungalow*   NRHP:1997
A modified L-plan stucco bungalow residence with a front facing gable, arched openings around entry, and a low stucco wall.

347 S. Parker — *1924 Bungalow*   NRHP:1997
A single-story box plan bungalow with stucco siding and multi-gabled roof with a projecting gabled porch. A decorative arch spans the driveway leading to the garage.

352 S. Parker — *1927 Mediterranean Revival*   NRHP:1997
A single-story stucco box plan Mediterranean revival residence with multi-gables and finished with flat tiles roof in rear. Large front facing arched windows with side panels enhance the front entry, which also contains a large front door with vertical sidelights.

355 S. Parker — *1938*

362 S. Parker — *1923*

377 S. Parker — *1928 Mediterranean Revival*   NRHP:1997
Two-story house designed in an unusual manner with Mediterranean Revival influences. Main portion of house is on a square plan with flat roof and parapeted walls. A smaller gable extension forms another wing of the house. Porte cochere extends from the side of the house. It and a hood above the French doors at the entry are of adobe tiles. Multi-paned casement windows are located around the house.

435 S. Parker — *1925 Mediterranean Revival*

PARKER STREET — NORTH

129 N. Parker — *1924 Bungalow*

139 N. Parker — *1925 Bungalow*

179 N. Parker — *1923 Mediterranean Revival*

Pine Street — South
—Pine is named for one of the horticultural trees—

137 S. Pine — *1905c Transitional*   NRHP:1997
A large, two-story house with clapboard siding and multi-gable roof. The most notable feature of the house is the complex roofline contrasted by the large, wrap-around porch supported by classical columns. The main portion of the roof is defined by a large, side-facing gable and a front-facing gable with a return at the eaves. French doors and a slatted balcony balustrade define the front portion of the house. The original door is present and flanked by sidelights.

147 S. Pine — *1920c Mediterranean Revival*   NRHP:1997
This is the Imanuel Lutheran School and is comprised of a large, single-story structure with stucco siding and a flat roof of adobe tiles. The main entry is articulated by a large, arched recessed opening with ornamental parapet above.

152 S. Pine — *1905c Hip Roof Cottage*   NRHP:1997
A small, single-story clapboard house with pyramidal roof. A full-width porch is present on the front facade, defined by a separate roof extension supported by wood posts connected by a slatted balustrade.

172 S. Pine — *1934 Bungalow*   NRHP:1997
A single-story bungalow with a single-gable roof staggered as three-front-facing gables. The house has since had its original siding covered with asbestos.

176 S. Pine — *1920 Bungalow*   NRHP:1997
A single-story house with single, shallow-pitched, front-facing roof. What was originally a recessed porch to the entry has since been enclosed.

184 S. Pine — *1925 Craftsman Bungalow* NRHP:1997
A single-story bungalow with double, shallow-pitched, front-facing gable roof. Forwardmost gable forms the entry porch overhang supported by wide elephantine concrete piers.

PINE STREET — NORTH

127 N. Pine — *1923c Mediterranean Revival*   NRHP:1997
A single-story, box plan house with stucco siding on the facades and with a flat roof. A front entry portico is formed by a rectilinear projection with large arched openings. Both the porch portico and main house have raised parapets, particularly at the corners, which emphasize the southwestern feel of the house. Adobe tile hoods are present above each of the windows on the front facade.

130 N. Pine — *1905 Gable Roof Cottage*   NRHP:1997
A single-story house with predominately shiplap siding and with steep-pitched gable roof. The main portion of the house is covered by a single side-facing gable. A smaller front-facing gabled dormer is embellished with ornamental shingles. Forward porch was previously present on the house but has since been enclosed. The porch roof and piers are still present.

138 N. Pine — *1914 Bungalow*   NRHP:1997
A single-story bungalow with wide lap siding and single front-facing, gable roof. A full-width porch is recessed beneath the main roof supported by tapered piers above a low porch wall. Cross-ties embellish the upper gable face .

143 N. Pine — *1922 Bungalow Rudolph Stade*   OTPA:1997
A single-story clapboard bungalow with shallow-pitched, gable roof. Roofline is comprised of two counter-posing gables, one a side-facing gable which extends forward and forms an entry porch overhang. This is supported by piers comprised of brick bases and wood posts on top. The front-facing gable acts as an attic dormer.

146 N. Pine — *1921 Bungalow*   NRHP:1997
A single-story clapboard bungalow with shallow-pitched, multi-gable roof. The main entry is via a corner recessed doorway. Siding is shiplapped with

front facade displaying two sets of picture windows flanked by double-hung windows.

151 N. Pine — *1924 Bungalow*   NRHP:1997
A single-story clapboard bungalow with double, front-facing gable roof. The forwardmost gable forms the entry porch overhang and is supported by wide, round columns.

157 N. Pine — *1925 Bungalow*   NRHP:1997
A single-story clapboard bungalow with multi-gable roof. The projecting, front-facing gable forms a wide entry porch overhang supported by tapered piers.

160 N. Pine — *1921 Bungalow*   NRHP:1997
A single-story bungalow with wide lap siding and multi-gable roof. Entry is via a corner recessed porch in the front-facing gable. The porch overhang is supported by a wide wood post. The front-facing gable is clipped at the peak.

163 N. Pine — *1924 Bungalow*   NRHP:1997
A single-story bungalow with lap siding and double, front-facing gable roof. The forwardmost gable forms the entry porch overhang supported by tapered piers.

172 N. Pine — *1920 Mediterranean Revival*   NRHP:1997
A single-story house with modified L-plan, stucco siding on the facades and a flat roof. A high cupola rises above the main roof, with arched openings below, to form the entry portico. A grouping of three arched, mullioned window s is present on either side of the front facade. The cupola is crowned with adobe tiles. Hoods are present on the remaining portions of the front facade.

173 N. Pine — *1924 Bungalow*   NRHP:1997
A single-story bungalow with multi-gabled, shallow-pitched roof. The original clapboard siding has since been covered by asbestos shingles. The main portion of the house is covered by a single, side-facing gable roof. A smaller front-facing gable forms an entry porch

overhang supported by round columns.

181 N. Pine — *1924 Bungalow*   NRHP:1997
A single-story clapboard bungalow with gable roof, largely a single front-facing gable. A full-width porch across the front facade is supported by piers with brick bases.

192 N. Pine — *1923 Spanish Colonial Revival*   OTPA:1997
TREE: California Redwood *Sequoia gigantea*
OWNER: Charles W. Liken
A single-story house with stucco facades and adobe tiled roof. The house is comprised of an irregular plan built on a symmetrical format, emphasis being on the center entry portico. This is comprised of a gabled overhang with large , arched opening. The main door is a large wood door with sidelights flanking it on either side. A pair of casement windows on either side of the entry portico features an ornamental ball relief picturing a vase with fruits. A low wall with brick capping surrounds the front portion of the house.
SAVI: weir-box, located on the corner.

Charles W. Liken Home

193 N. Pine — *1928 Spanish Colonial Revival*   NRHP:1997
GROWER: Joe Handcock
Wilber Crist bought this home from Handcock upon Crist's retirement after he sold his groves here in

Orange. Crist and his wife raised five daughters since coming to Orange in 1889.

A single-story house with stucco facades and multi-gable roof with adobe tiles. The tiling on the roof is the ornamental Dutch tile variety. Two steep-pitched, front-facing gables are present, the forwardmost of which slopes out to form an entry portico with large arched openings. Arched windows are present across the main portions of the front facade.

205 N. Pine — *1923 Provincial Revival*   NRHP:1997
Duncan Clark House
While built in the 20s, a string of tenants left this house without a continuous resident until the 1940s. Some twenty years later, Duncan & Alice Clark bought the home in 1967; Duncan, the grandson of one of the founders of the SAVI, was born in Orange in 1912 and passed away in 1998.

This is a single-story house with Tudor Revival influences. The house has an overall Hansel and Gretal appeal derived from a very steep-pitched, gable roof with clipped gables. Half-timbering is in the upper gable faces. Arched windows and porch openings embellish the lower facades. The house is built on a box plan with stucco facades.

206 N. Pine — *1929 Spanish Colonial Revival*   NRHP:1997
This is a large, two-story house with stucco facades and adobe tiled, hip roof. The house is built on a box plan with a symmetrical emphasis derived by the centrally located, recessed entry portico. A balcony with iron railing is located above.

213 N. Pine — *1922 Bungalow*   NRHP:1997
A single-story clapboard bungalow with gable roof. Two small, front-facing gables rise out of the front portion of the roof. Below there is a full-width porch formed by the extension of the main roof and supported by round Colonial-like columns. The large picture windows in front have ornamental glass

transoms.

214 N. Pine — *1926 Spanish Colonial Revival*   NRHP:1997
A large, two-story house with modified rectangular plan, stucco facades and adobe tiled, gable roof. Entry is on the south end of the front facade and is noted by a large rectangular projection with an arched opening on the first story for the main door and an arched opening above for a balcony entrance. Globed lights are present in their own lodge on either side of the main entry.

221 N. Pine — *1926 Mediterranean Revival*   NRHP:1997
A single-story box plan house with stucco facades and flat roof. A raised, stepped parapet is present along the front facades. The main entry is via an arched opening which leads to a recessed entry portico. Adobe tile hoods are above the front windows.

222 N. Pine — *1926 Spanish Colonial Revival*   NRHP:1997
A single-story house built on an L-plan with stucco facades and adobe tiled, gable roof. The main entry is via two large, arched openings which form a modified arcade along the front inner portion of the front facade. A large, arched mullioned window is present on the front-facing gable facade.

229 N. Pine — *1923 Mediterranean Revival*   NRHP:1997
A single-story house built on a modified U-plan with stucco facades and flat roof. Raised parapets on both the main house and the entry portico suggest Southwest influence. Entry is via a large arched opening into an entry portico. Adobe tiled hoods are present over the front windows.

237 N. Pine — *1924 Mediterranean Revival*   NRHP:1997
A single-story house built on a modified U-plan with stucco facades and flat roof. Entry is in the inner portion of the U beneath an adobe tiled hood. The main door is of double, mullioned glass.

240 N. Pine — *1936 Spanish Colonial Revival*   NRHP:1997

A single-story house built on an L-plan with stucco facades and adobe tiled, gable roof. Entry is at the apex of the ell. An arcade with arched openings is located in the extension of the front-facing gable.

245 N. Pine — *1924 Mediterranean Revival*   NRHP:1997
A single-story house with stucco facades and flat roof. The house is built on the symmetrical plan with centrally located entry beneath the rectiline projection with rectangular opening. Raised parapets suggest the Pueblo influence.

253 N. Pine — *1923 Bungalow Roy Cavett*   OTPA:1997
A single-story bungalow with· clapboard siding and multi-gable roof. The roofline profile is determined by two crossing gables, one a side-facing gable which extends forward to form the entry porch overhang. It is supported by wood piers of caste concrete and wood posts on top. The front-facing gable acts as a small attic dormer.

261 N. Pine — *1923 Bungalow nrhp:1997*
A single-story clapboard bungalow with cross-connecting front and side-facing gables. The side-facing gable extends forward to form the entry porch overhang supported by piers of caste concrete and wood posts on top. The front-facing gable acts as a small attic dormer.

262 N. Pine — *1923 Bungalow*   NRHP:1997
A single-story clapboard bungalow with tri-gable roof. The main portion of the house is covered by a single, side-facing gable roof. The front-facing gable forms the entry porch overhang supported by piers of wood posts atop brick bases.

269 N. Pine — *1922 Bungalow*   NRHP:1997
TREE: Australian Brush Cherry *Eugenia paniculata*
A single-story clapboard bungalow with multi-gable roof. The main portion of the house is covered by a single, side-facing gable. A small, front-facing, clipped gable is on the ridge of the roof along with a front-

facing, gabled entry porch. The porch is now supported by iron piers, a replacement for the original.

270 N. Pine — *1920c Altered Bungalow*   NRHP:1997

A single-story clapboard bungalow with gable roof. A centrally located, front-facing gable with clipped peak and return at the eaves forms an entry porch overhang supported by tapered piers with brick bases. The main entry beneath is flanked on either side by sidelights.

277 N. Pine — *1921 Bungalow*   NRHP:1997

BLDR: Oscar Leichtfuss CPA

Oscar built this home from 1921-22 while working for the Ehlen & Grote Co., becoming a CPA at the time the firm closed in 1938. Although he passed in 1946, his wife stayed until the 1970s.

A single-story clapboard house with shallow-pitched, multi-gable roof. A large, corner wrap-around porch is beneath the gable projections, supported by shallow, elephantine piers atop high concrete bases. The original door with plate glass windows is still present.

278 N. Pine — *1923 Bungalow*   OTPA:1997

OWNER: Perry Heikes

A single-story bungalow with wide lap siding and steep-pitched, multi-gable roof. A small, front-facing gable forms the entry porch overhang which is supported by tapered piers with ornamental brick bases and wood on top.

285 N. Pine — *1924 Mediterranean Revival*   NRHP:1997

A single-story box plan house with stucco facades and a flat roof. A rectilinear projection with arched openings forms the entry portico in the center of the front facade. Both the main house and entry portico feature stepped parapets. Adobe tiled hoods are over each of the windows on the front.

304 N. Pine — *1905 Gable Roof Cottage*   NRHP:1997

A two-story house built on an L-plan with shiplap siding and multi-gable roof. What was originally a full-width porch has since been partially enclosed and altered in an incompatible manner. The original porch was defined by a roof overhang at the first story supported by slim wood posts.

305 N. Pine — *1922 Bungalow*   NRHP:1997
A single-story house with lap siding and multi-gable roof. Two small, front-facing gables define the front facade. The main, side-facing gable roof extends forward to form a large entry porch supported by tapered piers on brick bases.

318 N. Pine — *1904 Victorian Cottage*   NRHP:1997
A single-story house with L-plan and combination steep-pitched, hip and gable roof. The original siding has been covered with asbestos shingles. Entry is at the apex of the ell with a separate porch overhang supported by ornamental trimmed posts. Porch posts and configurations suggest the Victorian Period, while the large picture window next to the main door in the roofline profile suggests the Classical/Revival, turn-of-the-century styles.

323 N. Pine — *1920c Bungalow*   NRHP:1997
A single-story bungalow with wide single, front-facing gable roof. The original siding has been covered by asbestos shingles. Main entry is via a small corner, recessed porch supported by wood posts.

325 N. Pine — *1919 Bungalow*   NRHP:1997
A single-story bungalow with lap siding and gable roof. A centrally located, front-facing gable forms the entry porch overhang supported by pairs of wood posts.

333 N. Pine — *1908 Hip Roof Cottage*   NRHP:1997
A single-story box plan house with clapboard siding and steep-pitched, hip roof A small hipped dormer is present on the front facade. Entry is via a corner recessed porch supported by clapboard posts. Wide eaves are embellished with ornamental brackets.

334 N. Pine — *1903 Hip Roof Cottage*   NRHP:1997
A single-story house with shiplap siding and combination steep-pitched, hip and gable roof. Front-facing gable is embellished with ornamental shingles. The house originally incorporated a L-plan with an entry and porch formed in the apex of the ell.

340 N. Pine — *1910 Board & Batten Cottage*   NRHP:1997
Gable Roof This is a small cottage scale house which, very likely, was hand built without architect or contractor assistance. The house is a small, simple, box plan format with single-gable roof. A full-width porch is present with its own separate overhang and slim wood posts. The house is sided in board and batten, indicating hand construction.

349 N. Pine — *1922 Bungalow*   NRHP:1997
A one-story L-plan bungalow with gable roof and wide lap siding. Entry is at apex of ell. The house is simple and unadorned.

355 N. Pine — *1914*

365 N. Pine — *1904 Hip Roof Cottage*   NRHP:1997
A single-story box plan house with steep-pitched, hip roof. The original clapboard siding has since been covered with asbestos shingles. A small hipped dormer is on the front of the roof. Entry is via a corner recessed porch now supported by an ornamental iron pier, a replacement for the original.

366 N. Pine — *1917 Altered Bungalow*   NRHP:1997
A single-story clapboard bungalow with single, front-facing gable roof. No porch is present, though one may have been located on the front of the house originally but has since been enclosed. The house is simple and unembellished .

373 N. Pine — *1909 Hip Roof Cottage*   NRHP:1997
A single-story house with combination steep-pitched, hip and gable roof. The house is built on a box plan. Original siding has since been covered with asbestos

shingles. No porch is present, though what was once a porch may have since been enclosed.

374 N. Pine — *1920c Bungalow*   NRHP:1997
A single-story house built on a rectangular plan with clapboard siding and single, side-facing gable roof. Entry is beneath a small gabled portico. The presence of two doors indicate the house was built as a duplex.

383 N. Pine — *1922 Bungalow*   NRHP:1997
A single-story bungalow with lap siding and multi-gable roof. A large corner, wrap-around porch is located beneath the main roof supported by tapered piers on ornamental brick bases. A slatted balustrade connects the piers.

384 N. Pine — *1910*

393 N. Pine — *1922c Bungalow*

—Out of Old Towne—

522 N. Pine — *1926 Spanish Colonial*   NRHP:1997
A Spanish colonial residence with stucco and wood siding on a rectangular plan. Large arch-framed multi-paned wooden windows with lintel openings are present on front facade. An arched entry portal with classical door surround is present. The roof is red tiled with molded tile cornice and multi gables.

523 N. Pine — *1924 Mediterranean Revival*   NRHP:1997
Modified Style A stucco house built on an irregular rectangular plan. The roof consists of two gables, one facing side to side and the other front to back. The front to back gable meets the other at its center and is several feet higher. The street side of the side to side gable frames the shed roof of the entry portico. The entry portico and the side wall extending over the driveway have attached openings.

525 N. Pine — *1926 Mediterranean Revival*   NRHP:1997
A Mediterranean Revival home with multi-gabled red Spanish tile roof and plaster siding. Scroll like decorative treatment at gable end corners. Arched

entry is covered with a tower like area with matching arched treatment near chimney. Large front window has mullions and two sidelights. Low stucco wall accents front rectangular plan.

533 N. Pine — *1925 Mediterranean Revival*   NRHP:1997
Modified Style - A combination gabled and parapet roof, rectangular plan stucco house. A front facing gable extends to form an entry portico. The portico has 9 rectangular openings. A portion of the side to side gable forms the remaining front facade. The roof is covered with adobe tiles.

536 N. Pine — *1939 Mediterranean Revival*   NRHP:1997
An irregular L-plan house with stucco siding and multi-gabled roof. Two forward facing, wood siding, gables and a side facing gable built over the driveway dominate the facade. The front mast portion of the house contains a mullioned window. A suspended shed roof overhang covers the entry which is set in the apex of the main house and its front most portion.

543 N. Pine — *1925 Provincial Revival*   NRHP:1997
A square plan stucco house. The parapet and portico roof are covered in adobe tiles. The portico has arched openings. The mullioned door is original and matches the mullioned picture window.

552 N. Pine — *1926 Mediterranean Revival*   NRHP:1997
Modified Style - A rectangular plan house with stucco siding and parapet and gabled roof. The side facing and front facing gabled have adobe tiles. The entry is centered in the front facade. The front facing gable wall contains a metal roofed bay window.

553 N. Pine — *1925 Spanish Colonial Revival*   NRHP:1997
A rectangular plan stucco house with parapet roof. The front porch extends the full length of the facade and the wall extends on both sides to form side walls. The large porch has a tiled roof and is delineated from the house by a decorative parapet wall.

Pixley Street — South

*—Pixley is named for pioneer Dewitt Clinton Pixley,
business owner—*

130 S. Pixley — *1920s Bungalow*

140 S. Pixley — *1907c Western False Front Pressed Tin*

144 S. Pixley — *1925 California Bungalow*

148 S. Pixley — *1924 Bungalow*

154 S. Pixley — *1904 Victorian Cottage Hip Roof*

164 S. Pixley — *1904 Cottage, Hip Roof*

170 S. Pixley — *1900c Victorian Cottage*

178 S. Pixley — *1910 Bungalow*

188 S. Pixley — *1910 Vernacular*

194 S. Pixley — *1910 Vernacular*

320 S. Pixley — *1937*

323 S. Pixley — *1936*

331 S. Pixley — *1927c Provincial Revival* OTPA:1997
OWNER: Charles Oldfield
A rectangular plan, stucco sided provincial revival
residence with front facing chimney and roof gable.
The facade contains several sets of vertical windows
and front entry is enhanced with an arched opening, a
large front door and 2 small accent windows.

332 S. Pixley — *1927 Provincial Revival*   NRHP:1997
A provincial revival residence with brick facade and
2 front facing deep gables, enhanced with small wood
slatted openings. Front entry has low brick wall
protecting front door with matching vertical side
lights. Large front arched window highlights the front
facade.

340 S. Pixley — *1925 Mediterranean Revival*   NRHP:1997
Single-story, Mediterranean Revival bungalow with
stucco facade and flat roof. Most notable are the
angled facade extensions and the stepped parapet with

tiled ridges. A separate tile hooded projection with large arched opening forms the entry porch.

348 S. Pixley — *1926 Provincial Revival*   NRHP:1997
A wood sided rectangular plan provincial revival residence with 2 front-facing gables and matching set of windows. Entry is protected by low brick wall. Front door has matching sidelight doors.

352 S. Pixley — *1927 Spanish Colonial Revival*   NRHP:1997
Single-story, U-plan house combining Spanish Colonial Revival and Provincial influences. Roof is gabled with tile facing. Arched picture windows on front facade emphasize Spanish Colonial influence.

353 S. Pixley — *1928 Bungalow*   NRHP:1997
A small, rectangular plan bungalow with a single, front-facing gable roof. A smaller, central gable overhang in front forms the entry porch and is supported by a grouping of wood posts.

362 S. Pixley — *1927 Spanish Colonial Revival*   NRHP:1997
Single-story bungalow-scale house built on an L-plan with front gable face incorporating a large arched, multi-paned window and ornamental tiles along the roof eave. Apex of ell has separate arcaded entry with two large, arched openings and a tile hooded roof.

365 S. Pixley — *1928 Bungalow*   NRHP:1997
Clapboard bungalow influenced house with single-gable roof and smaller, clipped front-facing gable.

368 S. Pixley — *1938*

369 S. Pixley — *1925 Mediterranean Revival*   NONC

375 S. Pixley — *1937*

404 S. Pixley — *1925 Pueblo*   NRHP:1997
A pueblo styled residence with flat roof and tile accentuating the roof line. Front entry is covered with decorative wrought iron treatment and matching single windows.

407 S. Pixley — *1924*   NONC

411 S. Pixley — *1924 Bungalow* NRHP:1997
A small, clapboard box with single gable roof which extends forward to form a full-width porch. Entry is at center with a sash window on either side.

412 S. Pixley — *1923*

416 S. Pixley — *1928 Bungalow* NRHP:1997
A very small bungalow cottage with double, front-facing gables. Original siding is covered with asbestos shingles. Forwardmost gable forms entry overhang and is supported by wood posts.

427 S. Pixley — *1924*

428 S. Pixley — *1922 Bungalow* NRHP:1997
A single-story multi-gabled Bungalow with side entry and 3-paneled window facing front. Front facade is enhanced with double panel windows.

434 S. Pixley — *1929 Bungalow* NRHP:1997
A single-story, clapboard bungalow with unusual combination of double, front-facing gables. Front facade is in an L-format, and entry is at apex of ell. Large picture window on frontmost gable face has multi-pane transom.

435 S. Pixley — *1924 Bungalow* NRHP:1997
Single-story clapboard bungalow with double, front-facing gable. Forwardmost gable forms entry porch overhang and is supported by elephantine piers.

442 S. Pixley — *1923 Bungalow* NRHP:1997
Single-story clapboard bungalow with double, front-facing gables. Front most gable forms entry porch overhang and is supported by elephantine piers embellished with ornamental brick bases.

449 S. Pixley — *1924 Bungalow*

450 S. Pixley — *1923 Bungalow* NRHP:1997
Single-story, box plan clapboard bungalow with main roof comprised of a front-facing gable. Smaller, front-facing gable extends forward to form porch overhang.

This is supported by elephantine piers highlighted by ornamental brick bases.

459 S. Pixley — *1924 Bungalow*   NRHP:1997
Single-story clapboard bungalow with double, front-facing gables. Forwardmost gable forms entry porch overhang and is supported by elephantine piers highlighted by ornamental brick bases.

460 S. Pixley — *1928 Spanish Colonial Revival*   NRHP:1997
Single-story stucco house with gable roof and side extension of gable forming arcaded entry. The entry features a large, arched opening which is complemented by a large, arched picture window on the front facade. Ornamental tiles highlight eaves of roof.

467 S. Pixley — *1924 Bungalow*   NRHP:1997
Single-story, clapboard bungalow with double, front-facing gables. Forwardmost gable forms entry porch overhang and is supported by tapered piers.

475 S. Pixley — *1936 Bungalow*   NONC
Single-story, box plan clapboard bungalow with single, front-facing gable roof. A smaller, gabled portico is located symmetrically in center of front facade and forms entry porch overhang. Simulated Mediterranean look.

483 S. Pixley — *1924 Bungalow*   NRHP:1997
TREE: Avocado *Avocado*. The largest Avocado in Orange, came from a seedling.
Single-story, rectangular plan bungalow with single, shallow-pitched, side-facing gable roof. The contrasting front-facing gable projection forms entry porch overhang and is supported by wood posts.

PIXLEY STREET — NORTH

115 N. Pixley — *1905 Post Victorian*

127 N. Pixley — *1905c Cottage, Hip Roof*

128 N. Pixley — *1910 Vernacular*

140 N. Pixley — *1920 Bungalow*

141 N. Pixley — *1920s Bungalow*

150 N. Pixley — *1920 Bungalow*

154 N. Pixley — *1923 Bungalow*

158 N. Pixley — *1924 Bungalow*

166 N. Pixley — *1925 Bungalow*

170 N. Pixley — *1919 Bungalow*
BLDR: Charles Labahn Grower Built by Labahn and son Charles Jr. who grew walnuts for some years.

This house is in original condition with upstairs windows and elephantine porch piers. Front brickwork has been added to the Bungalow, typical of the era.

174 N. Pixley — *1924 Bungalow*

176 N. Pixley — *1924 Bungalow*

River Avenue — East
—River Avenue is named for the Santiago Creek—

119 E. River — *1915c Bungalow*   NRHP:1997
A small, single-story clapboard bungalow with rectangular plan and single, front-facing gabled roof. The house is very simple and unadorned. Entrance is from the side beneath a small gabled portico.
Nutwood Place 1906 Arroyo Stone Marker

126 E. River — *1915 Bungalow*
Nutwood Place 1906 Arroyo Stone Marker

127 E. River — *1919 Craftsman Bungalow*   NRHP:1997
A small, single-story bungalow with a single, front-facing gabled roof. The original siding is still present on the forwardmost gable, but the remainder of the house has since been covered with asbestos shingles. A front-facing, projecting gable forms the entry porch overhang and is supported by piers with wide concrete bases and smaller wood posts on top. To either side of the main entry door is a pair of sash windows.

133 E. River — *1910c Cottage*

137 E. River — *1915c Craftsman Bungalow*   NRHP:1997
A single-story house with single, side-facing gabled roof. The original siding has since been covered with asbestos shingles. A wide shed dormer is present on the front portion of the roof. One-half of the front facade is devoted to a recessed porch supported by piers with brick bases.

213 E. River — *1921 Bungalow*   NRHP:1997
A small, single-story bungalow with wide lap siding and single, front-facing gabled roof. One-half of the front facade is devoted to a recessed porch supported by wood posts. The original door with mullioned-pane, plate glass windows is still present. An unusual sunray embellishment adorns the upper front gable face.

225 E. River — *1904 Vernacular*   NRHP:1997
TREE: 1786c California Sycamore *Platanus racemosa* 68" 95'

110'. This Sycamore is natural and graced the edge of Santiago Creek, for which River Ave. is named. River Ave. is the only one way street in Orange - due to the tree. In the 1940s National Geographic came and determined the age of the tree.

Harper Fruit Co
A packing house operator, Harber eventually opened his own firm. The style of this house is very difficult to pinpoint, since it appears that the house has undergone modifications over the years, particularly in the period prior to 1925.

The house is very large and is built on a box plan, which incorporates a steep-pitched, side-facing gabled roof with a full-width front porch typical of the Craftsman period. The roof slopes forward at an unusual angle and features two small shed dormers on the front portion.

315 E. River — *1939*

327 E. River — *1919*

330 E. River — *1920c Bungalow*   NRHP:1997
A single-story bungalow with shallow-pitched, multi-gabled roofline. The original siding on the facades has been covered with asbestos shingles. The front entry is characterized by a projecting gable supported by slender wood posts. The entry door, which is not original, is flanked on either side by picture windows with transoms. A pergola is located to the side of the porch entry .

334 E. River — *1924 Vernacular Simpson*   OTPA:1997
A small rectangular box pan with low-pitched gabled roof and exposed rafters. The small partial-width porch matches the front facade and front gable. The entry door is flanked by single double-hung windows.

337 E. River — *1919*

338 E. River — *1914*

SHAFFER STREET — SOUTH
—Shaffer is named for pioneer Peter J. Shaffer, grower—

133 S. Shaffer — *1920 Hip Roof Cottage*   NRHP:1997
A single-story clapboard house with combination hip and gable roof resulting in an L-plan. The short leg of the ell is the gable portion which is comprised of a front-facing gable with a return at the eaves. A small, ornamentally framed, louvered transom is visible. The entry porch is located in the apex of the ell. It has its own separate roof extension supported by ornamentally turned posts.

133 S. Shaffer — *1905c Cottage, Hip Roof*

184 S. Shaffer — *1927 Mediterranean Revival*   NRHP:1982
Walker Memorial Hall
This is the Walker Memorial which, along with the St. John's Lutheran Church, has been made a part of the St. John's complex of buildings, listed on the NRHP. Walker Memorial Hall is built in the then popular Mediterranean Revival style with strong Renaissance Revival influences. The building includes a 600-seat auditorium, kitchen, dining room, meeting room and lobby. The building is constructed in brown brick with a large, prominent entry defined by a rectilinear tower and adobe tiled roof. A canopy hangs above the entry which features a raised entrance with an ornamental iron balustrade. The south half of the front facade includes a stepped parapet; the north half features an arched parapet. Renaissance arches house the mullioned casement windows which occur in a regular pattern across the facade. The building is in excellent condition and well maintained.

226 S. Shaffer — *1902 Hip Roof Cottage*   NRHP:1997
A single-story house with lap siding and a steep-pitched hip roof. A small hip dormer is present on the front portion of the house. Entry is via a corner recessed porch which has since been enclosed but was originally supported by wood posts.

227 S. Shaffer — *1921 Craftsman Bungalow*   NRHP:1997
A single-story bungalow with double, front-facing, gable roof and facades which are now covered by stucco. The frontmost gable forms a full-width entry porch overhang supported by tapered piers with ornamental brick bases and wood posts on top.

236 S. Shaffer — *1920c Bungalow*   NRHP:1997
This bungalow incorporates Period Revival influences, notably English or Provincial. The house is defined by a steep-pitched, multi-gable roof and stucco siding with shingles present in the upper gable faces. A front-facing gable defines the entry which is comprised of a multi-pane door inside a small, recessed entry portico. Ornamental purlins and a reversed spire on the gable peaks are notable embellishments. Since the 1982 survey, this structure has been altered with inappropriate window replacements.

260 S. Shaffer — *1920 Prairie Influence*   NRHP:1997
Built by J.H. McConnell, this unusual home has been bought and traded by several owners and has had many families as residents up until 1928. After an extensive remodel, it became the permanent home of Louis Luhr and his wife.

A single-story stucco house with flat roof and raised parapet and pilasters. Entry is via a porch projection with wide opening. Horizontal banding and the overall horizontal quality of the house are indicative of the Prairie School Residential architecture established by Frank Lloyd Wright.

262 S. Shaffer — *1922 Craftsman Bungalow*   NRHP:1997
A single-story clapboard bungalow with double, front-facing gable roof. The forwardmost gable forms the entry porch overhang and is supported by tapered piers.

312 S. Shaffer — *1903 Bungalow*

328 S. Shaffer — *1907 Vernacular*   NRHP:1997

A small, single-story house with a single, side-facing gable roof with a sloping angle to the gable. A small shed dormer is present on the front. What was probably a full-width porch has since been enclosed. This house is simple and unembellished. Since the 1982 survey, this structure has been altered with appropriate reopening of the front porch.

336 S. Shaffer — *1917 Bungalow* NRHP:1997
This is a single-story house with double, front-facing gable roof and ornamental lap siding. The forwardmost gable originally formed the entry porch overhang which has since been enclosed.

344 S. Shaffer — *1905 Hip Roof Cottage* NRHP:1997
A single-story clapboard house with a steep-pitched hip roof and corner recessed entry porch. The porch has since been screened in but originally was supported by Classical columns. Since the 1982 survey, this structure has been altered with inappropriate siding and aluminum windows.

362 S. Shaffer — *1920 Bungalow* NRHP:1997
A single-story bungalow once of clapboard, now covered by asbestos siding. A multi-gable roof with parallel, front-facing gables define the front portion of the house. The forwardmost gable forms the entry porch overhang and is supported by tapered piers.

368 S. Shaffer — *1920 Craftsman Bungalow* NRHP:1997
A single-story bungalow with wide lap siding and double, front-facing gable roof. The forwardmost gable forms the entry porch overhang and is supported by piers with wood posts on top. The upper gable faces are ornamented by widely spaced, exposed beams.

373 S. Shaffer — *1920c Bungalow* NRHP:1997
This is a simple, small clapboard bungalow with single, side-facing gable roof. No porch is present. Entry is directly from the front facade. Two, three-part windows are also present on the front facade.

374 S. Shaffer — *1911 Craftsman Bungalow*   NRHP:1997
A single-story house with wide lap siding and double, front-facing gable roof. The forwardmost gable originally formed the entry porch overhang but has since been enclosed. The original slim, tapered piers are still visible. The eaves are embellished with triangular bracket supports; louvered attic transoms are present on both of the gable faces.

375 S. Shaffer — *1923 Bungalow*   NRHP:1997
A single-story simple clapboard bungalow with single, side facing gable roof. No porch is present. Entry is directly from the front facade. Two, three-part windows are also present on the front facade.

380 S. Shaffer — *1910 Craftsman Bungalow*   NRHP:1997
A single-story clapboard bungalow with double, front-facing gable roof. The forwardmost gable forms the entry porch overhang and is supported by slim tapered piers. Triangular bracket supports grace the eaves; the upper gable faces are defined by louvered attic venting.

394 S. Shaffer — *1915 Craftsman*   NRHP:1997
A one and one-half story Craftsman house with combination board and batten and lap siding. The main roof is comprised of a single gable with side-facing gables contrasted by a front-facing gable dormer. What was originally a full-width porch supported by arroyo stone piers has since been screened in. Ornamental purlins and louvered venting with diamond-pane transoms ornament the dormer gable. Also notable is the porte cochere which extends from the side of the house and has a gable overhang supported by arroyo stone piers.

404 S. Shaffer
SAVI: located on the corner.

425 S. Shaffer — *1919 Vernacular*   NRHP:1997
This unusual, one-of-a-kind house is distinguished by steep-pitched, multi-gable roof and ship lap siding.

The entry is via a porch formed by one of two parallel, front-facing gables; the porch overhang is supported by slim wood posts. The house shows signs of having been much modified over the years.

445 S. Shaffer — *1921 Bungalow*   NRHP:1997
A small, single-story clapboard bungalow with single, front-facing gable roof. What was probably a recessed corner porch has since been enclosed. The house is simple and unembellished.

447 S. Shaffer — *1923 Bungalow*   NRHP:1997
A single-story clapboard bungalow with double, front-facing gable roof. The smaller, forwardmost gable forms the entry porch overhang and is supported by thin posts.

462 S. Shaffer — *1920*

470 S. Shaffer — *1925 Bungalow*   NRHP:1997
A small, single-story bungalow with tri-gable roof and siding now covered by asbestos. Center frontmost portion of the house is comprised of a front-facing gable which forms entry porch overhang supported by wood posts.

478 S. Shaffer — *1910 Transitional*   NRHP:1997
An unusual, two-story clapboard house with single, front-facing gable roof. A full-width porch is located beneath the second story and is supported by fluted tapered piers. The original hardwood door with oval pane is still present.

484 S. Shaffer — *1923 Bungalow*   NRHP:1997
A small, single-story bungalow with clapboard siding and single, front-facing gable roof. A smaller, front-facing gable forms the entry portico and is supported by wood posts.

Shaffer Street — North

133 N. Shaffer — *1913 Craftsman*   OTPA:1997
OWNER: August Dusin
A one and one-half story rectangular plan house with
lap siding and single, side-facing gable roof. A small,
front-facing gabled dormer is also present in the front
and features an ornamental transom. The main roof
extends forward to form a full-width porch supported
by piers with brick bases. Triangular bracket supports
in exposed beams adorn the eaves around the house.

143 N. Shaffer — *1912 Bungalow*   NRHP:1997
TREE: Coastal Redwood *Sequoia semperviren* 30" 75' 25' -
very few in Orange.
A single-story house with wide lap siding and multi-
gable roof. The front facade is comprised of a double,
front-facing gable with a forward roofline, the
forwardmost of which forms the entry porch overhang.
This is supported by tapered piers.

146 N. Shaffer — *1903 Classic Box*   OTPA:1997
OWNER: Wilber Welch
A high, two- story clapboard house with box plan and
flattened, hip roof. A large, corner wrap-around porch
on the first story is supported by ornamental, turned
columns, harking back to the Victorian Period. Wide
eaves are adorned with pairs of ornamental brackets.
Since the 1982 survey, this structure has undergone
restoration.

151 N. Shaffer — *1887 Vernacular*   OTPA:1997
Pioneer Henry Grote
A single-story house with shiplap siding and single,
front-facing gable roof. No porch is present, but the
high, narrow windows, inner-framing define the house
as being from the Victorian Period. Since the 1982
survey, this structure has been appropriately altered.

154 N. Shaffer — *1887c Gable Roof Cottage*   NRHP:1997
A small, single-story house with wide-lap siding and
steep-pitched, multi-gable roof. Across the front

facade is a full-width porch with its own separate roof overhang supported by wood posts. These posts are connected by a slatted balustrade. Entry is at center, flanked on either side by a pair of sash windows.

164 N. Shaffer — *1911 Craftsman*   NRHP:1997
A large, one and one-half story house with lap siding and single, side-facing gable roof. A large hipped dormer with a balcony and accompanying overhang are present on the front portion of the roof. The main roof extends forward to form a full-width porch supported by fluted piers. Entry is at center, flanked on either side by windows.

169 N. Shaffer — *1889 Victorian Italianate*   OTPA:1997
Henry & Wilhelmina Grote
BLDR: F.W. Gelderman Ehlen & Grote (Grote St., now Cleveland,) half owner of the largest business building in Orange, built this large home on 15 acres bounded by Shaffer, Chapman, Maple and Cleveland. He and his wife had 10 children.

A large, two-story house with box plan, shiplap siding and flattened hip roof. The windows are ornamentally framed with jigsawn wood; the entry is at center on the first story. Originally a large, ornamental porch surrounded this entry but has since been removed. The house has an elaborate cornice defined by wide eaves and pairs of ornamental brackets. Since the 1982 survey, this structure has undergone partial restoration.

Grote, half owner of the largest business building in Orange, built this large home on 15 acres bounded by Shaffer.

172 N. Shaffer — *1912 Bungalow*   NRHP:1997
A single-story bungalow with wide lap siding and double, front-facing gable roof. The forwardmost gable forms the entry porch overhang supported by tapered piers on arroyo stone bases. The exposed beams are

fashioned as triangular bracket supports which add ornamentation to the eaves of the house. The main door is flanked by sidelights. Windows on the front facade feature ornamentally mullioned, upper sashes.

182 N. Shaffer — *1913 Bungalow*   NRHP:1997
A single-story bungalow with double, front-facing gable roof. The original siding has been covered by asbestos shingles. The forwardmost gable forms the entry porch overhang supported by wood posts atop a low porch wall. Exposed beams, used both as triangular bracket supports and as ornamentation on the front facade, are on the upper gable faces.

192 N. Shaffer — *1905 Victorian*   NRHP:1997
This is a large, two-story house with clapboard siding and combination hip and gable roof. The house features a large, elaborate, corner wrap-around porch supported by classical columns. Pedimented gable with ornamental woodwork in the gable faces adorn each entry to the porch. Sizing and formatting of the windows and columns, the siding and roofline, all suggest the Classical Revival influences; the wrap-around porch and ornamentation in porch gables suggest Victorian influences.

195 N. Shaffer — *1914 Craftsman*   NRHP:1997
A large, two-story Craftsman house with clapboard siding and a single, side-facing gable roof. A large, front-facing gabled dormer with balcony is on the front portion of the roof. The main roof extends forward on the front and sides to form a full-width front and wrap-around porch. The porch is supported by fluted, tapered piers. Main entry is at front center—a door with plate glass windows flanked by complementary side lites on either side. Also, to either side of the front door is a large, three-part picture window with mullioned transoms.

222 N. Shaffer — *1920 Bungalow*   NRHP:1997
A single-story clapboard bungalow with multi-gable

roof. The house is built on a modified L-plan with the entry in the apex of the ell. The roof extends over the entry to form a large entry porch supported by piers with a connecting slatted balustrade.

227 N. Shaffer — *1914 Bungalow*   NRHP:1997
A single-story bungalow with wide-lap siding and double, front-facing gable roof. The main roof extends forward to form the entry porch overhang supported by tapered piers on top of brick bases. Ornamental purlins and lattice grace the upper gable faces.

232 N. Shaffer — *1920 Bungalow*   NONC
A single-story bungalow with double, front-facing gable roof. The forwardmost gable forms the entry porch overhang supported by piers with wood posts on top. The house has been considerably modified through the use of stucco siding on the facades and ornamental masonry on the frontmost gable and porch. The original door with plate glass panes is still present.

235 N. Shaffer — *1895c Gable Roof Cottage*   NRHP:1997
What was originally a Victorian frame house was substantially remodeled in 1909 to reflect the then popular bungalow style. Generally, the house has a bungalow appearance, but closer scrutiny reveals the original Victorian details . Shiplap siding and a multi-gable roof are present with a centrally located, front-facing gable forming the entry porch overhang supported by tapered piers. The door is clearly Victorian and is treated in the Victorian manner. To the side is a bay window of high, narrow windows characteristic of the Victorian styling.

240 N. Shaffer — *1905 Hip Roof Cottage*   NRHP:1997
A single-story clapboard house with combination hip and gable roof. The house is built on an L-plan, featuring a large corner, wrap-around porch supported by classical columns. Entry is beneath in the apex of

the ell. The original door is still present.

241 N. Shaffer — *1929 Bungalow*   NRHP:1997
A single-story clapboard bungalow with single, front-facing gable roof. A one-half size corner porch is formed beneath the main portion of the house and is sheltered by a shed roof extension supported by wood posts. The original door with plate glass window is still present.

248 N. Shaffer — *1909 Bungalow*   NRHP:1997
A single-story house with wide lap siding and double, front-facing gable roof. The forwardmost gable forms the entry porch overhang supported by wood posts atop a low porch wall. Ornamental purlins and cross-ties embellish the upper gable faces. The main door is flanked on either side by a three-part window with multi-paned transom.

251 N. Shaffer — *1914 Bungalow*   NRHP:1997
A single-story house with double, front-facing gable roof. The original siding has since been covered with asbestos shingles. The forwardmost gable forms the entry porch overhang supported by tapered piers atop masonry bases.

256 N. Shaffer — *1909 Bungalow*   NRHP:1997
A single-story clapboard bungalow with multi-gable roof. The house is built on a modified L-plan with the short leg of the ell extending forward to form an entry porch. The foundation is skirted in such a manner as to give the house a special flair. The porch is supported by a trio of wood posts atop a clapboard porch wall. Ornamental brackets and a bay window to the side of the porch further highlight the house.

259 N. Shaffer — *1915 Craftsman*   NRHP:1997
A two-story Craftsman house with ornamental lap siding on the facades and shallow-pitched, multi-gable roof. The house is distinguished by a second story portion, primarily over the rear half of the house, and

a large corner, wrap-around porch supported by wood posts. Entry is beneath the porch roof at center, and the original wood door with plate glass windows is still present and is flanked on either side by large picture windows with mullioned transoms.

264 N. Shaffer — *1915c Craftsman* NRHP:1997

A one and one-half story house with single, side-facing gable roof and wide lap siding. A front facing, gabled dormer features a three-part transom window. Main roof extends forward to form a full-width porch which is supported by arroyo stone piers. Square bay windows on the sides of the house, which can note Craftsman homes, are present.

265 N. Shaffer — *1913 Bungalow* NRHP:1997

A single-story bungalow with double, front-facing gable roof and combination clapboard and shingle siding. The forwardmost gable forms the entry porch overhang supported by tapered wood piers. Large transomed picture windows are featured on the front facade.

272 N. Shaffer — *1915c Bungalow* NRHP:1997

A single-story bungalow with wide lap siding and double, front-facing gable roof. The forwardmost gable forms the entry porch overhang supported by tapered wood piers. Upper gable faces are distinguished by cross-ties. Original door with plate glass windows is still present and flanked on either side with large, three-part picture windows.

275 N. Shaffer — *1913 Bungalow* NRHP:1997

A single-story bungalow with wide lap siding and multi-gable roof fashioned in an L-plan. The front-facing gable forms the entry porch overhang supported by wide elephantine piers. A large picture window with mullioned transoms is present on the front facade.

280 N. Shaffer — *1910 Bungalow* NRHP:1997

A single-story bungalow with single, front-facing gable roof. The original clapboard siding has since been covered with asbestos shingles. A full-width, recessed porch is supported by tapered piers. The original door with plate glass panes is still present. Ornamentally exposed beams adorn the lower portion of the upper gable face. Since the 1982 survey, this structure has been altered by a two story addition.

283 N. Shaffer — *1914 Altered Bungalow*   NRHP:1997
A single-story bungalow with lap siding and double, front-facing gable roof. The forwardmost gable forms the entry porch overhang supported by slender wood posts. The low porch wall is faced with arroyo stone.

288 N. Shaffer — *1910 Craftsman*   NRHP:1997
A one and one-half story house with wide lap siding and single, side-facing gable roof. A shed dormer with casement windows is on the front of the roof. What was originally a full-width porch beneath the main roof extension has since been albeit in a compatible way. The front facade of the house now features almost solid, multi-paned windows.

291 N. Shaffer — *1916 Craftsman Bungalow*   NRHP:1997
A single-story craftsman bungalow with ornamental lap siding and multi-gable roof. Main portion of the house is covered by a single-gable roof with side-facing gables. A centrally located front-facing gable forms an entry porch overhang. The overhang and pergolas to either side of it are supported by very wide, concrete columns. Entry is at center beneath the overhang.

306 N. Shaffer — *1920 Bungalow*   NRHP:1997
A single-story bungalow with ornamental lap siding and shallow-pitched, multi-gable roof. The house is distinguished by a large, corner wrap-around porch beneath an extension of the main roof and supported by elephantine piers with concrete bases. Two smaller, front-facing gables with vertical slatting are attic

dormers.

314 N. Shaffer — *1921 Bungalow*   NRHP:1997
A single-story bungalow with wide lap siding and clipped, tri-gable roof. Main portion of the house is covered by a single-gable roof. The central, front-facing gable forms the entry porch overhang supported by elephantine piers. Lattice work in the upper gable face distinguishes its facade.

317 N. Shaffer — *1922 Bungalow*   OTPA:1997
OWNER: Henry Beck
A single-story bungalow with ornamental lap siding and shallow-pitched, multi-gable roof. The roof is fashioned in a semi-L-plan with the front-facing gable forming the entry overhang supported by piers of ornamental brick bases with wood posts on top. The original door, featuring a single, plate glass window, is beneath its center entry.

322 N. Shaffer — *1907 Hip Roof Cottage*   NRHP:1997
A single-story house with modified L-plan and combination steep-pitched, hip and gable roof. Separate roof overhang defines porch located in the apex of the ell. A front-facing gable features a return at the eaves. Since the 1982 survey, this structure has been altered with appropriate siding restoration .

325 N. Shaffer — *1914 Bungalow*   NRHP:1997
A single-story clapboard bungalow with single, front-facing gable roof. A full-width porch, supported by tapered, wide fluted piers on the exterior and slender tapered piers near the entry, is recessed beneath the main portion of the house.

330 N. Shaffer — *1917 Bungalow*   NRHP:1997
A single-story clapboard bungalow with single, front-facing gable roof. Entry is via a corner recessed porch supported by slim wood posts.

333 N. Shaffer — *1904 Hip Roof Cottage*   OTPA:1997
OWNER: Dinah Stinson

A single-story clapboard house with combination steep-pitched, hip and gable roof. A full-width porch on the front facade is defined by a separate roof overhang supported by slender wood posts. Entry is beneath at center. The boxy, symmetrical quality of the house is typical of the Classical Revival homes of the period, although this house does not incorporate the reform embellishment .

341 N. Shaffer — *1936 Provincial Revival*   NRHP:1997
A single-story house with modified L-plan, wide lap siding and steep-pitched, gable roof. Two front-facing gables articulate the front facade joined by a wide brick chimney. No porch is present. The house echoes the format and massing of the Provincial Revival houses, although it does not incorporate the embellishment typical of that style.

342 N. Shaffer — *1920c Bungalow*   NRHP:1997
A single-story house with single, front-facing gable roof. The original siding has since been covered with asbestos shingles. Main entry is at center covered by a gabled portico with an inner arch. Large, double-hung windows are on either side of the entry.

349 N. Shaffer — *1905c Bungalow*   NRHP:1997
A single-story bungalow with wide lap siding and single-front-facing gable roof. One-half of the front facade is defined by a recessed entry porch now supported by ornamental iron piers, a replacement of the original. Cross-ties and purlins ornament the upper gable face.

352 N. Shaffer — *1912*

357 N. Shaffer — *1905c Gable Roof Cottage*   NRHP:1997
A single-story house built on an L-plan with steep-pitched, gable roof. Original siding has been covered with asbestos shingles. Entry is at the apex of the ell and has its own separate overhang supported by slender wood posts. Two high, ornamental brick

chimneys are present and emanate from the central portion of the house.

358 N. Shaffer — *1910 Altered Bungalow*   NRHP:1997
A single-story clapboard bungalow with single, front-facing gable roof. A smaller, front-facing gable with a shallower pitch articulates a full-width entry porch overhang supported by concrete base piers with wood posts on top. Since the 1982 survey, this structure has been altered with inappropriate porch rail, posts and stickwork.

382 N. Shaffer — *1925*

383 N. Shaffer — *1911 Vernacular*   NRHP:1997
A single-story box plan house with clapboard siding and steep-pitched, hip roof. Entry is via a recessed portico at the center. The house originally had a recessed corner porch but has since been enclosed and the original porch posts are still visible. Since the 1982 survey, this structure has been altered with inappropriate gable roof.

390 N. Shaffer — *1910 Bungalow*   NRHP:1997
A one and one-half story house with combination clapboard and shingle siding. Clapboard is on the lower portion, while the upper gable face is adorned with ornamental shingles. The roof is comprised of a single, front-facing gable with a side-facing gabled dormer. Entry is via a recessed corner porch supported by a clapboard pier. Exposed beams are fashioned as triangular braces and further ornament the upper portions of the house.

393 N. Shaffer — *1906 Gable Roof Cottage*   NRHP:1997
A one and one-half story clapboard house with single, side-facing gable roof. The smaller, front-facing dormer is on the front portion of the roof. The main roof extends forward to form a full-width porch supported by round columns in the Classical fashion. Entry is beneath at center. The house incorporates an

unusual combination of Classical Revival and Craftsman elements. Formatting is Craftsman while columns and windows are typical of the Classical period.

406 N. Shaffer *1909 Craftsman*   OTPA:1997
OWNER: Charles Bentley
A one and one-half story Craftsman house with wide lap siding and single, side-facing gable roof. Front-facing gabled dormer is also present. This dormer is ornamented with a little balcony balustrade, mullioned transom window, cross-ties and ornamental purlin. The main roof extends forward to form a full-width porch supported by piers with brick bases and wood posts on top. Entry is beneath at center and flanked on either side by a large picture window with mullioned transom.

409 N. Shaffer — *1909 Craftsman Finley*   NRHP:1997
This home was used in the 1945 film "Fallen Angels" by Otto Preminger. This is a two-story house built in the Craftsman style with added details which make the house unique.

The house is built on a modified box-plan and includes a multi-gable roof. Siding is clapboard. A large, wrap-around porch is on both the street-facing sides. An attached roof provides the porch overhang supported by elephantine piers. An ornamental balustrade connects these piers. The main entry is on the corner of the house and includes an angled format for the door and flanking sidelights. The second story includes a sleeping porch with sloping roof, elephantine piers, an ornamental balustrade and curved latticework along the sides. Ornamentally carved rafter tails are beneath the eaves and the porch roof. The house is in excellent condition and in its original architectural state.

440 N. Shaffer — *1922 Bungalow*   NRHP:1997
A single-story clapboard bungalow with double, front-

facing gable roof. Forwardmost gable forms the entry porch overhang supported by tapered piers of ornamental brick bases with wood posts on top. Large picture windows with mullioned transoms are on the front facade.

444 N. Shaffer — *1921 Spanish Colonial Revival* NRHP:1997
A single-story house built on an L-plan with stucco facades and adobe tiled, gable roof. Entry is at the apex of the ell where a recessed portico is formed with an ornamental arched opening. Combination arched and rectilinear windows are on the front facade.

456 N. Shaffer — *1922 Bungalow* NRHP:1997
A single-story clapboard bungalow with double, front-facing gable roof. Forwardmost gable forms the entry porch overhang supported by classical round columns. Since the 1982 survey, this structure has undergone major restoration.

461 N. Shaffer — *1925 Provincial Revival* NRHP:1997
A single-story house with wide lap siding and steep-pitched, gable roof. The house has Provincial Revival influences, although it does not incorporate the embellishment typical of that style. The house is built on a slight L-plan with the entry in the apex of the ell. The front-facing gable has an extended slop to form the entry portico.

464 N. Shaffer — *1923 Bungalow* NRHP:1997
A single-story clapboard house with shallow-pitched, multi-gable roof. The house is built on a modified L-plan with the front-facing gable extending forward to incorporate a recessed entry porch. This gable and adjacent pergola are supported by brick piers which may not be original.

469 N. Shaffer — *1933*

472 N. Shaffer — *1925 Mediterranean Revival* NRHP:1997
A single-story house with stucco facades and combination flat and gable roof. Entry is via a recessed

portico with a large arched opening. The stepped parapet incorporates adobe tiled ridges which are complemented by the adobe tile window hood on the front facade.

477 N. Shaffer — *1922 Mediterranean Revival*   NRHP:1997
A single-story house with stucco facades and flat roof. The house is built on a slight L-plan with the entry in the apex of the ell. A separate addition was included and forms a recessed portico with arched opening and adobe tiled hood. Roof ridges also are adorned with adobe tiles.

482 N. Shaffer — *1929 Provincial Revival*   NRHP:1997
Modified Style
A single-story house with ornamental lap siding and steep-pitched, multi-gable roof. The house is clearly fashioned after the Provincial Revival style but does not incorporate the typical embellishment of that style. Entry is in the apex of the ell beneath an independent gable projection supported by a Classical column. The original door with plate glass window is still present, flanked on either side of the front facades by a pair of double-hung windows.

496 N. Shaffer — *1924 Bungalow*   NRHP:1997
A single-story bungalow with wide lap siding and single, front-facing gable roof. Smaller, centrally located, projecting gable forms the entry porch overhang supported by wood posts.

525 N. Shaffer —
TREE: 1873c Tulip Tree *Liriodendron.*
Although this school was built in the 1950s, this tree has been listed as the oldest planting in Orange.

766 N. Shaffer —
TREE: Monkey Puzzle *Araucaria imbricata* 33" 90' 30'.

840 N. Shaffer — *1911*   OTPA:1997
Owner: John Campbell

SYCAMORE AVENUE — EAST

—Sycamore is named for one of the horticultural trees—

407 E. Sycamore — *1910*   NRHP:1997
A small boxed shape stucco sided home with recessed entry and small stucco overhangs over side windows. Windows and doors accented with ornamental wood mullions.

419 E. Sycamore — *1928 Bungalow*   NRHP:1997
A single-story bungalow with lap siding and single, front-facing gable roof. The second, front-facing gable, centrally located on the front facade, forms a slight entry porch overhang supported by wood posts. The original door with plate glass windows is still present.

419 E. Sycamore — *1928 Bungalow*

420 E. Sycamore — *1920c Altered Bungalow*   NRHP:1997
This is a typical City of Orange bungalow which originally had clapboard siding but has since been stuccoed over. This detracts from the original architectural integrity of the house. The house is built on a basic box plan with a single, front-facing gable roof. Entry is at the center of the front facade beneath the shed porch overhang supported by wood posts. A large, double-hung window flanks either side of the main entry.

425 E. Sycamore — *1928 Bungalow*   NRHP:1997
A single-story house with lap siding and single-gable roof with side-facing gables. The front entry is at the center of the front facade beneath a large gabled portico with an inner arched opening. This portico is supported by wide piers.

425 E. Sycamore — *1928 Bungalow*

724 E. Sycamore — *1919*   NRHP:1997
Small box-shaped Bungalow with small covered porch entry and matching double hung front windows. Concrete walls front garden area.

802 E. Sycamore — *1922*

Sycamore Avenue — West

145 W. Sycamore — *1923c Western Gothic Revival* NRHP:1997
A two-story church building with a gable roof and clapboard siding. The entry is defined by a rectilinear tower with a small gable portico. The windows have a mullioned upper pane and transoms above. It is simple and unadorned.

145 W. Sycamore — *1923c Western Gothic Revival*

209 W. Sycamore — *1923 Bungalow*   NRHP:1997
A single-story house with shallow-pitch, gable roof. A front-facing gable formes the entry porch overhang and is supported by wood posts. The original clapboard siding has been covered with asbestos shingles.

209 W. Sycamore — *1923 Bungalow*

215 W. Sycamore — *1923 Bungalow*   NRHP:1997
A single-story bungalow with wide lap siding and double front-facing gable roof. The forwardmost gable forms the entry porch overhang and is supported by wood posts.

223 W. Sycamore — *1914*

TOLUCA AVENUE — EAST
—Toluca may be named for Toluca Lake CA—
(The only other such placename in the US)

325 E. Toluca — *1915 Craftsman*   NRHP:1997
This house incorporates both Craftsman and Colonial Revival bungalow features. The house is unusual for the way that it incorporates a full two-story with single, side-facing gabled roof. The main entry is articulated by a centrally located projecting gable which forms a small entry overhang. This is supported by Colonial columns. This entry porch is treated in the same manner as was done on the Colonial Revival bungalows.

327 E. Toluca — *1915c Vernacular*

334 E. Toluca — *1939*

405 E. Toluca — *1935*

Van Bibber Avenue — East
—Van Bibber is named for an early pioneer—

504 E. Van Bibber — *1919 Bungalow*   NRHP:1997
A single-story clapboard bungalow with multi-gable roof. Main portion of the house is covered by a single, side-facing gable roof. The center, front most portion of the house features a front-facing gable which extends downward to form the entry porch overhang supported by wood posts. Behind this porch is a smaller, front-facing gable which acts as the attic dormer.

505 E. Van Bibber — *1920 Bungalow*   NRHP:1997
A single-story bungalow with lap siding and multi-gable roof. The front facade is defined by a large, front-facing gable projection and includes a grouping of three pairs of multi-pane, casement windows.

511 E. Van Bibber — *1919 Bungalow*   NRHP:1997
A single-story bungalow with multi-gable roof and siding which is now covered with asbestos. The main portion of the house is covered by a single-gable roof with side-facing gables, but a third gable, which is front-facing, forms the entry porch overhang and is supported by wood posts. The upper porch gable face is adorned with slatting. The original front door with multi-pane windows is still present.

512 E. Van Bibber — *1927 Bungalow*   NRHP:1997
A single-story clapboard bungalow with multi-gable roof; each gable is clipped. The front half of the house is comprised of a forward gable extension which forms the entry porch overhang; this is supported by wide piers with concrete bases and wood posts on top. Wide vertical slatting adorns the upper gable.

520 E. Van Bibber — *1922 California Bungalow* NRHP:1997
A single-story clapboard bungalow with single-gable roof with side-facing gables. A small, front-facing gable forms the entry portico and is supported by ornamental brackets. Front entry is at center, flanked

on either side by a pair of double-hung windows.

525 E. Van Bibber — *1919 Bungalow*   NRHP:1997
A single-story bungalow with wide lap siding and single, front-facing g able roof. Entry is via a corner recessed porch which is supported by a wood post. An angled bay window in the front features a hood roof and window on each plane.

528 E. Van Bibber — *1920c Craftsman Bungalow* NRHP:1997
A single-story bungalow with wide lap siding and multi-gable roof. The front facade is comprised of three, front-facing gables. The center gable is located over the main portion of the house; on either side two smaller, front-facing gable extensions form porch overhangs which are supported by tapered wood piers. Beneath each porch gable is an entry, indicating duplex usage.

529 E. Van Bibber — *1919*

530 E. Van Bibber — *1920c Craftsman Bungalow*

535 E. Van Bibber — *1919 Bungalow*

536 E. Van Bibber — *1920 Craftsman Bungalow* NRHP:1997
A single-story clapboard bungalow with shallow-pitched, multi-gable roof. The roof is arranged in an L-plan with the frontmost leg of the ell extending forward to form an entry porch overhang supported by wide piers with concrete bases and tapered wood posts on top.

539 E. Van Bibber — *1922 California Bungalow* NRHP:1997
A single story bungalow with tri-gable roof. The main portion of the house is covered by a single-gable roof with side-facing gables. A narrower, front-facing gable extension forms an entry portico. It is supported by Colonial columns. The main entry is at center, flanked on either side by sidelights. To either side of the porch is a large, three-part window.

545 E. Van Bibber — *1921 Bungalow*   NRHP:1997
A single-story clapboard bungalow with multi-gable

roof. One-half of the front facade is articulated by a front-facing gable extension which forms an entry porch overhang and is supported by wood posts. The main entry door is beneath, flanked by sidelights.

546 E. Van Bibber — *1924 Provincial Revival*   NRHP:1997
A single-story house with stucco siding and multi-gable roof in the Provincial Revival tradition. The house is built on an L-plan and features many multi-pane windows. Rolled eaves distinguish the roofline.

551 E. Van Bibber — *1922 Bungalow*   NRHP:1997
A single-story clapboard bungalow with a shallow, front-facing gable roof. The main roof extends forward to form a full-width porch and is supported by wood posts atop a brick porch wall. Entry is at center and flanked on either side by a double-hung window.

552 E. Van Bibber — *1915 Bungalow*   NRHP:1997
A single-story bungalow with ornamental lap siding and double, front-facing gable roof. The forwardmost gable originally formed an entry porch overhang but has since been enclosed. The original tapered wood piers are still in evidence. Since the 1982 survey, this structure has been altered with appropriate redesign of porch windows.

559 E. Van Bibber — *1922 Bungalow*   NRHP:1997
A single-story clapboard bungalow with double, front-facing gable roof. The forwardmost gable forms the entry porch overhang and is supported by tapered piers. A large picture window with multi-pane transom is present on either side of the main entry.

560 E. Van Bibber — *1910 Bungalow*   NRHP:1997
A single-story bungalow with lap siding and single, side-facing gable roof. No porch is present, but two small, front-facing gables adorn the roof with matching double-light small windows. The front door is flanked by dual double hung wood windows.

567 E. Van Bibber — *1921 Bungalow*   NRHP:1997

A single-story bungalow with lap siding and multi-gable roof. The main portion of the house is covered by a single-gable roof with side-facing gables. A smaller, front-facing gable projection forms the entry porch overhang in the front, now supported by wrought iron piers which are a replacement of the original.

568 E. Van Bibber — *1923 Craftsman Bungalow* NRHP:1997
A very small bungalow cottage with clapboard siding and double, front-facing gable roof. The smaller, forwardmost gable forms the entry porch overhang and is supported by round columns. A pergola is to the side. Both the front door and two windows on the front facade are mullioned.

575 E. Van Bibber — *1920 Craftsman Bungalow* NRHP:1997
A single-story clapboard bungalow with shallow-pitched, multi-gable roof. The house is arranged on a modified L-plan with the entry at the apex of the ell. The roof extends forward at this point to form an entry porch overhang supported by tapered piers.

576 E. Van Bibber — *1908 Craftsman Bungalow* NRHP:1997
A single-story bungalow with wide lap siding and single, front-facing gable roof. A full-width, recessed porch on the front facade is supported by wood piers with diagonal braces. Triangular bracket supports and an ornamental transom are featured on the front facade.

584 E. Van Bibber — *1921 Bungalow*   NRHP:1997
A single-story bungalow with wide lap siding and single-gable roof with side-facing gables. A small entry portico is formed by a front-facing gable extension and is supported by wood piers.

590 E. Van Bibber — *190 Victorian*   NRHP:1997
A two-story house with shiplap siding and multi-gable roof. The front facade is distinguished by a full-width porch with its own separate roof overhang which

results in a small gable with inner arch at center front. Porch supports include ornamental wood posts connected by ballustrade with ornamental ballisters.

637 E. Van Bibber — *1917c Bungalow*   NRHP:1997
A bungalow with lap siding and gable roof with projecting beams and a brick end chimney. This was on the same property as 639 East Van Bibber but is now a separate lot.

639 E. Van Bibber — *1917 Bungalow*   NRHP:1997
A single-story bungalow with wide lap siding and single-gable roof with side facing gables. No porch is present, but a small pergola-like structure at the center front shelters the entry. To one side is a pair of multi-pane casement windows; to the other side is an arrangement of six, small casement windows, each with a multi-pane transom.

WALNUT AVENUE — EAST

—Walnut is named for one of the agricultural grove trees—

420 E. Walnut — *1921 Spanish Colonial Revival* NRHP:1997
A single-story house with modified box plan, stucco facades and combination flat and gable roof. Entry is via an arcade which covers half of the front facade and features three large, arched openings. A tiled hood articulates this arcade. Both the roof ridges and front-facing gable are faced with adobe tiles.

524 E. Walnut — *1925 Bungalow*   NRHP:1997
A single-story, clapboard bungalow with single, side-facing gable roof. A smaller, front-facing gable forms the entry porch overhang supported by Colonial columns. A pergola on either side of this porch entry is also supported by Colonial columns.

528 E. Walnut — *1937 Bungalow*

538 E. Walnut — *1939 Bungalow*   NRHP:1997
A single-story bungalow with wide lap siding and single, side-facing gable roof. A smaller, front-facing gable forms the entry porch overhang supported by piers.

548 E. Walnut — *1929 Bungalow*   NRHP:1997
A single-story, clapboard bungalow with single, front-facing gable roof. A small, front-facing gabled portico, supported by wood posts, forms the entry porch. The original door with plate glass window is still present.

604 E. Walnut — *1927 Provincial Revival* NRHP:1997
A single-story house with stucco facades and steep-pitched, multi-gable roof. Two front-facing gables articulate the front facade, the smaller of which forms an entry portico with large arched opening. A large, wide chimney is adjacent to the entry portico. On the upper gable is half-timbering.

612 E. Walnut — *1926 Mediterranean Revival*   NRHP:1997
A single-story, box plan house with stucco facades and stepped parapet. A rectilinear projection, on the

center portion of the front facade with three large arched openings, forms the entry portico. Entry is beneath and flanked on either side by a three-part window with tile hood.

620 E. Walnut — *1926 Provincial Revival* NRHP:1997
A single-story house with stucco facades and steep-pitched, multi-gable roof. The house clearly tries to emulate the Provincial Revival style but does not incorporate the typical detailing of the period. Rolled eaves, however, are characteristic of the style.

638 E. Walnut — *1930 Provincial Revival* NRHP:1997
A single-story house built on a U-plan with stucco facades and steep-pitched, multi-gable roof. The two front-facing gables are on either leg of the U, the larger of which features a large picture window with ornamental brick molding. Entry is in the inner portion of the U, and an ornamental brick chimney is on the side of the house.

705 E. Walnut — *1927*

715 E. Walnut — *1924 Bungalow* NRHP:1997
A single-story, clapboard bungalow with multi-gable roof featuring clipped gables. The main portion of the house is covered by a single-gable roof while a centrally located, front-facing gable forms an entry porch overhang. This is supported by piers with brick bases. A brick chimney is located to the side of the porch.

733 E. Walnut — *1926 Mediterranean Revival* NRHP:1997
A single-story, box plan house with stucco facades and flat roof. A recessed entry with a large arched opening and tile hood articulates the front facade. Brick on the lower foundation wall may not be original.

803 E. Walnut — *1924 Provincial Revival* NRHP:1997
A single-story house with shiplap siding and steep-pitched, multi-gable roof. A small, front-facing gable forms an entry portico supported by iron piers, a

replacement of the original. A wide stepped chimney is on the front facade.

815 E. Walnut — *1924 Bungalow*   NRHP:1997
A single-story, clapboard bungalow with single-gable roof with side-facing gables. A centrally located, front-facing gable forms the entry porch overhang supported by piers with ornamental brick bases. All of the roof gables are clipped.

823 E. Walnut — *1924 Bungalow*   NRHP:1997
A single-story, clapboard bungalow with tri-gable roof. The main portion of the house is covered by a single-gable roof with side-facing gables. A centrally located, front-facing gable forms the entry porch overhang supported by piers with ornamental brick bases and wood posts on top. The original door with three plate glass windows is still present.

833 E. Walnut — *1924 Bungalow*   NRHP:1997
A hip roof bungalow residential structure with front porch featuring Romanesque porch columns and a hip roof porch overhang. Wood shiplap siding and wood 6/1 and 4/1 windows are present.

WALNUT AVENUE — WEST

132 W. Walnut — *1922 Bungalow*   NRHP:1997
A single-story bungalow with parallel front-facing gables. The forward most gable forms a full-width entry porch and is supported by wood posts.

140 W. Walnut — *1919 Bungalow*   NRHP:1997
A single-story bungalow with ornamental lap siding and shallow-pitch gable roof. A centrally located, front facing gable forms the entry porch overhang and is supported by wood piers on concrete bases.

150 W. Walnut — *1915c Bungalow*   NRHP:1997
A single-story clapboard bungalow with single side-facing gable roof with gables being clipped. The shed dormer is present on the front portion of the roof. The central portion of the front roof extends forward to shield a recessed entry. The main door features mullioned plate glass and is flanked on either side by 3-part transomed windows.

224 W. Walnut — *1905 Hip Roof Cottage*   NRHP:1997
A single-story house with clapboard siding and steep-pitch, hip and gable roof. The house is built on a modified L-plan with the apex of the ell being devoted to what was once probably a large wrap around porch but now only covers the front portion of the facade. The porch overhang is supported by Classical columns.

311 W. Walnut — *1923 Bungalow*   NRHP:1997
A single-story bungalow with single side-facing gable roof. The original siding has been covered with asbestos shingles. One-half of the front facade is devoted to a recessed entry porch which is supported by wood posts.

WASHINGTON AVENUE — EAST

118 E. Washington — *1920c Vernacular*   NRHP:1997
A small, single-story cottage with single-gable roof
and siding now covered with asbestos. The gable is
elongated on one side while the entry is on the side
facade and has its own small, gable portico projection.

205 E. Washington — *1920c Craftsman Bungalow* NRHP:1997
A single-story bungalow with wide lap siding and
multi-gable roof. The house is located on a corner lot
and has a double entry, indicating duplex usage
originally. The main front facade has a centrally
located gable projection which forms the entry porch
overhang supported by piers with wood posts and a
connecting balustrade. Exposed beams in the gable
face and slatted venting provide embellishment. An
identical gable projection is located on the side of the
house as well.

214 E. Washington — *1915c Craftsman Bungalow* NRHP:1997
A single-story, tri-gable bungalow with siding now
covered by asbestos. The main portion of the house is
covered by a single-gable roof with side-facing gables.
A centrally located, front-facing gable on the front
facade provides an entry porch. This is supported by
tapered piers with a connecting, low porch wall. Two
doors are located beneath the porch, indicating duplex
usage. Original doors with window panes are still
present.

217 E. Washington — *1920c Bungalow*   NRHP:1997
A single-story house with wide lap siding and single,
front-facing gable roof. The main entrance is via a
corner recessed porch which is supported by a wood
post and has a connecting slatted balustrade.

226 E. Washington — *1904 Hip Roof Cottage*   NRHP:1997
A single-story house with box plan, hip roof and siding
now covered by asbestos. One-half of the front facade
is defined by a corner recessed porch which is now
supported by wrought iron piers, a replacement of the

original. A small pedimented gable on the front portion of the roof features a louvered transom. The wide eaves of the main roof are adorned with ornamental brackets.

230 E. Washington — *1915 Bungalow*   NRHP:1997
A single-story bungalow with wide lap siding and single, front-facing g able roof. What was originally a recessed corner porch has since been enclosed, but the original wood piers and slatted balustrade are still present.

236 E. Washington — *1907 Hip Roof Cottage*   NRHP:1997
A single-story clapboard house with modified L-plan and combination gable roof. The entry is via a corner porch formed by an extension of the main hip roof and is supported by Classical columns with Corinthian capitals. The remaining half of the front facade is articulated by a front-facing, pedimented gable. Wide eaves throughout are ornamented with brackets. The original front door and accompanying screen door are still present.

306 E. Washington — *1904 Transitional*   OTPA:1997
OWNER: A.C. & Ida Hamilton
A two-story house with a single, front-facing gable roof and siding now covered by asbestos. A full-width front porch is present on the first story. This has its own separate roof overhang supported by Classical columns. Entry is at center. The original front door is still present.

323 E. Washington — *1916 Bungalow*   NRHP:1997
A single-story bungalow with lap siding and double, front-facing gable roof. The forwardmost gable forms the entry porch overhang and is supported by ornamental columns. Cross-ties and triangular bracket supports adorn both front gable faces.

326 E. Washington — *1920c California Bungalow* NRHP:1997
A single-story clapboard house with single-gable roof

with side-facing gables. Either side of the front facade is defined by a small gabled entry portico with diagonal brace supports. Double entry indicates duplex usage.

426 E. Washington — *1922 California Bungalow* NRHP:1997
A single-story clapboard bungalow with multi-gable roof. Main portion of the house is covered by a single-gable roof with side-facing, clipped gables. The front-facing gable in the center portion of the front facade forms the entry porch overhang and is supported by round columns. A pergola is located on either side and is also supported by wide, round columns. The main entry is at center, flanked on either side by side vents.

504 E. Washington — *1908 Hip Roof Cottage* OTPA:1997
TREE: Camphor *Cinnamomum camphora* 30" 40' 60'.
OWNER: Henry W. Duker
A single-story clapboard house with hip roof and corner recessed porch. The porch is supported by a singular column. The front portion of the roof also features a small gable projection which is embellished with ornamental shingles and jigsawn work.

Henry W. Duker Home

505 E. Washington — *1904 Hip Roof Cottage* NRHP:1997
This single-story cottage-scale house embodies both Victorian and turn-of-the-century features. The box

plan and pyramidal roof are clearly turn-of-the-century, while the porch posts and front pedimented gable ornamentation are Victorian. The house incorporates a full-width porch across the front facade which is supported by ornamental turned posts. A small pedimented gable on the front of the roof features ornamental shingles and an ornamentally framed transom. It should be noted that the wood shake shingles are not original and are a later addition.

513 E. Washington — *1914 Craftsman Bungalow* NRHP:1997
A single-story clapboard bungalow with double, front-facing gables. The forwardmost gable forms the entry porch overhang and is supported by wide piers. The house has been modified in more recent years to include stucco siding and a brick veneer at the foundation wall. Neither is original.

514 E. Washington — *1920 California Bungalow* NRHP:1997
A single-story clapboard bungalow with single, shallow-pitched gable roof with side-facing gables. An additional front-facing gable is located on the center portion of the front facade and forms the entry portico.

521 E. Washington — *1909 Hip Roof Cottage*   NRHP:1997
A single-story box plan house with clapboard siding and hip roof. Entry is via a corner recessed porch which has been modified to include wrought iron posts. Front-facing, pedimented gable is located on the front portion of the roof and features ornamental shingles and an ornamentally framed attic vent.

524 E. Washington — *1909 Hip Roof Cottage*   NRHP:1997
A single-story, box plan house with clapboard siding and hip roof. Entry is via a corner recessed porch supported by a single, Classical column. A small, pedimented gable is present on the front portion of the roof. Also notable is the double entry with original screen doors.

532 E. Washington — *1909 Bungalow*   NRHP:1997

A single-story clapboard bungalow with single, shallow-pitched, front-facing gable roof. What was once a corner recessed porch has since been enclosed. The house is simple and unembellished.

535 E. Washington — *1909 Bungalow*   NRHP:1997
A single-story house with wide lap siding and hip roof. Present on the front facade are two, front-facing gable faces, the smaller of which forms an angled bay window, and the larger of which supports a second, smaller gable which forms an entry portico. These gables give the house an unusual distinction.

537 E. Washington — *1909 Bungalow (in rear of 535 E.)*

539 E. Washington — *1915c Hip Roof Cottage*   NRHP:1997
A single-story, box plan clapboard house with hip roof. Front facade is articulated with a small entry porch overhang.

540 E. Washington — *1911 Hip Roof Cottage*   NRHP:1997
TREE: Big Cone Pine *Pinus coulteri.* Planted by Wanda Pears coulteri is named for Don Coulter.
A single-story, box plan house with clapboard siding and hip roof. A front-facing, gable dormer is present on the front of the roof. The house features wide eaves but no porch is present.

541 E. Washington — *1915c Cottage, Hip Roof (in rear of 539 E.)*

548 E. Washington — *1909 Hip Roof Cottage*   NRHP:1997
A single-story, box plan house with clapboard siding and hip roof. Entry is via a corner recessed porch, though no porch support is present. A small, pedimented gable is present on the front portion of the roof and is embellished with an ornamentally framed attic vent.

604 E. Washington — *1919 Craftsman Bungalow* NRHP:1997
OWNER: Henry & Dora Peters
BLDR: Orange Contracting & Milling Co.

A single-story bungalow with wide lap siding and double, front-facing gable roof. The forwardmost gable forms the entry porch overhang and is supported by tapered piers. Ornamental purlins grace the eaves.

Henry & Dora Peters Home

605 E. Washington — *1905c Hip Roof Cottage*   NRHP:1997
A single-story, box plan house with clapboard siding and hip roof. One-half of the front facade is articulated by a corner recessed porch and is supported by a Classical column with Corinthian capital. A small, pedimented gable, attic dormer is present on the front portion of the roof and has an ornamentally framed, transom vent.

610 E. Washington — *1910 Hip Roof Cottage*   NRHP:1997
A single-story house with modified box plan, clapboard siding and multi-hip roof. The house features a staggered front facade with the frontmost portion extending into a full-width porch supported by four Classical columns. A dormer gable is present just above the porch overhang. The original door and screen door are still present on the house.

622 E. Washington — *1907 Hip Roof*   NRHP:1997
A rectangular plan single story residence with hipped roof and a small front facing gable which is ornamented by vertical wooden slats. The entry is

beneath a corner of the hipped roof. A classical column and small window are present at the porch.

623 E. Washington — *1915 Craftsman*   NRHP:1997
A one and one-half story house with clapboard siding and single-gable roof with side-facing gables. A smaller, front-facing dormer gable is also present. It is ornamented with jigsawn brackets and an ornamentally framed vent. The main roof extends forward to form the full-width porch overhang and is supported by piers with concrete bases and wood posts on top. Entry is just off center and is flanked on either side by a large, fixed-pane picture window with transom.

629 E. Washington — *1914 Bungalow*   NRHP:1997
A single-story clapboard bungalow with a multi-gable roof fashioned in an L-plan. The short leg of the ell results in a front-facing gable porch overhang and is supported by wood posts.

630 E. Washington — *1913 Craftsman*   NRHP:1997
A one and one-half story clapboard house with single, side-facing gable roof and small, front-facing gable dormer. The dormer is embellished with ornamental bracket supports and a beveled glass transom. One-half of the front facade is occupied by a recessed porch supported by a tapered pier atop a low porch wall.

637 E. Washington — *1935 Mediterranean Revival* NRHP:1997
A low-to-the-ground, single story, stucco bungalow with box plan and flat roof. The house is otherwise simple and unembellished except for the gabled entry portico, large arched opening and tile hood.

712 E. Washington — *1919 Craftsman Bungalow* NRHP:1997
A single-story bungalow with wide lap siding and double, front-facing gable roof. The forwardmost gable forms the entry porch overhang and is supported by wood posts. Exposed beams adorn the upper gable faces.

720 E. Washington — *1921 Bungalow*   NRHP:1997
A small, single-story clapboard bungalow with single, front-facing gable roof. A smaller, gable projection on the center front facade forms an entry porch overhang supported by wood posts.

728 E. Washington — *1921 California Bungalow* NRHP:1997
A single-story, clapboard bungalow with tri-gable roofline, each gable being clipped. The main portion of the house is covered by a side-facing gable roof; a centrally located, front-facing gable projection forms the entry porch overhang supported by thin wood posts. Entry is at center, flanked by sidelights. To either side of the porch is a grouping of three windows with transoms.

736 E. Washington — *1917 Craftsman Bungalow* NRHP:1997
A single-story, clapboard bungalow with a single, front-facing gable roof. A smaller, front-facing gable is located at the center front facade and forms the entry porch overhang supported by thin wood posts.

742 E. Washington — *1919 Craftsman Bungalow* NRHP:1997
A single-story bungalow with wide lap siding and multi-gable roof. The front facade is articulated by a smaller, front-facing gable running parallel to the main gable and forming the entry porch overhang. This is supported by piers with brick bases and wood posts on top and features slatting and beams arranged in an ornamental fashion.

804 E. Washington — *1917 Gable Roof Cottage*   NRHP:1997
A single-story house with single, front-facing gable roof with a side extension. Siding is asbestos. A smaller, front-facing gable porch overhang is present on the front facade supported by wood posts. Entry is beneath at center and flanked on either side by multi-pane casement windows.

812 E. Washington — *1921 Worker Housing*   NRHP:1997
An irregular plan modest worker house with multi-

gables, wide shiplap siding, and double hung windows. The structure sits in rear of lot with the main portion of the house framed by a side facing gable. The garage is attached to the home by a shed roof.

818 E. Washington — *1928 Provincial Revival*   NRHP:1997
A single-story stucco house with steep-pitched, multi-gable roof fashioned in the Provincial Revival manner. Popular at this time were Provincial influences on the housing stock, and this house incorporates the typically used rolled eaves and large arched windows and arched openings.

828 E. Washington — *1919 Craftsman Bungalow* NRHP:1997
TREE: Red Flowering Gum *Eucalyptus ficifolia* 30" 35' 45'.
A single-story bungalow with wide lap siding and front-facing gable roof. The main roof extends forward to form a full-width porch and is supported by tapered piers. The upper gable face is ornamented with vertical slatting and exposed beams arranged in an ornamental fashion.

838 E. Washington — *1922 Bungalow*   NRHP:1997
A single-story clapboard bungalow with single, front-facing gable roof. What was originally a full-width porch has since been enclosed, but the original porch piers are still present.

WAVERLY STREET — SOUTH
—*Outside Old Towne Orange*—

143 S. Waverly — *1926 Spanish Colonial Revival* NRHP:1997
A single story house built on an L-plan with stucco facades and an adobe tiled gable roof. The main entry is formed by an extension of one roof and is articulated by arched opening bay window with mullioned windows present on the front facade.

144 S. Waverly — *1925 Mediterranean Revival* NRHP:1997
A single story box plan residence with stucco facade and flat roof raised parapets are on both the main house and the entry porticos (garage also). The side entry portico mirrors the front one. Front facade has two pairs of triple windows and porch the whole length of the house.

151 S. Waverly — *1940 Provincial Revival*

156 S. Waverly — *1929 Tudor Revival* NRHP:1997
OWNER & BLDR: Al Eisenbaum
Built by Eisenbaum for his new bride, he operated his father's Tin Shop on North Orange.

A one and a half story Tudor Revival with a multi-gabled clipped roof and stucco sidings. Multiple mullioned windows are on the facade inclusive of asset of three mullioned picture windows. A chimney rests against the south side gable. A small extension of the roof provides an uncovered structural entry. There is an art studio in the apex of the roof.

159 S. Waverly — *1939 Provincial Revival* NRHP:1997
A hipped roof, stucco sided house in a modified box plan, with recessed, angled entry. The small front extension has its own smaller hipped roof. A wide decorative trim accents bottom portion of front roof.

167 S. Waverly — *1938 Mediterranean Revival* NRHP:1997
A parapet multi-gabled adobe tiled roof house with stucco siding on an L-plan. A front facing gable extension farms the entry porch. Through adobe vents

placed above a large picture window on front facade. A small parapet roof garage is present.

174 S. Waverly — *1938 Mediterranean Revival*   NRHP:1997
A Mediterranean Revival residence with parapet roof and adobe tiled, multi-gables roof on an L-Plan. A large concrete tapered chimney is present on the side of the house. An extension of the roof forms the entry. Varying sizes of mullioned windows are present on front facade.

175 S. Waverly — *1937 Provincial Revival*   NRHP:1997
Provincial Revival residence with a steep pitched multi-gabled roof on a smooth stucco rectangular plan. One of the two front facing gables forms an entry portico with a large arched opening. A large stucco chimney is present on front facade.

182 S. Waverly — *1931 Bungalow Cottage*   NRHP:1997
Modified Style A multi-gabled Bungalow with wood lapped siding. A front facing gable forms the entry porch which is supported by wooden supports on concrete piers. The original porch appears to have been enclosed. The steep gables have an ornamental element in peak.

183 S. Waverly — *1937 Provincial Revival*   NRHP:1997
A stucco-sided L-Plan residence with steep pitched single-story gable roof. The two front facing gables are joined and one forms an entry portico with an arched opening. A large stucco chimney is present on the side. Two pairs of double hung mullioned windows are present on facade. The rear gable is higher than the front gable and forms a slight peak on roof.

Waverly Street — North

121 N. Waverly — *1935 Mediterranean Revival*   NRHP:1997
A single-story Mediterranean Revival residence with stucco siding and front facing gable which forms the entry portico and is accessed by an arched opening. Roof is adobe tile. A large picture window flanks the front entrance.

131 N. Waverly — *1923 Dutch Colonial Revival*   NRHP:1997
A single-story Dutch Colonial Revival with wood lap siding and multi-gabled clipped roof. The main portion of the home is covered by a single-gabled roof with side facing gables. The centrally located front facing gable forms an entry porch overhang with pergolas to the entry porch and the end of the pergolas. Matching mullion windows are present on the front door with side lights and two pairs of windows on either side of the front facade

139 N. Waverly — *1923 Mediterranean Revival*   NRHP:1997
A single-story Mediterranean Revival stucco residence, originally with rectangular floor plan. The front facade is articulated by a hip roof and also a flat parapet roof. The entry portico is formed by a shed roof extension from the wall. This portico is enhanced by three arched openings on the side and a large arch opening as the entry. An elaborate picture window is present.

140 N. Waverly — *1926 Provincial Revival*   NRHP:1997
A single story clapboard house with steep pitched multi-gable roof. Entry is recessed between gables with covered porch. Front facing picture window flanked by two mullioned smaller windows. The other gabled extension has same smaller mullioned windows. An extension of front gable forms a wing wall.

147 N. Waverly — *1937 Provincial Revival*   NRHP:1997
A single story, stucco sided Provincial Revival residence with L-Plan. A steep pitched front facing gable covered with wide wood lapped siding forms the

entry. No porch is present. A mullioned window with thirty lights enhances the forward facing facade.

148 N. Waverly — *1923 Gable Roof Cottage*   NRHP:1997
A single story Cottage with wood lap siding and multi-gabled roof. Main portion of the home is covered by a single gable roof with side facing gables. The centrally located front facing gable forms an entry porch overhang with pergolas to either side, supported by wooden columns. Two pairs of vertical mullioned windows flank the entry.

155 N. Waverly — *1924 Craftsman Bungalow*   NRHP:1997
A single story Bun~~ ' ~~ ith multi-gabled roof and wood lap ~~ ~~ ~~ ~~. ~~ ~~ ne forward mist gable is an extension of the home. A low shed roof forms the entry porch. The front door is accented by sidelights.

156 N. Waverly — *1936 Provincial Revival*   NRHP:1997
A one-story stucco residence with two front facing gables trimmed with wide wood lap siding at the peaks which is carried forward to the garage. A covered entry and small side entrance enhances the home. A mullioned picture window with twenty lights enhances the front facade. The smaller mullioned windows are near the entry.

163 N. Waverly — *1924 Mediterranean Revival* NRHP:1997
A single story box plan Mediterranean Revival residence with stucco facade and flat roof. Raised parapets are on both the main home entrance and side entrance, and the garage entry portico.

166 N. Waverly — *1933 Spanish Colonial Revival* NRHP:1997
A single-story Spanish Colonial Revival with stucco siding and multi-gabled roof line home built on a modified L-Plan with front facing gables which form an entry portico which is accessed by an arched opening. Roof is sided in adobe tiles. Large rounded windows enhances the front facade. Rear garage emulates rounded arch styles with door openings.

173 N. Waverly — *1924 California Bungalow*   NRHP:1997
A Bungalow style residence of irregular floor plan, stucco sided single story structure. Combination of gabled and shed roofs. The home is set back on lot with a brick garage in front.

174 N. Waverly — *1923 Transitional Prairie*   NRHP:1997
A Prairie style single story residence with stucco siding and flat roof. Entry is via porch which projects forward the full length of the front facade. A pair of picture windows flanked by two double hung windows is visible on t he front facade. Top of parapet trimmed in wood with rounded vent openings. The side entrance is recessed.

182 N. Waverly — *1930 Craftsman Bungalow*   NRHP:1997
A single story Craftsman Bungalow with wood lap siding and a tri-gable roof. The house features two entries, indicating the intention for original duplex use. Each entry is articulated by a shallow to medium pictured gable portico supported by piers with wood posts. The front has two symmetrical sets of windows.

183 N. Waverly — *1924 Craftsman Bungalow*   NRHP:1997
A large two story Craftsman with multi-gabled roof and wood lap siding. A front facing gable forms the entry porch. This gable is supported by piers with concrete bases. Angled brackets and exposed rafter tails are visible.

216 N. Waverly — *1948 Craftsman Bungalow*   NRHP:1997
A multi-gabled Bungalow residence with wide wood lapped siding, in a box plan. One of the front facing gables forms the entry. Classical columns on ornamental, placed on brick, piers surround the entry porch. The gables are enhanced by short returns at eaves. A small side entry porch forms an extension of the roof. A pair of picture windows flanked by small double hung windows are present on the front facade.

232 N. Waverly — *1924 California Bungalow*   NRHP:1997

A small multi-gabled Bungalow with wood lapped siding. The plan is rectangular with two large picture windows on the front facade. A small front entry is covered with another gable, showing four gables on front facade. A pergola entry is present on the side.

252 N. Waverly — *1924 Craftsman Bungalow*   NRHP:1997
A single-story multi-gabled roof Bungalow with wood lap siding. A large shallow front facing gable forms an entry porch which extends the full length of the house. The porch is supported by wooden columns supported by ornamental placed brick piers.

272 N. Waverly — *1923 California Bungalow*   NRHP:1997
A single-story, L-plan, multi-gabled Bungalow with wood lap siding. A front facing gable forms the entry porch supported by a wood columns and brick piers. The front entry door is flanked by sidelights. A mullion side entry door is visible.

282 N. Waverly — *1924 California Bungalow*   NRHP:1997
A single-story L-plan Bungalow with multi-gable roof and wood lap siding. A shed roof forms the front porch. Two brick piers with wood columns support the overhang. Two double hung picture windows flank the door. A south side gable covers the entry porch.

292 N. Waverly — *1924 California Bungalow*   NRHP:1997
A single-story multi-gabled Bungalow with wood lap siding on a rectangular plan. A front facing gable forms the entry porch supported by a set of three wooden columns atop ornamentally placed brick piers. Two transom picture windows flank the entry.

BIBLIOGRAPHY

National Register of Historic Places, The Plaza Historic District, Orange Community Historical Society, 1982

Santa Fe Depot Area Specific Plan, City of Orange, 1993

Old Towne Orange, A Walk Through History & Brochure, Kathleen Less and Philip Brigandi, 1992

Orange California History, A Compilation Of Various Sources, Orange Public Library, 1995

Color It Orange, A Selection of Stories About the City of Orange, Orange Community Historical Society, 1993

A Place Called Home, Orange's Architectural Legacy, Phil Brigandi and Karen Wilson Turnbull, 1990

A New Creation, The Incorporation of the City of Orange 1888, Phil Brigandi, 1988

Growth and Progress of Orange, Chamber of Commerce Report, August 1959

City of Orange General Plan Historic Preservation Element, City of Orange Planning Department, 1983

Historic Inventory Old Towne - Photo Records Volumes I - V, City of Orange Planning Department, 1982

Historic Preservation Design Guidelines for Old Towne Orange, California, City of Orange, August 1985

Historic Preservation Design Guidelines for Old Towne Orange, California, City of Orange, August 1995

City of Orange Historic Building Inventory Update, Final Report, AEGIS, October 1991

City of Orange Directories, Florence Flippen Smiley, City of Orange, CA Old Towne Orange Historic Resources Base Map, City of Orange Planning Department, 1996

Local History Ephemera Files, Orange Public Library, City of Orange, CA

Orange Addition Vol 1-5, Paragon Agency Publishers, 1994

GLOSSARY

alabasters	any structure made of gypsum
arcaded	two or more arches
archivolts	beam on top of a column support, carried around a curve
baluster	a verticle element, supporting a rail
balustrade	a group of balusters
barge board	decorated board at the end of a gable
board & batton	verticle wall board seams are covered with battons
ballard	low solid post landscape feature
Beaux Arts	style of classic lines; Greek/Roman columns
Bungalow	style an outgrowth of Craftsman style; smaller, single story with sleeping porches and river rock.
canopy	decorative roof structure, extending from a wall
Classic Box	style of squared off and box-like home.
Craftsman	style almost exclusively domestic; simple box-like shapes; low pitched roofs, stucco, clapboard, shingles or board and batten; river boulder sheathing of lower portion of walls; exposed structural roof rafters
cupola	cup form on top of a vault
curvilineear	curved form lines
dentils	small, repitition of teeth like blocks, found under an eave
dormer	small, gable-like room roof-cover on a sloping roofline
eave	edge on the low side of a roof or gable
elephantine	any structure large and massive
ell	the spelling of 'L'
entablature	entire horizontal composition of the edge of a column form
facade	entire front of a building (façade)
gable	peak roofline extension
Hip Roof Cottage	style of small homes with steep rooflines

Mediterranean	style with tiled roofs, stucco faces; some flat roofs with parapets and towers.
Mission	style with arched openings with pier, arch and surface of buildings treated as a single smooth plane; bell towers, covered with tiled hip roofs.
Moderne	style with curved aerodynamic form of ships or airplanes; stucco boxes, with rounded corners; horizontal banded surfaces; glass brick, round windows and steel railings.
muntins	horizontal dividers of a multi-paned window
mullions	verticle dividers of a multi-paned window
Palladian	a window style after Palladia; arched top with vertical side windows
parapet	edge around a flat roof like a short wall
pergola	small arbor or horizontal trellis, like a covered walkway
porte cochère	covered drive-through
portico	roofed door
Paririe	style of stucco boxes with horizontal emphasis; horizontal patterns of openings; bands of windows placed directly under the roof.
Provinical	style of French country homes; peaked roofs over doorways; high rooflines.
rake board	end of the edge of a single sloping roof
rectilinear	straight form lines
romanisque	an arch by design somewhere between Roman and Gothic
rusticated	groovs cut into stone; faux brick
shiplap	grooved side board, overhanging onto the one below
sidelap	simpler side board overhang
slumpstone	concrete block with the curved effect of adobe
stucco	a wall plaster of exterior portland cement

transom	horizontal feature over a door
transom window	horizontal window over a door; may open
truss	triangulated horizontal support
turret	small tower; may be attached to a larger tower
vaulted	arch over a space
veneer	lamination over a surface; for better appearance
Vernacular	style: regional; specific to a location
Victorian	style referencing Queen Victoria of England; ornate, stylized in several interpretations:

Italinate: Villa and High Victorian; irregular mass tower placed within the ell of two major wings or single volumetric form, richly articulated by sharp angular details.

Gothic: Volumes covered by high pitched roofs; use of barge boards on gable cornices, pointed windows, open arches, and board and batten walls.

Queen Anne: Highly irregular form with special emphasis on the picturesque silhouette of the roof. Gables, dormers, high chimneys, towers, turrets and pinnacles.

weather board	horizontal board covering a sill
window dormer	verticle face of a window on a dormer

NOTES

SpecialBooks.com

Special Books provides unique historical and unusual books on topics as diverse as Custer's Last Stand and the Titanic. From replicas of historic pieces, to newly authored selections of varied interest. New titles will be added later this year.

A first hand account of Custer's Last Stand, written down in cards and letters by 2nd Lt. Wallace - an actual survivor of the famous Battle of the Little Big Horn. -22 transcripts from 1876; Glossary; 100pgs. **$18.76**

A reprint of the first book on the Titanic. Originally published weeks after the tragic sinking, this book contains first hand reports from eye-witnesses. -66 Illustrations; 350pgs. **$19.12**

Capistrano Nights is a delightful tale of the people who lived around the Mission San Juan Capistrano. Written by Father John O'Sullivian some seven decades ago, these stories tell of the Mission's society 100 years ago. **$12.95**

You can contact us at:
The Paragon Agency • P.O. Box 1281
Orange, CA 92856
(714) 771-0652 • www.SpecialBooks.com

— Copy this form and send it in to OTPA —

OTPA Membership Application

Learn how to preserve
Join OTPA Today!

Your membership entitles you to vote at general membership meetings and to receive copies of Orange Preserves Newsletter.

Dues:	
1 year membership:	
Individual	$8.00
Family	$15.00
Senior	$5.00
Sustaining	$25.00
Lifetime	$150.00

Name: _____

Address: _____

_____

Phone #: _____   Email: _____

I'm particularly interested in _____

Mail to: OTPA • P.O. Box 828, Orange, CA 92856
Make checks payable to OTPA   www.oldtowneorange.com